Felix Dzer
a biogra

New Outlook Publishers

1808 Hylan Blvd Suite #1009

Staten Island, New York 10305-1934

www.newoutlookpublishers.net

Table of Contents

INTRODUCTION

The Soviet people undertaking enormous effort in all areas of the work to build communism have already achieved great successes in developing productive forces, economic and social relations, socialist democracy, and culture, and in moulding the new man. The world's first socialist country has entered the stage of developed socialism. The attainments scored by the Party and the people have been recorded in the updated edition of the CPSU Programme adopted by the 27th Party Congress.

The historic achievements of the Soviet people in building a new society, their victory in the Great Patriotic War of 1941-45, the country's confident advance towards higher stages of social, economic and cultural progress, and the growth of the Soviet Union's influence on the course of world development are inseparably linked with the Communist Party s activities. It is the inspirer and organiser of the creative endeavour of the people, Soviet society's leading and guiding force. Today, the Party has advanced the strategy of accelerating the country's socio-economic development which is aimed at accomplishing a qualitative change in all aspects of the Soviet people's life.

The impressive social and economic changes that have taken place in the country and the peaceful creative work of the Soviet people have embodied the dreams and truly heroic efforts or many generations of revolutionaries, above all, political figures and statesmen of the Leninist school who have entered the political arena in the revolutionary epoch.

Felix Dzerzhinsky, one of the great revolutionaries, was a steadfast Communist, a staunch defender of the revolution, a fighter for a better future for his own country and people and the whole of mankind. He was a man to be feared by the enemies of the revolution, a man whose life was a never-ending struggle to realise the ideals of communism. Though short, his life was full and eventful. A convinced BolshevikLeninist[1], who had spent eleven years—a quarter of his life— in prison and exile, Dzerzhinsky helped govern the world's first socialist state of workers and peasants. He was a truly

3

popular hero who struck terror into the bourgeoisie. Fellow-Bolsheviks nick-named him "iron Felix", paying tribute to his loyalty to the cause of revolution.

Dzerzhinsky joined the ranks of fighters for the emancipation of the working class at the age of 17. His career as a revolutionary began in the working-class environment of Kaunas and Vilnius in Lithuania. Soon, he was a professional revolutionary, a leader of the working-class movement in the Northwest of the Russian Empire and in Poland. His dedicated work had done much to unite the Polish and Russian revolutionary movement, enhance internationalism among the Polish working class, bring the two fraternal proletarian parties closer together, and strengthen the Bolshevik Party.

Dzerzhinsky was a consistent and firm Leninist. He became personally acquainted with Lenin in 1906 at the Fourth Congress of the Russian Social-Democratic Labour Party (RSDLP)[2] in Stockholm. But at a much earlier time he had "met" Lenin through his works. Dzerzhinsky thought highly of Lenin's activities as an organiser of the Communist Party and the fact that he consistently championed a truly revolutionary strategy and tactics in the working-class movement.

Dzerzhinsky was directly involved in the preparation and accomplishment of the October 1917 armed uprising in Petrograd. He was one of the members of the Party Centre directing it, and was personally in charge of key sectors of the revolutionary struggle which effectively foiled the counterrevolutionary plans of the bourgeoisie.

After the revolution, Dzerzhinsky was appointed by the Party and by Lenin personally as head of the AllRussia Extraordinary Commission to Combat Counter-Revolution, Sabotage and Profiteering (Vecheka). Since its establishment, the Commission acted as an alert and capable guardian of the young Soviet

Republic, and it is as its head that Dzerzhinsky's qualities as an organiser and staunch Bolshevik were most clearly revealed.

Since March 1919, Dzerzhinsky had headed the People's Commissariat for Internal Affairs, alongside with the Extraordinary Commission, and actively participated in the creation of the Soviet state apparatus. He made an important contribution to the establishment and maintenance of revolutionary law and order throughout the country.

In April 1921, Dzerzhinsky was also appointed head of the Commissariat for the Transport. He personally did a great deal to rehabilitate the country's transport, and especially the railways, an essential condition for overcoming economic dislocation, famine and territorial isolation.

Another responsible position held by Dzerzhinsky was that of Chairman of the Supreme Economic Council. In that capacity, he made a great personal contribution to the implementation of Lenin's ideas and the Party's economic policy of the country's industrialisation. He was directly involved in the establishment of ferrous and non-ferrous metallurgy, the aviation industry, and tractor- and agricultural machine-building. Dzerzhinsky stressed the importance of scientific research and was known for his efforts to promote science in the Soviet Union.

From the very first days of the existence of the Soviet state, Dzerzhinsky was repeatedly elected a delegate to congresses of the Soviets, and to the All-Russia Central Executive Committee and the USSR Central Executive Committee (since 1924), the highest body of the country's state authority. He was actively involved in solving various issues of state-building in the young republic, distinguished himself again as head of the All-Russia Central Executive Committee commission on the improvement of the condition of children. This work revealed his kindness and humanitarian qualities.

Felix Dzerzhinsky's career was fruitful, multifaceted and scrupulously honest. A Bolshevik of the Leninist school, he was in charge of key sectors of the Party's political and organisational work. Needless to say, he invariably enjoyed the complete confidence of fellow Bolsheviks.

Dzerzhinsky's work as a state, public and economic leader was terminated unexpectedly. He died on July 20, 1926—a soldier killed in battle. The Party Central Committee and the Central Control Commission stated in an address to all Party members, the working people, and the Red Army and Navy: "In the torture-chambers of tsarist Russia and in Siberian exile, during the interminable years of penal servitude, in prison and during the years of freedom, in underground work and when holding government jobs, in the Extraordinary Commission and at the head of construction work— Felix Dzerzhinsky was forever in the line of fire..."

* * *

We offer the reader a scientific biography of Felix Dzerzhinsky, which, we believe, can give a complete and accurate idea or his life and versatile work. It is based on the works of Lenin, the documents of Party congresses and conferences, plenary meetings of the CPSU Central Committee, the Social-Democracy of the Kingdom of Poland and Lithuania and the Communist Party of Poland (1918-1938), and the writings of Dzerzhinsky (letters to relatives and Party comrades, a prison diary, reports on Party work, speeches at Party congresses and conferences and statements to the press, etc.). The authors have extensively researched archival documents, numerous memoirs devoted to him (in Russian and Polish), his earlier biographies (especially those written by his first biographers, many of whom knew him personally: Jakub Hanecki, Yu. Krasny, Felix Kon, Adolf Warski), and other works dealing with the various aspects of Felix Dzerzhinsky's career. The book At the Time of Great Battles, written by Dzerzhinsky's wife, Sofia, provided much useful information. It was published in the Soviet Union and was also published in the Polish People's Republic. It is valuable not only by virtue of the personal reminiscences of the one who probably stood closest to Dzerzhinsky, but also because of the wealth of facts it contains which describe the epoch and the people who worked side by side with this great man.

The authors have also used extensive literature on the history of the CPSU, the USSR, and the international communist movement.

The book contains a list of major landmarks in Dzerzhinsky's career and name index.

The biography was written by a team of authors, including Sejriyon Khromov (editor-in-chief), Hya

Doroshenko, Sofia Dzerzhinskaya, Alexander Khatskevich, Vassily Korovin, Mikhail Kozichev, Isabella Mishakova, Velmira Nevolina, Alexander Solovyov, Alexei Velidov, Nina Vinogradova and Rozaliya Yermolayeva.

Notes

[1]Bolsheviks—followers of Lenin who received the majority (bolsbinstvo in Russian) vote at the elections to the leading Party bodies at the Second RSDLP Congress. Their opponents were called the Mensheviks (members of the menshinstvo, minority).

[2]The name of the Communist Party of Russia and then of the Soviet Union between 1898 and 1917

.

Chapter One

CHILDHOOD AND YOUTH. EARLY CAREER AS A REVOLUTIONARY

At the end of the 19th century, the revolutionary working-class movement in Russia entered a new period of development. It became a massive one in scope, and in addition, since the mid-1890s social-democracy in Russia had become not only an ideological trend but an active political force closely associated with the working-class struggle.

In the autumn of 1893 Lenin moved to St. Petersburg, where he began the historic trail along which he led the proletariat, all working people of Russia to the overthrow of the autocracy and bourgeoisie, the victorious socialist revolution.

That was the background of Felix Dzerzhinsky's youth.

His father, Edmund Dzerzhinsky, came from the Polish poor small gentry and worked as a schoolteacher. Out of the ten Dzerzhinsky brothers, only Edmund and Felicjan managed to obtain a higher education. In 1863, Edmund graduated from the physics and mathematics department of St. Petersburg University and three years later moved with his family to Taganrog, where he taught physics and maths at both a girls' and boys' grammar schools.

Edmund was consumptive, and hard work made his health rapidly deteriorate. In 1875, he took his family back to his native parts, the Dzerzhinovo estate near the Nalibokskaya Pushcha where, on August 30 (September 11, New Style) 1877[1], in the small house [2] by the rapid Usa River, Felix Dzerzhinsky was born.

His mother, Helena, nee Januszewska, came from the intelligentsia. For many years, her father was a professor at St. Petersburg Railway Institute, and her two brothers were transport engineers.

Edmund gave free lessons to peasant children, teaching them reading, writing, arithmetic and physics. Local peasants, who were brutally oppressed by landowners, kulaks (wealthy peasants) and the police, felt free to appeal to him for advice at any time. He had a reputation as a just man. He died of

consumption in 1882 at the age of 42, leaving a 32-year-old widow with eight children. They subsisted on

Edmund's small pension and the tiny rent they received for Dzerzhinovo. Luckily, Helena's mother, Kazimiera Januszewska, was able to assist her daughter financially; the sum, though not large, was regular.

From earliest childhood, the Dzerzhinsky children were used to working quite hard, to doing things for themselves, and to helping each other. The atmosphere in the family was warm and friendly. Helena did her best to bring up her children strong in health and in spirit. In summer, her sons took long boating trips along the Usa, a tributary of the beautiful Niemen, and went on hiking tours to the distant fairy-tale corners of the Nalibokskaya Pushcha. They had many friends among village children.

Felix was a high-spirited and sensitive child. Though sometimes naughty, he was never cruel or rough. He was fond of animals and could not bear to see them maltreated. He loved nature and enjoyed wandering in forests, picking flowers, berries and mushrooms, swimming in the river, and catching fish and crabs. The boy's contributions were a welcome addition to family meals.

From his friends—village children mostly—he learned how hard the poor peasants' and young hired labourers' lives were, and it is probably at that time that the seeds of protest against social injustice were sown in his soul...

Need did not prevent Helena, an intelligent and morally strong woman, from giving her children adequate opportunities for physical, moral and intellectual development. Family life, and especially the example set by his mother, were among the major formative influences on Felix. Later, writing to his sister Aldona on the subject of family upbringing, Dzerzhinsky wrote: "Love makes its way into the soul and makes it strong, kind and responsive, while fear, pain and shame only warp it. Love is the source of all that is good, noble, strong, warm and bright."

When Felix was a child, the 1863 uprising for the national emancipation of Poland and Lithuania was still fresh in people's memories. It was not easy to forget the reprisals instituted by the tsarist General Muravyov against Poles, Byelorussians, and Lithuanians, as well as against the Russian officers and men who sympathised with the insurgents. Felix was aware of the oppressive policies of the autocracy and the inhuman way the landowners and kulaks treated the poor peasants. All this made a strong impression on the sensitive boy.

Many years later, in a letter to his wife written on June 11, 1914, Dzerzhinsky remarked: "I remember the nights at our small country house when our mother told us stories by the light of a lamp, and the trees were whispering outside ... her stories about the indemnities levied against the people, the reprisals against them, and vexing taxes... This was the moment of truth. This, among other things, led me to choose the road that I later traversed, and every violent act I learned about, I felt as an act of violence against me personally."

That Dzerzhinsky deeply loved his mother is evident: "Our mother is immortal through us. She has given me my soul and filled it with love, opened my heart and won a place for herself in it forever."

At the age of six, Felix learned to read and write, first in Polish and then, at the age of seven, in Russian. His first teacher was his mother. Later, his elder and favourite sister, Aldona, prepared him for attending school in 1887. It was at that time that the family moved to Wilno (now Wilnius, the capital of the Lithuanian SSR).

The family spent the summer in Dzerzhinovo. Felix went there for the last time before the revolution in 1892. He would never lose his love for wild life and the memory of Dzerzhinovo. In prison and exile, he would dream about the time when the autocracy would fall, and he could go back home to join the people he loved. Characteristically, he wrote later: "I can remember that the beauty of nature ... almost invariably made me think about our idea... That beauty, that nature should never be rejected. It is the temple of the wanderers ... who have happened to find themselves homeless but will gain a whole world if they follow the road of the proletariat."

From 1889 to 1895 Felix attended a boarding school. He and his brothers lived under the watchful eyes of school headmasters and supervisors, whose goal was to turn out loyal servants of tsarism. There were constant drills and strict rules; and also tale-bearing, informing and cramming. Felix found it all exceedingly difficult to bear. He fearlessly rose in defence of those unjustly punished and persecuted and earned himself a reputation of being constantly dissatisfied, a young man critical of the school customs and traditions. The most reactionary tutor, the German master, even demanded that Felix be expelled altogether.

He read a lot at school. He loved books, especially poetry, and tried his hand at writing verse. He had a good knowledge of the Polish and Russian classics—Adam Mickiewicz, Marja Konopnicka, Ludwik Kondratowicz, Boleslaw Prus, Alexander Pushkin, Mikhail Lermontov and Nikolai Nekrasov. He also liked to read Nikolai Gogol and Mikhail Saltykov-Shchedrin, and studied the works of Vissarion Belinsky and Alexander Herzen.

Having many friends among workers in Wilno, Dzerzhinsky gained a close view of the condition of the working class and could not help trying to find the answer to the obvious question: why the masses must work, and even so many still starve to death, while a handful of exploiters enjoy a life of leisure?

Beginning with the sixth grade, his faith in God began to waver, and in the seventh, it crumbled altogether. Since that time, Dzerzhinsky was an avowed atheist who did his best to grasp the laws of social life and find radical ways to put an end to injustice.

At that time, Marxist literature was banned. It was hard to find, being distributed mostly illegally. Dzerzhinsky wrote about that period: "I had to grope my way without guidance, without a hint from anyone." But the works of Marx, Engels and Lenin, which he somehow managed to obtain and thoroughly studied, clarified many things. The Marxist philosophy became his credo and shaped his world outlook.

At the age of 17, as a seventh-grader, Dzerzhinsky joined an illegal students' social- democratic self- development group. This is when he first read the Manifesto of the Communist Party written by Marx and

Engels, The Origin of the Family, Private Property and the State by Engels, Plekhanov's The Development of the Monist View of History, and the Erfurt Programme of the German SocialDemocracy, among others.

Dzerzhinsky's letters to relatives and friends reveal how he came to profess the positions of scientific communism and Marxism.

Since his childhood Dzerzhinsky had been devoted to his people, loved Polish literature and art, and had a good knowledge of Polish history. But even as a child he had many occasions to witness how Polish landlords and capitalists, who existed hand in glove with the Russian autocracy, exploited and maltreated the working masses, regardless of their nationality.

Even as a youth Dzerzhinsky was a consistent and convinced internationalist. He appreciated the strength and significance of the revolutionary movement in Russia, and was aware of the character of Poland's and Lithuania's capitalist way of development. He realised that only in collaboration with the Russian proletariat could the working people of Poland and Lithuania attain social and political freedom. Lenin wrote in 1914: "The Polish Social-Democrats were therefore quite right in ... pointing out that the national question was of secondary importance to Polish workers.... in proclaiming the extremely important principle that the Polish and the Russian workers must maintain the closest alliance in their class struggle."[3]

Having joined the revolutionary movement, Dzerzhinsky soon became an experienced agitator and populariser well versed in the methods of secret work. He was the organiser of youth study groups at the girls' school and technical high school, among Wilno's factory apprentices, handicraftsmen and workers. He livened up the meetings by discussing interesting topics. Even then, he realised the need to link working conditions at a particular factory with the more general goals of the class struggle, and to give the men a motive for joining the struggle.

12

While still at the boarding school, Dzerzhinsky strictly observed the rules of secrecy and was very cautious. It was at that time that he developed the traits essential for underground work: reserve, ability to swiftly assess a situation, and to act daringly and resolutely.

Dzerzhinsky's associate in the underground work, a working-class poet Andrzej Gulbinowicz, thus described him: "Comrade Jacub (Dzerzhinsky's underground alias.— Ed.) was a fiery eager youth. At meetings, he did not deliver long speeches or reports. He spoke concisely and clearly and willingly plunged into the work... He was indefatigable and it rubbed off on us."

The year 1894 marked a crucial turning point in Dzerzhinsky's life. This was when he, together with a small group of friends, swore on the Mountain of Gediminas in Wilno to devote his entire life to the struggle against evil and injustice, and for the freedom and happiness of the working people. It was an oath he would keep until his final heartbeat.

The year 1895 was a notable one in the history of the Russian revolutionary working- class movement: in St. Petersburg, Lenin set up the League of Struggle for the Emancipation of the Working Class, the nucleus of a proletarian party which opened up a new, proletarian stage in the liberation movement in Russia. The League, headed by Lenin, soon began to conduct mass activities among the workers, and succeeded in uniting Marxism with the working-class movement.

In the autumn of 1895 at the age of 18 years, Dzerzhinsky joined the Social-Democratic Party of Lithuania. His propaganda and organisational work was gaining in scope, and e remained active among the handicraftsmen and workers of Wilno. At that time, he had several Party pseudonyms, but his favourite one was Jacek. That was the name given him by the young railroad workers of Wilno whom he instructed at youth group meetings.

In October 1895 his grandmother, Kazimiera Januszewska, moved to Wilno. She took a house at 26 Poplawska St., and her grandchildren came to live with her. It was with great relief that Felix and his brothers left the loathsome boarding school.

Felix used the wing attic to print illegal leaflets. He and his fellow-revolutionaries plastered them around the city at night. The strictest secrecy was maintained, and no one ever learned about the existence of an underground press in his grandmother's house.

But Felix did not spend all his time writing and mimeographing leaflets. In the basement of St. Bernardinu Cathedral, he equipped another underground press. "At night, we used a hectograph to print pamphlets and leaflets," reminisced Maria Voitkevich-Krzhizhanovskaya. "The secrecy of the surroundings ... made us closely watch every movement and listen to every sound. Our nerves were strained. Felix, who was totally engrossed in what he was doing, looked inspired." Felix set up another hectograph in another district not far from a police station, where no one ever thought of looking for subversive activity.

In December 1895 he represented the Lithuanian youth at the congress of illegal students' groups in Warsaw. Their purpose was to study Polish (which was banned at educational establishments) and the history of Poland, and to involve young people in the struggle against the autocracy. The majority of congress delegates, as well as its leaders, held nationalistic views. Dzerzhinsky's speech at the congress established him as a resolute champion of proletarian internationalism. He spoke with confidence of an inevitable victory, was adamant in his demands and filled with revolutionary enthusiasm. According to Bronislaw Koszutski, who thought like Dzerzhinsky, their position at the congress was shared by only three or four other delegates belonging to a small group of left-wingers.

Persistent work in educating the masses about revolutionary theory finally yielded results. In 1896, Dzerzhinsky organised the first (in Wilno) congress of social-democratic students, which approved a curriculum for students' groups drawn up with Dzerzhinsky's active participation.

At that time, his mother's health began to fail. More than once Felix escorted her to Warsaw for treatments. He was devoted to her, and her illness disturbed him deeply. He frequently came to visit her in hospital. "I fervently hope that mother will be all right in about a month," he wrote to his sister Aldona.

But Helena grew worse and worse, and died on January 14, 1896. It was a severe blow for Felix, however, he refused to be overcome by grief and redoubled his efforts as a Party member.

Dzerzhinsky was doing well at school, but the atmosphere of the establishment made him detest it. Studies took up a great deal of his time and interfered with his work in the revolutionary movement. But his mother had wanted him to get an education and, not wishing to upset her, Felix carried on at school.

However, after her death and having given serious thought to his future, he decided to leave school in the spring of 1896, his last, eighth year. The school management had no idea of his illegal activities and was unable to accuse him of anything undesirable.

Having made his decision to leave school, he once walked into the tutors' room and openly attacked one of the most hated and reactionary tutors, chauvinist Mazikov. The flabbergasted tutors had to listen to his views of education in tsarist Russia.

Felix's aunt Zofja Pilar requested the headmaster to allow her nephew to leave school. She was given a certificate stating that student of the 8th grade of the First Wilno School Felix Dzerzhinsky terminated his studies in accordance with his aunt's request. The certificate gave Felix the right to take his graduation exams in another town and enter a university without entrance exams.

After leaving school, Dzerzhinsky became a full-time professional revolutionary. "Faith must be followed by deeds, and one must be closer to the masses and learn together with them," he wrote later in his autobiography. His activities were mostly among the working class. He lived the life of workers and fought for their interests. On August 29, 1916, he wrote to his brother Wladyslaw that he had become a part of the broad proletarian masses and shared all their strivings, torments and hopes with them. He also stated that he felt he had found a way straight to the people's hearts and seemed to sense them beating. The social conditions in which Felix worked gave him the opportunity to gain invaluable experience of the revolutionary struggle, and to study the theory, strategy and tactics of Marxism, the international doctrine of the proletariat.

Throwing himself wholeheartedly into his work, Jacek asked to be sent to the people, to carry out assignments that would be more fulfilling than teaching students' groups. "I managed to become an agitator," he wrote in his autobiography, "to get to the working-class strata which had hitherto been untouched by revolutionary propaganda."

Among Dzerzhinsky's closest friends were Aleksander, Wincenty and Mikolaj Birinczyk, agitators with a working-class background, Waclaw Balcewicz, a shoemaker and revolutionary Social-Democrat, and Andrzej Gulbinowicz.

Felix and his friends were working against great odds. Wilno workers were mostly employed at small factories or in workshops scattered all over the city, so agitation and propaganda consumed a great deal of time and energy. The disunited proletarian masses had to be helped to evolve a socialist consciousness and roused to take part in concerted action. At the same time, it was essential to combat the Polish Socialist Party (PSP),[4] which was doing its best to take advantage of the workers' political backwardness and lack of unity to extend its influence over them.

Wilno workers celebrated May Day 1896 in secret gatherings out of town. They were sponsored and organised by Social-Democrats, including Dzerzhinsky. Preserved in the manuscript section of the archive of the Central Library of the Lithuanian SSR is Dzerzhinsky's speech which he himself wrote down. The contents reveal quite clearly that at that time he was already a competent propaganda worker trying to elevate the workers' class-consciousness. He effectively promoted the masses' political education and involved the working-class strata into the revolutionary movement. In his speech, Dzerzhinsky levelled criticism against the PSP accusing it of chauvinism, setting workers of different nationalities against each other, and failure to fight for working-class interests. He emphasised that a mass proletarian movement was instrumental in this struggle.

16

On May 1, the First Inaugural Congress of the Social-Democratic Party of Lithuania (SDPL) was held at the flat of doctor Anton Damaszewicz. Here a difference of opinion on the national question became apparent. The Marxist, revolutionary wing of the SDPL was represented by true internationalists Felix Dzerzhinsky, Aleksander Birinczyk, Waclaw Balcewicz, J. Janulewicz, G. Malewski and others. Anton Domaszewicz and Alfons Morawski, who headed the Party, and held erroneous views, were instrumental in having a petty-bourgeois and nationalist programme adopted.

Dzerzhinsky took part in the work of the congress as a representative of the Social- Democratic youth. He vigorously championed the Marxist principles of the class struggle and proletarian internationalism, but he and his supporters were in the minority.

In Wilno and later in Kowno (now Kaunas, Lithuanian Soviet Socialist Republic) Dzerzhinsky worked to bring the Lithuanian Social-Democrats closer to the Russian Social-Democrats and the Russian workingclass movement, and did a great deal to introduce the principles of proletarian internationalism. He took part in a mass campaign aimed at giving the workers a correct understanding or pressing political and economic issues and the more general goals of the class struggle.

After the death of his mother in 1896, Dzerzhinsky made his home for a while with his sister Aldona. But in January 1897, not wishing to further inconvenience her, he rented a room in a workers' suburb in Zarechnaya St., where he lived up to February 1897.

The revolutionary outbursts in the spring and summer of 1897 had begun to annoy the police in Wilno. The gendarmes were particularly interested in the activities of Felix Dzerzhinsky—Jacek—who was very popular among Wilno workers. His arrest seemed imminent.

With the upswing in the revolutionary movement, the Party sought to extend its activities to other Lithuanian towns, especially the industrial town of Kowno, which did not have a social-democratic organisation. It was decided to send Dzerzhinsky there since he was the best propagandist and organiser. Leaving Wilno in early March 1897 Dzerzhinsky registered himself in Kowno as an aristocrat from Wilno Gubernia who was himself a student and instructed others. And that was the truth. In Kowno he had acquired a great deal of knowledge as a political leader and organiser of workers.

Dzerzhinsky's task was by no means easy. Informers were everywhere-, the police had recently disbanded the organisation of the PSP; factories and workshops employed workers of many nationalities—Lithuanians, Byelorussians, Jews, Poles, Russians, and Letts; workshops had from two to five workers, while large factories, for instance those belonging to Tilmans and Rekos, employed from 500 to 800 workers, many of whom were poverty-stricken, ignorant people. There was a great deal for Dzerzhinsky to do in Kowno.

To gain the workers' confidence, he got a job at a bookbinder s shop, naturally, without informing either the police or his landlord. This work allowed him to develop the skills required for secret activities. He learned to "do up" various documents (i.e., conceal them in book bindings) for the use of SocialDemocrats who were forced to work underground.

At the workshop Dzerzhinsky had the opportunity to procure paper and paint for printing revolutionary leaflets and newspapers. Besides, his work as a bookbinder gave him a means of subsistence, although a very meagre one. His working hours were long and the wages extremely low. Not infrequently he went hungry. To earn a little extra money, he gave lessons. Speaking about that time, Dzerzhinsky said, "The smell of pancakes or something else made my mouth water more than once when I went into a worker's flat. Sometimes, I would be invited to dinner, but I refused, saying that I had already eaten, although my stomach was empty."

During the five months of his stay in Kowno Felix demonstrated his tremendous capacity for work, ability to think quickly and clearly, and a gift for attracting people, getting to understand them, stirring them to action and inspiring faith in the final victory of the proletariat.

In his work as an agitator and propagandist, Dzerzhinsky repeatedly focused on the struggle waged by workers of other

18

nationalities, particularly the citizens of St. Petersburg. Exposing the nationalist ideology and policies .of the PSP, he tried to make it clear to the workers that only joint action with the Russians would enable Lithuanians, Poles and other nationalities to abolish the autocracy and capitalist oppression and exploitation, and gain true freedom.

Dzerzhinsky's work in Kowno demonstrated his political maturity and his competence as an organiser and populariser. At factories and workshops, he singled out and trained the most promising workers, both men and women, who were later to make up the nucleus of the social-democratic organisation in Kowno. "The work went well and yielded good results. Contacts were established with all factories," reminisced Dzerzhinsky later. His closest associate at the time was Juzef Olechnowicz.

Dzerzhinsky knew how to efficiently use oral and written propaganda. Arriving in Kowno in March 1897 he published the first (and, unfortunately, last) issue of the illegal paper Kowienski Robotnik (Kowno Worker) as early as April 1. The newspaper was small, written and mimeographed by Dzerzhinsky himself. On one of his numerous visits to Wilno, the Wilno Committee of the Social-Democratic Party discussed the issue of the Kowienski Robotnik he had brought with him.

"We noticed," wrote Andrzey Gulbinowicz, "that the first pages were written in a clear and elegant hand, the others, in very small and often illegible print... He [Felix] explained that he had been pressed for time, having to write the entire paper himself, and that he also had to print and distribute it running from factory to factory and talking to workers."

The articles printed in the paper vividly reflected the situation prevailing at Kowno factories, where workers had to toil for 13-14 hours for a pittance. The paper depicted their hard and hopeless existence and urged them to take action to protect their rights.

Forced to work with the utmost secrecy due to the threat of police reprisals, Dzerzhinsky was of course unable to openly advocate the establishment of a social- democratic organisation. But the meaning of his essays was clear enough. He also wrote and mimeographed the memorable illegal leaflet "May Day Workers' Holiday", which was distributed in Kowno and Wilno. "Let every worker with an advanced consciousness explain to his brothers what we should do, what we can attain and how, and what sort of force we shall represent when everyone comes to understand our cause and express solidarity with us, i.e., when everyone will stand up for all, and all for one ... let the fraternal ties of unity be established among us from this day; let this holiday be the day of our rebirth!"

Dzerzhinsky also wrote for the Wilno Echo Zycia robotniczego (Echo of Workers' Life) and for the Robotnik Litewski (Lithuanian Worker) printed abroad. His articles discussed pressing issues of the working-class movement.

In his party work, Dzerzhinsky emphasised the political education of the proletariat and its class struggle against the autocracy and bourgeoisie. In an essay entitled "The Schmidt Factory", Dzerzhinsky wrote: "Political freedom is our watchword in the struggle against the government. And when we shall overthrow the tsarist government, when we shall have a chance to unite and openly discuss our affairs, when we shall have an opportunity to openly enlighten our uninformed comrades, then the solidarity and strength of the working class will grow, and, having put an end to the rule of tsarism, we shall then also put an end to the rule of capitalists. Factories, mines, railways, all land and implements of labour will become the property of all, everyone will work as much as necessary—socialism will come. The whole working world is striving towards socialism—let us, too, strive for emancipation!"

While in Kowno, Dzerzhinsky kept up the proletarian struggle with many strikes, trying to make them organised and directed towards clearly defined goals. He wrote in his autobiography: "At that time, I received the practical experience needed to stage a strike." A strike Dzerzhinsky organised in Aleksot, a Kowno suburb, was particularly successful: the working day was reduced by three hours. That strike had not only economic but major political significance for Kowno workers, and for the entire Lithuanian proletariat.

Dzerzhinsky's contributions to the Kowienski Robotnik and the leaflets he wrote helped to enhance the workers' class consciousness, urged them to join forces and act in an organised manner, and promoted proletarian solidarity. In his addresses to workers, he always urged them to link their concrete economic demands with the pressing political tasks of the proletariat.

In his article "How Should We Fight?", he stated that strikes were very efficient and discussed how to stage them. He stressed the need for strict organisation, explained the negative consequences of spontaneous outbursts, and the senselessness of destroying equipment and machinery.

Another important article written by Dzerzhinsky, "April 16", praised the struggle of the Russian proletariat, particularly the activities of St. Petersburg workers. Dzerzhinsky pointed out the important contribution of their organised strike movement to improving the conditions of workers throughout the country, including Lithuania, and called upon Lithuanian workers to follow in the steps of their St. Petersburg comrades.

While in Kowno, Dzerzhinsky worked with extreme caution. Even at that early stage of his career as a revolutionary, he realised the grave danger posed by political provocations staged by tsarist authorities, and the need to combat the actions of agent-provocateurs. "There must not be traitors in our midst who betray their brothers to our foe... Let the tyrants perish, let the blood-suckers perish, let the traitors perish, and long live our holy workers cause!" he wrote in the leaflet "May Day Workers' Holiday".

The upsurge of the workers' campaign in Kowno factories annoyed the police and factory-owners. Gendarmes suspected that an experienced propagandist and organiser was operating in the town. For quite a long time the police were unable to track Dzerzhinsky down due to the secrecy of the underground work, and the efforts of the workers to protect their leader. However, on July 17, 1897, the gendarmes managed to capture him with the assistance of an agent provocateur. In Kowno, he was arrested and served a prison sentence for the first time in his life.

According to the report of a police colonel, a search of Dzerzhinsky's flat yielded clippings from "permitted and banned" papers, and legal and illegal literature: about strikes, unrest, and clashes between the workers, on the one hand, and the police and the troops, on the other, both in Russia and abroad. Dzerzhinsky's notes of his talks with workers, and a list of Kowno factories with the number of workers employed at them. Also found was a postal sheet stating the condition of peasant holdings in Russia, as well as a handwritten excerpt from the poem "The Sun of Truth Shall Rise after a Bloody Dawn". Dzerzhinsky had a small library (36 books in all) of popular scientific books and fiction, up to 5 copies of each, and a catalogue.

A search of the arrested workers' rooms conducted on August 11, 1897, revealed that some had books from Dzerzhinsky's library, and he was charged with distributing banned literature. But the incriminating materials were insufficient for a conviction, partly because Dzerzhinsky was still a minor. However, even during the investigation "that dangerous political criminal" was in fact kept under the harsh regimen of penal servitude. He was repeatedly locked up in the punishment cell without food or water, and several times he was beaten unconscious.

There were endless confrontations, intimidation, threats, blackmail and promises designed to force Dzerzhinsky to reveal his contacts. He spent about a year in prison before trial, and behaved honourably during his first severe ordeal. He retained his cheerful disposition and his belief in a brighter future for his people. His brother Stanislaw sent him books, and he began to learn German.

Trying to cheer up his sister Aldona, he wrote: "Although I am here in prison, I am not depressed... Prison is frightening only for those who are weak in spirit."

Dzerzhinsky secretly slipped out letters and essays for the Echo Zycia robotniczego, in which he described the harsh prison life. When he learned that Domaszewicz was trying to engineer a split in the working-class movement, he lashed out against nationalist views and did what he could to unite the SDPL and the RSDLP. Despite the restrictions of prison life, he managed to keep in touch with people outside.

On June 10, 1898, the superintendant of the Kowno prison informed Dzerzhinsky that, in conformity with the "royal command" issued by Tsar Nicholas II, Dzerzhinsky was to be exiled, without a court hearing, under police surveillance to Vyatka Gubernia for a term of three years. On June 13, he was to begin his journey.

Aldona waited for him by the prison gates the entire night of June 12. Finally, the sun rose, and, bound together, the prisoners began to troop out surrounded by mounted and unmounted guards. Felix was thin and pale, but his head was raised as proudly as ever. His eyes lit up with joy at the sight of his sister. She ran up to him but a gendarme pushed her roughly aside. Aldona ran along the pavement trying to keep up with Felix, tears streaming down her face. "Don't cry, sister, I am all right, I'll write to you," said Felix in a loud and firm voice.

The prisoners travelled in overcrowded convict coaches. Political prisoners were kept together with murderers and thieves. I spent more time in prison cells than on the road," wrote Dzerzhinsky. But the worst of the journey began after the stay in Kaluga prison. The prisoners were kept in the tightly closed hold of a ship. They suffered from thirst and hunger; many were unable to bear the privations and died on the way. "I sailed along the Oka, Volga and Kama. We were locked up in the so-called 'hold' like sardines in a tin. There was not enough light and air." Thus Dzerzhinsky was becoming acquainted with the tsarist empire's system of eliminating "dissidents" which was approved by law and the church.

The number of political prisoners continued to grow. Dzerzhinsky made friends with some of them and, as an old-timer, tried to make things easier for them. In turn, new arrivals told him about the latest revolutionary developments in Russia. Thus Dzerzhinsky came to know Russian Social-Democrats and was later able to establish contacts with the Bolsheviks.

On July 27, 1898, Dzerzhinsky arrived in Vyatka (now Kirov). Governor Klingenberg assigned him to the small town of Nolinsk. But the ship that he was to sail on failed to arrive because of low water.

Nearly all his comrades had already been sent on their way, but Dzerzhinsky remained under guard. He was exhausted by the journey and fell ill.

On August 6 he wrote to the Governor requesting that he be allowed to travel to Nolinsk at his own expense. Finally, on August 14, he was released from prison, and on the 15th received permission to sail on a small private steamer unescorted and paying his own fare. A Polish engineer, one Zawisza, who was working at a railroad construction site, helped him to get hold of some money and clothes.

Nolinsk was a small town of about 5,000 residents with a tobacco factory, a library and a hospital. There, Dzerzhinsky met and became friendly with Margarita Nikoleva, also a political exile.

On December 1, 1898, Dzerzhinsky began to keep a diary, which now makes profoundly moving reading. It just shows how strong and honourable young Dzerzhinsky was, how he devoted his life to the cause of revolution, and how critically he judged himself. Writing about Nikoleva, he said: "It seems to me that she puts the personal soul, personal qualities above all else. She believes that the important thing is to develop personal feelings, such as compassion, responsiveness, truthfulness, etc. ... Perhaps I'll be able to awaken a person of action in her, a fighting person, a person who is actively looking for real life... " And he did help her to understand many complicated issues, such as social relations.

On Wednesdays the exiles assembled to discuss political questions, the latest development, and new books. Dzerzhinsky was the centre of these gatherings thanks to his intelligence, extensive knowledge and firm principles.

Soon after his arrival in Nolinsk, he found a job at the tobacco factory as a cloth- printer. Working hours were from 6 a.m. to 8 p.m., and the wages extremely low. Tobacco dust made his eyes smart and ate into his lungs. But he was happy—he felt at home among the workers and enjoyed trying to awaken their desire for social emancipation. His popularity among the exiles, local residents and factory workers evoked the sharp displeasure of the police and the factory owners, and he was fired.

Dzerzhinsky was kept under constant open police surveillance in Nolinsk. Gendarmes often broke into his room, eavesdropped, and instructed his landlords to observe the activities of their tenant and his visitors. It was an intolerable existence and he was forced to change flats often.

"As I am forever changing flats," he wrote to his sister, "don't write to me at my home address but straight to the post office in Nolinsk."

Constant hunger and poor living conditions aggravated his illnesses. His trachoma grew worse: he was threatened with blindness. Finally, he ended up at the local hospital. However, even there the police did not leave him alone. At the Governor's order he was forcefully evicted from the hospital and, in freezing weather, taken to the village of Kaigorodskoye, 400 versts (some 265 miles) north of Nolinsk. With him went Alexander Yakshin. Dzerzhinsky had spent about five months in Nolinsk.

On the eve of year 1899, Dzerzhinsky found himself in the farthermost corner of Vyatka Gubernia. In winter, it was bitterly cold (the temperature dropped below 40°C; in spring and autumn, the roads were completely impassable, and the summer was scorching hot. The village stood in the midst of bogs which emitted a putrid miasma. Clouds of gnats and midges made life miserable. Kaigorodskoye was a truly god-forsaken hole, which seemed to have no contact with the outside world. The pub and church were the "spiritual centres" of the settlement, which consisted of about a hundred ramshackle huts sitting low in a hollow.

Dzerzhinsky suffered tremendously. The climate was making him very ill, and neither a doctor's services nor drugs were available. He lived in constant need, did not have enough to eat and was poorly clothed.

The worst thing, however, was the isolation from his friends and from revolutionary work. Afterwards, Dzerzhinsky remarked that the time in Kaigorodskoye was the worst of all. But even during that period he remained an optimist, still believing in a brighter future and continuing to further his education. His eyes hurt, but he read all the same. "The future will require that we be knowledgeable," he wrote to Margarita Nikoleva on January 29, 1899.

Despite the constant surveillance and strict censorship, Dzerzhinsky managed to keep in touch with his friends outside. Through exiles living in Nolinsk and Slobodskoye, he received news of the activities of Party comrades. Although thousands of kilometres lay between him and Wilno, he tried to remain part of his friends' struggle.

Dzerzhinsky's letters from Kaigorodskoye describe his first exile, his interests, his Marxist world outlook, and personal qualities of integrity.

On November 5, 1898, he wrote to Aldona, "My views are quite established ... life can destroy me ... but it will never change me ... only the grave will terminate my struggle."

His letters to Margarita Nikoleva reveal that the young revolutionary had gained a clear understanding of the complex questions of social life, political economy, philosophy, and ethics. He thoroughly studied the second volume of Marx's Capital. "Recently I've been doing mostly political economy," he wrote to Nikoleva on January 21, 1899. "I'm terribly interested in the law of equalisation of general rate of profit, i.e., average rate of profit, and the way the theory of value (i.e., surplus value.—Auth.) relates to it."

A knowledge of Marxism enabled him to level bold and well-founded criticism against such a distinguished bourgeois scholars as the British subjectivist philosopher John Stuart Mill, the Russian "legal Marxist" Bulgakov, and liberal Narodniks (Russian Populists).

Critically analysing Mill s utility theory, Dzerzhinsky also set forth his own views of psychology and ethics. "I am interested in morality as a social phenomenon. From this point of view, morality is a product of social development, the development of social relations among the people stemming from economic relations, which in their turn depend on the development of productive forces and the technical form of these forces. My view proceeds from my overall world outlook... It is not the consciousness of men that determines their existence; but their social existence that determines their consciousness."

Dzerzhinsky worked out a plan for the systematic study of fundamental works. Of great interest are his synopses of the second volume of Capital and Mill's works which he sent to Nikoleva and which reveal his ability to deal with complicated issues.

Dzerzhinsky thought highly of group discussions, and sympathised with Margarita Nikoleva in one of- his letters: It is, however, not very pleasant to study on one's own. I know this from my own experience." And indeed, his very serious studies must have required a great deal of time and energy, especially in the remote Kaigorodskoye, where he had neither books nor friends. From time to time he managed to obtain permission to travel to the bigger village of Slobodskoye (and sometimes went secretly), where SocialDemocrats, including the Marxist Pyotr Stucka, were living in exile.

Dzerzhinsky's notes on the condition of peasant holdings in Russia that had been found and confiscated during the search of his Kowno flat show that he had carefully studied rural economics. While in Nolinsk and Kaigorodskoye, he continued to work on this question. His letter to Aldona written from Nolinsk on November 5, 1898, contains an exhaustive description of the country's agriculture and its development trends, and notes, among other things, the ruin of many peasant farms and the growing tendency among the peasantry to leave the land and seek employment elsewhere.

Criticising liberal Narodniks, Dzerzhinsky pointed to the process of stratification under way among the peasantry. "Village life-what is it really like? It is a life full of ignorance, full of petty cares, a life that is not the same for everyone ... life of gradual impoverishment of the majority and its enslavement by the kulaks."

While in Kaigorodskoye, Dzerzhinsky spent much time among local peasants. Frequently, he could be seen helping them to take in the harvest or lay in a supply of fodder. He tried to awaken their consciousness and make them see the need for protesting the exploitation and arbitrary rule of the tsarist authorities. The peasants changed his first name to Vassily, which sounded better to the

Russian ear. Dzerzhinsky helped the peasants as much as he could, mostly by drawing up requests for the division of land or property. He was always ready to come to the aid of a friend. He lent moral support to Margarita Nikoleva when she was feeling low, and was invariably attentive and considerate towards A. Yakshin, whose life had been full of hardships, Dzerzhinsky did his best to bolster his faith in his own strength and the ultimate victory of revolution.

Dzerzhinsky was a man of principle, and one of the things he could never accept was grovelling before the police authorities. He was self-critical and constantly worked to eradicate his own weaknesses. He would closely analyse his behaviour, desires, feelings and attitude to people. "To be strong, one must throw away everything unworthy," he wrote to Nikoleva. "I will become, and am becoming, a better man, and if at times I feel terrible—well, that means that the struggle goes on, and it is a good thing, since I will emerge from it ready for action. I will live for the cause alone."

Even at the beginning of his revolutionary career, Dzerzhinsky's views of morality, family, friendship and love stemmed from his world outlook. He was convinced that man's personal happiness rested on his public activities. "It's not as if there was just one feeling. There are two vital feelings: a personal feeling and its support and basis—a public feeling.' He believed that love and friendship are a great source of energy and strength, building up a person's will and fortitude in the struggle. But, he said, not every feeling gives strength. "We can allow only that feeling that strengthens the will."

On February 15, 1899, Dzerzhinsky was given a medical examination and declared unfit for military service. He was told he would certainly die young. But that horrible prognosis failed to crush his will. He was not afraid of death and would not humble himself to beg the Governor to transfer him to another, healthier, place of exile.

What tormented him, though, was his belief that he had done too little for the emancipation of the people. "It is indeed a bitter, an unbearably painful thought: to have lived and done nothing, to have brought nothing with me... No, this will not be," he wrote to Margarita Nikoleva. And so he decided to escape in order to accomplish as much as he could in the time that was left him. "I shall try to arrange my short life so as to live it as fully as possible," he wrote in another letter. Soon it became apparent that the medical board's report had been made for a reason: to prevent the dangerous rebel from coming into contact with servicemen.

As spring drew near, Dzerzhinsky began to prepare his escape in earnest. He went on long hunting trips so that his guards would not get alarmed at a long absence. This also gave him a chance to thoroughly acquaint himself with the locality and map out his escape route, and to somewhat improve his health.

More than anything else, Dzerzhinsky missed taking part in revolutionary activities. He was spoiling for a fight. In a letter to Aldona, he wrote, "I missed my homeland ... the homeland that has so grown into my soul that nothing can tear it out, for it is a part of my heart... Passing before my eyes were the images of the past and still more vivid pictures of the future... This life ... was poisoning me... I gathered my last strength and escaped."

Not later than August 27, 1899, he fled unnoticed from Kaigorodskoye, though the police were keeping an eye on everyone. On October 30, a circular from the police department instituted a search for Dzerzhinsky throughout the Russian Empire.

The escape route mapped out by Dzerzhinsky was not an easy one, and quite different from what the police expected. Alone, he courageously sailed a small boat along the upper reaches of the Kama, whose banks were overgrown by thick forests. After safely reaching a railway station, he boarded a train and arrived in Wilno much earlier than the arrival of the police circular ordering a search for the " dangerous criminal".

"So I was back at Wilno," he wrote in his autobiography. "The Lithuanian Social- Democrats were engaged in talks with the PSP on the subject of unification. I was the most resolute opponent of nationalism... When I got back to Wilno my old comrades were already in exile, and students were calling the tune. I was kept away from the workers and told to go abroad." However, Dzerzhinsky did not go abroad but rather travelled secretly to Warsaw.

Thus ended an important stage in the life of Felix Dzerzhinsky—six years of serious studies, the assimilation of Marxism, and constant revolutionary struggle.

September 1899 opened a new page in his career; he became actively involved in the Polish revolutionary working-class movement.

* * *

Notes

[1]Old Style is used in the book up to February 14, 1918.

[2]In 1880, a nephew, architect Justyn Dzerzhinsky, helped Edmund build a new and larger log house with a garret, where Felix spent his childhood.

[3]V. I. Lenin, "The Right of Nations to Self-Determination", Collected Works, Vol. 20, Progress Publishers, Moscow, 1964, pp. 433-34.

[4]The Polish Socialist Party-a reformist nationalist party established in 1892. In 1906 it split into the PSP Left-wing (Polish Socialist Party-Lewisa) and the PSP Right-wing, so-called "revolutionary" faction. The PSP Left-wing, which was under the influence of the Social-Democracy of the Kingdom of Poland and Lithuania and the growing working-class revolutionary movement gradually adopted a revolutionary stand. In December 1918, it joined the Social-Democratic Party of the Kingdom of Poland and Lithuania to form the united Communist Workers' Party of Poland (CWPP).

Chapter Two

PARTY WORK ON THE EVE OF AND DURING THE FIRST RUSSIAN REVOLUTION (1899-1907)

By the time Dzerzhinsky had arrived in Warsaw, the major industrial and cultural centre of the Kingdom of Poland,[1] the revolutionary Polish working-class movement had gained substantial experience in its class struggle. In March 1893, a Marxist workers' party had been formed—the Social-Democracy of the Kingdom of Poland (SDKP). Its organisers and theoretical leaders were Rosa Luxemburg, Julian Marchlewski, Leon Jogiches (Jan Tyszka) and Adolf Warski.

Its central organ, Sprawa Robotnicza (printed in Paris), as well as leaflets and appeals urged the Polish workers to fight the autocracy and capitalism in collaboration with the Russian proletariat, popularised the Marxist principles of the class struggle and of proletarian internationalism, and directed sharp criticism against the nationalist programme and tactics of the PSP, whose leadership was spreading mistrust and hostility against the revolutionary working-class movement in Russia and substituting the ideas of socialism and proletarian internationalism with a bourgeois chauvinistic programme.

After 1896, the work of the SDKP was seriously crippled as a consequence of mass arrests and the effective banning of the activities of most of its branches.

When Dzerzhinsky arrived in Warsaw, the SDKP organisation there was practically nonexistent. Propaganda work among the workers was conducted by the PSP and the Bund.[2] The Social-Democrats who had escaped arrest did not carry out any organisational activities among the masses but confined themselves to working in isolated workers' and students' groups. Dzerzhinsky soon found his bearings in the situation, got in touch with the leading social- democratic workers (specifically, shoemaker Jan Rosol and his son Antek), and set out to restore the Social-Democratic organisation. His very first talks, which he gave under the name of the Astronomer, demonstrated that many worker members of the PSP did not really support that party's programme and tactics. They had joined it only in the absence of a socialdemocratic organisation and because they could have access to banned literature. Together with Jan and Antek Rosol, Dzerzhinsky initiated a campaign among the working-class members of the PSP to win them over to the side or Social- Democracy. Their efforts were the most successful among shoemakers, who numbered about 45,000 in Warsaw at the time.

The shoemakers worked mostly at home, taking the finished footwear to their contractor once a week. Generally the whole family was involved with the work. The conditions of their life and labour were abysmal. They worked 14-18 hours a day but earned barely subsistence wages. Given this sort of exploitation, even the workers' most elementary needs were not being met. Dzerzhinsky studied the conditions of their life and work and. gathered them for talks. One such gathering attracted some 200 people (during a strike at Eisenhorn's company). In his speech Dzerzhinsky tried to explain in simple and concrete terms the essence of capitalist exploitation. He suggested ways in which the workers should conduct talks with the management and talked about the need to link the workers' campaign for better wages with the struggle to overthrow tsarism.

One of the men at the gathering, Jan Lesniewski, wrote later: "The meeting has forever remained in my memory. It was the first such large-scale meeting between Felix Dzerzhinsky and the shoemakers of Warsaw. He won the confidence and affection not only of shoemakers but other workers of Warsaw."

After four months of propaganda work, Dzerzhinsky and the Rosols managed to get away from the PSP a large number of workers—carpenters, metalworkers, shoemakers and bakers and, in the autumn of 1899, to restore the Social-Democratic organisation under the name of the Working-Class Union of SocialDemocrats.

The principal goal was to win over the rest of the working-class members of the PSP. With this end in view, Dzerzhinsky wrote a popular essay containing well-considered criticism of the nationalist programme advanced by the PSP and set forth the goals of Social-Democrats. He also touched on the question of Poland's independence, which the PSP liked to play up, and proved that PSP leaders were employing the slogan of Polish independence as a smoke-screen for their activities, that they were intentionally silent on the issue of political rights that the "independent democratic Polish republic" was supposed to grant the workers.

Dzerzhinsky wrote: "Consequently, it is the socialist system that is the ultimate objective of our struggle, and it would be Utopian to think about its establishment in Poland now."

Under the conditions prevailing in the country at that time, the call to establish an independent Poland could only have an adverse effect on the working-class movement in Lithuania and Poland, where the working population was made up of Poles, Jews, Lithuanians, Letts, Germans and Russians.

Working-class agitators copied the essay in longhand and distributed it through the city in an attempt to acquaint the workers with the goals of the revolution.

The Warsaw Social-Democratic branch headed workers' strikes and meetings, mimeographed leaflets, and set up five study groups to train agitators—three among shoemakers and bakers and two among carpenters and metalworkers. The classes, which were conducted by Dzerzhinsky, studied the Party programme and tactics and discussed current affairs.

The organisation was in dire need of banned Marxist literature. Therefore, oral propaganda became very important. Despite the constant threat of arrest, Dzerzhinsky took an active part in this work. Daily, he spoke at workers' clandestine meetings. "I myself had to write, conduct propaganda, establish contacts with the intelligentsia and mimeograph," he wrote later. "Arrest was imminent, but I could not stop my work, for the workers' needs had to be satisfied."

He also kept in touch with Lithuanian Social-Democrats who held internationalist views in the hope of eventually uniting the Social-Democrats of Poland and Lithuania into a single party. In late December 1899 Dzerzhinsky held a meeting in Wilno with local Social-Democrats Mieczyslaw Kozlowski, Edward Sokolowski, and Piotr Sunkielewicz. There he set forth his plan of party unification and explained why he felt there was a need to decisively combat the PSP and consolidate the links between the working-class movement in Lithuania and the Kingdom of Poland on the one hand and the Russian proletarian movement on the other. It was also decided at this meeting that the Warsaw organisation of the SDKP, the Working-Class Union of Social-Democrats, would prepare and publish a draft programme of the united party, and an inaugural congress was mapped out for early 1900.

A provisional organisational centre was elected. It was headed by Dzerzhinsky and also included Jan Rosol, Mieczyslaw Kozlowski and Edward Sokolowski.

Upon his return to Warsaw, Dzerzhinsky mimeographed the draft programme. Thus work began to set up a party— the Social-Democracy of the Kingdom of Poland and Lithuania (SDKPP and L). The congress of the Party's groups abroad held in Leipzig in February 1900 approved the establishment of a united
party.

In January 1900 Dzerzhinsky and his comrades set out to organise an underground printing press.

However, their efforts were stopped short due to Dzerzhinsky's arrest. On the morning of January 23, 1900, at a meeting of one of the workers' groups, Dzerzhinsky was seized and locked up in No. 10 Block of the Warsaw Citadel. On the night of the same day, 18-year-old Antek Rosol, Dzerzhinsky's friend and associate, was arrested at his parents' flat.

The arrest of Dzerzhinsky and other active Social- Democrats dealt a severe blow to the young and still not very stable party. However, Jan Rosol and the activists who had managed to escape arrest soon relaunched the work of the Warsaw Social-Democratic branch. In June 1900, the Party committee consisting of five members was set up and prepared for its second congress.

In August of the same year, a congress of the Social-Democratic branches of the Kingdom of Poland and Lithuania was convened in Otwock (not far from Warsaw). It announced the establishment of a united party, the Social-Democracy of the Kingdom of Poland and

Lithuania. It also adopted a decision to establish closer contacts with the Russian Social-Democrats, and elected the Party's Main Board of five members.

According to the Rules, branches in the Kingdom of Poland and in Lithuania were autonomous, with each electing its own Central Committee of five members.

In the meantime Dzerzhinsky remained in prison (first in Warsaw and later in Siedlce) undergoing a preliminary investigation. Every effort was made to gather enough evidence to incriminate him.

His prison dossier reads, in part: "The leader of the gathering was aristocrat Felix Dzerzhinsky known as the Bookbinder, who delivered a speech on the need to unite the Polish workers' party with the Russian Social-Democrats in order to overthrow tsarism, and promised to supply those present with banned literature printed in St. Petersburg." The investigators tried to break the political prisoner, who was ill with tuberculosis, not only physically but morally, to make him "lose his illusions" and give up the revolutionary struggle. But they reckoned without sufficient knowledge of Dzerzhinsky's character. Although only 23 years old, he behaved with courage and dignity, and openly admitted that he was a convinced Social-Democrat and opponent of the autocracy, that he lived in Warsaw illegally and was engaged exclusively in popularisation activities among workers.

Proof of his moral strength and indomitable spirit is found in his letter to Aldona written from the Siedlce prison on October 8, 1901: "I am much younger than you are, but I think that in my short life I have absorbed so many different impressions that they would suffice for an old man... I cannot either hate or love half-heartedly. I cannot give away only half of my soul. I will either give it all, or give nothing. I have drained not only the bitter cup of life but its sweet cup, too, and if somebody says to me: look at your wrinkled forehead, your exhausted body, your present life, look and realise that life has broken you, I will reply: it is not life that has broken me but I who have broken life; it is not life that has drained me but I who have taken all I could from it."

These words accurately characterise the young revolutionary. Even as a child, he had never tried to appear anything than what he really was. "In this revolutionary," wrote Clara Zetkin,[3] "everything was genuine and honest: his love and his hatred, his enthusiasm and his wrath, his words and his deeds."

When the investigation was over, the Minister of Justice suggested that Dzerzhinsky be exiled to Archangel Gubernia under police surveillance for four years, counting the time of the preliminary investigation. However, the police department did not agree with this "lenient" sentence.

In early January 1902 Dzerzhinsky was transferred from the Siedlce prison to the Moscow central deportation prison, whence, following an Imperial decree, he was transported to Eastern Siberia for five years. The place of his exile was to be the town of Vilyuisk, 610 km north of Yakutsk. While in the Moscow prison, Dzerzhinsky had taken part in a manifestation of political prisoners to mark their solidarity with a group of political exiles being deported to Siberia. For this he was deprived of the right to write to his relatives and receive letters or visits from them for one month.

In late February, he was brought to the Alexandrovskoye deportation prison near the city of Irkutsk. On March 5, he wrote to Aldona that he was in Eastern Siberia, more than 6,000 km away from home, and that in spring, when the rivers would become navigable, he would be taken to Vilyuisk, another 3,0004,000 km to the north. A large number of prisoners at the Irkutsk prison were waiting for the authorities to name their destination.

The time passed slowly, and the gendarmes were in no hurry. Finally, Dzerzhinsky's patience came to an end. Together with a group of political exiles, he addressed a written appeal to the prison superintendent demanding to know where they were to be sent, and to be transported there immediately. The superintendent forwarded the letter to the Governor of Irkutsk.

It was almost May, but no reply was forthcoming. The prisoners, headed by Dzerzhinsky, demanded that their appeal be answered. Instead, the authorities sent in a group of rapists and murderers sentenced to penal servitude for life to deal with the political exiles. The political prisoners were not intimidated and surrounded the criminals. Dzerzhinsky knocked down the most formidable-looking man and wrenched a knife away from him. Having arrived at the scene, the prison superintendent ordered the criminal to be put in the punishment cell and "apologised" to the political prisoners for the "misunderstanding".

After the incident, the political prisoners were worse off than ever. Dzerzhinsky conceived a bold plan. Next morning, during their walk, the prisoners were to attack the wardens, disarm them and drive them outside the prison gates, thus placing themselves in charge. On the morning of May 6, 1902, the plan was brilliantly executed under Dzerzhinsky's leadership, and a red flag was hoisted over the prison, with the word "Freedom!" written on it. The territory of the prison was declared a "free republic", and Felix Dzerzhinsky elected its chairman.

In fright the prison authorities summoned the troops and mounted police, and the Irkutsk Vice-Governor arrived in the village of Alexandrovskoye.

News of the event reached St. Petersburg. The orders received were to deal with the conflict by peaceful means. For two days the authorities conducted talks with the prisoners over the prison fence. They were told to remove the barricade blocking the prison gates, take down the red flag, and return to their cells. But the prisoners, showing a great deal of courage and determination, refused to obey.

On the third day, special messenger informed Dzerzhinsky that the Governor had agreed to meet some of the insurgents' demands. However, Dzerzhinsky turned the offer down.

"There are 44 of us here," he replied, "and each would rather die than surrender until all our terms are met."

Fearing publicity, the prison authorities were obliged to give in and comply with the major demands of the political prisoners. Only after that, at 2 p.m. on May 8, the prison gates were opened, and the uprising was over.

On May 12, 1902, Dzerzhinsky and the other political prisoners temporarily detained at the

Alexandrovskoye prison were transported to Verkholensk via the Yakutsk road. On the way, they made a stop at the village of Kachug, about 25 km from Verkholensk. From that point, the Lena was navigable, so the exiles boarded a steamer which took them further north to Yakutsk. The men disembarked at the places to which they had been assigned by the authorities.

While still en route to his destination Dzerzhinsky was already considering an escape plan. He confided his intention to Henryk Walecki, a PSP member, and later a Social- Democrat, whom he had met during his imprisonment, in No. 10 Block in Warsaw and who met him in Kachug. It was decided that

Dzerzhinsky and Sladkopevtsev, an SR,[4] would stay on in Verkholensk feigning illness and supposedly awaiting the arrival of the next group of exiles. Preparations began. The men bought a boat which they would use to sail down the river at night to the village of Zhigalovo, from whence they would make their way to the Siberian railroad by the highway.

The escape was carried out on June 12, 1902. Dzerzhinsky and Sladkopevtsev left Verkholensk forever, and, having surmounted grave difficulties, were free once again. On the 17th day after the escape from Verkholensk, Dzerzhinsky was back in Warsaw. Then he went to Berlin, where the leaders of the SocialDemocracy of the Kingdom of Poland and Lithuania were residing. That was the first time Dzerzhinsky met Rosa Luxemburg, Julian Marchlewski, Jan Tyszka, Adolf Warski and Jakub Hanecki.

In Berlin, he had a chance to read the Russian Bolsheviks' newspaper Iskra, Lenin's work What Is to Be Done? and other literature. Since he had been unable to read contemporary political writings during his two years of imprisonment, Dzerzhinsky, in the words of Adolf Warski, attacked with gusto "the latest Marxist literature, swallowing books in Polish and Russian".

In August 1902, a conference of the Social-Democracy of the Kingdom of Poland and Lithuania was held in Berlin. Among the

38

proposals put forward by Dzerzhinsky and adopted by the conference were those to establish a Committee of the Party Abroad, found a Party newspaper, Czerwony Sztandar, build up Party branches in Warsaw, Lodz, Bialystok and other towns of the Kingdom of Poland and Lithuania, and step up Party activities among young people. The conference elected Dzerzhinsky a member of the Party Committee Abroad and appointed him its secretary. He had become one of the acknowledged and most popular leaders of the Social-Democracy of the Kingdom of Poland and Lithuania.

After the conference, friends persuaded Dzerzhinsky to go to Switzerland for a while to build up his health which had greatly deteriorated during his years in prison and exile. He reluctantly agreed, but even in Switzerland he continued his political education. "I don't do too much," he wrote to Aldona, "just work for about 6 or 8 hours a day, so there's plenty of time for walks, reading and taking it easy." When is health had improved somewhat, he moved to Krakow, a town on the border of the Russian Empire on the side of Austro-Hungary. Here he again became engrossed in Party work. His autobiography states: "I moved to Krakow to act as a liaison and assist the Party from abroad. Since that time I came to be known as Jozef."

While in Krakow and acting on Party orders, Dzerzhinsky launched the Czerwony Sztandar.[5] He also arranged for the newspaper and other banned literature to be smuggled into the kingdom of Poland, although this was certainly no easy matter. He established contacts with underground groups of the Party, and himself made frequent trips to Warsaw and other cities to recruit and train agitators on the spot, hold Party meetings and conferences, and conduct other preparations for forthcoming revolutionary activities. In Krakow, he set up a Party section embracing the Social-Democrats and engaged in propaganda work among the Polish émigrés. A heavy work schedule (18-20 hours a day) and the wet autumn weather, which was always a bad time for Dzerzhinsky, aggravated his tuberculosis. His old friend Bronislaw Koszutski, who at that time was employed as an assistant at the Fraternal Help sanatorium for students in the town of Zakopane, asked him to take a treatment there. Dzerzhinsky agreed and was admitted under the name of Yuzef Domansky, a dentist college student. Dzerzhinsky stayed in the sanatorium for two months, till late December 1902. Then, feeling somewhat better, he returned to Krakow and once more plunged into work.

At the order of the Party Main Board, he visited Party groups abroad to gain an idea of their work and to allocate tasks. He continued to keep an eye on the Czerwony Sztandar, attended sessions of the editorial board, suggested subjects, looked for suitable material, often worked as a proofreader, and found reliable ways to smuggle the newspaper across the border into the Kingdom of Poland. Dzerzhinsky corresponded with underground Party groups and provided the ciphers and new addresses. He worked from dawn till the early hours of the morning. It often happened that he had no time to write even a few lines to Aldona. When he did manage to write, he sometimes complained that he was homesick and that he would have been glad to leave Krakow; however, work required "that I be here, so I will be here".

During this time, Lenin, still in exile, and the newspaper Iskra he had founded, were conducting vigorous preparations for the Second RSDLP Congress. The Organising Committee asked the SDKP and L Main Board to send its delegates and acquainted them with the agenda.

A consistent advocate of joint action among all Russia's Social-Democrats, Dzerzhinsky, acting on his own and Warski's behalf, sent a letter on July 7, 1903 to the Committee of the Social-Democratic Party

Abroad proposing that a congress be convened to discuss the union of the Social- Democracy of the

Kingdom of Poland and Lithuania with the RSDLP and to elect delegates to the Second RSDLP

Congress. His suggestion was accepted, and the Fourth Congress of the Social-Democratic Party, held in

July 1903, adopted the following decision concerning the RSDLP: "It is desirable to have a joint SocialDemocratic organisation for a whole Russian state. This is the major task of the given moment and is of fundamental significance, in relation to which the organisational forms are a matter of detail."

The congress also stated that in all intra-party matters concerning agitation and organisation within the Kingdom of Poland and Lithuania, the Polish Social-Democrats should enjoy complete independence, and that the Central Organ (CO) of the RSDLP should include a Polish member. The decisions of the congress were to be outlined to the RSDLP Second Congress by Warski, Hanecki, and Dzerzhinsky. Dzerzhinsky was elected to the Main Board of the Social-Democracy of the Kingdom of Poland and Lithuania.

In July and August 1903, Brussels, and later London, became the site of the Second RSDLP Congress, which completed the unification of the revolutionary Marxist organisations of Russia along the ideological, political and organisational principles evolved by Lenin. A party of the new type was formed, a party of the working class, whose work was based on the principles of scientific communism and whose aim was to accomplish a socialist revolution and build a socialist and then communist society.

However, the Social-Democracy of the Kingdom of Poland and Lithuania and the RSDLP failed to unite due to the faulty position adopted by Warski and Hanecki on the nationalities question.[6] They protested against including the point on the right of nations to self-determination into the Party Programme.

Afterwards they left the congress, having submitted a statement substantiating their point of view.

The Second RSDLP Congress instructed the newly elected Central Committee to resume talks with the Social-Democrats of the Kingdom of Poland and Lithuania on the issue of uniting the two parties.

In 1903 and 1904 Dzerzhinsky continued his work in Krakow as a representative of the Party's Main Board. He made trips to Warsaw, Lodz and the Dabrowa coal-mining basin, where he headed Party conferences, spoke at workers' meetings, and frequently carried banned literature. Throughout this period, he persistently advocated uniting the Polish Social-Democrats with the RSDLP. He stated that the country was in great need of a single social-democratic party built on the principle of proletarian internationalism. He wrote that "there cannot exist a proletarian movement of individual nationalities, but must be a single proletarian movement, a single social-democratic party, which will strive to embrace all the proletariat irrespective of nationalities."

In January 1904, the Russo-Japanese war broke out. The Russian tsar hoped that a victory would bolster the autocracy and stifle the revolutionary movement. But things worked out differently.

Dzerzhinsky and other Party leaders shared Lenin's position, believing that the best thing would be the defeat of tsarism in a war that was unjust on both sides. The Czerwony Sztandar and the printed appeals of the Main Board distributed in the Kingdom of Poland exposed the imperialist nature of the war and called on the Polish proletariat to use the weakening of the autocracy to overthrow it by acting jointly with the Russian workers. "Down with the autocracy! Long live socialism! Let us declare war on war! We want bread and work!"—these were the slogans printed by the illegal Polish Social-Democratic Party press at the time of the Russo-Japanese war.

Dzerzhinsky wanted to organise an exhibition of propaganda and cartoons of tsarism in connection with its defeats in the war in the Far East. Ample material had been collected, but the Austrian authorities banned the exhibition for fear of offending a "friendly government".

Dzerzhinsky was anxious to join the front ranks of the revolutionary fighters. Early in 1905 he moved to Warsaw to directly guide the mass action. Warsaw workers remembered him from his work in 18991900. "In the Party environment," Sofia Dzerzhinskaya wrote, "he was known as the most fearless and selfless Party activist, and stories were told about his courage, about his daring escapes from exile."

Dzerzhinsky attracted the workers and Social-Democrats of Warsaw by his seemingly inexhaustible energy, revolutionary enthusiasm, courage, selflessness, and unshakeable faith in the proletarian victory.

Adolf Warski wrote: "Jozef, like Rosa Luxemburg, became the most popular, the most beloved leader of the Polish working class. And since that time, Polish Social- Democrats could not even imagine the Party without Jozef.

"Jozef never had enough time and strength to balance his profound 'faith' (in the victory of socialism – Auth.) and his deeds'; the day was too short for him, and human strength too limited. But as the movement advanced and the year 1905 drew nearer, Jozef demonstrated enormous reserves of will and energy. And when January arrived and he moved to Warsaw permanently, his strength increased tenfold; he was everywhere, filled with fresh initiative and energy; he was indefatigable and infected the others with his will and enthusiasm."

That was what Dzerzhinsky was like on the eve of the first Russian revolution of 190507. He was performing a great service enhancing the political awareness of the Polish proletariat and prepare it for the decisive battle with the Russian autocracy.

* * *

January 9, 1905, marked the beginning of the first Russian revolution. The news that peaceful demonstrators had been shot down by government troops at the Winter Palace in St. Petersburg spread throughout the Kingdom of Poland. Revolutionary activities there were headed by the Social-Democratic Party, which remained loyal to its internationalist revolutionary commitments.

Dzerzhinsky, who had just arrived in Warsaw, found himself in the midst of the workers' revolutionary action.

On Monday, January 10, Polish Social-Democrats had already issued a leaflet commenting on the events in St. Petersburg and urged support for the Russian revolution. In a show of solidarity, Polish workers stopped work at factories, railways and mines and announced a general strike in Warsaw, Lodz, Czestochowa and some other towns.

Lenin, who at that time was living in exile in Geneva, was closely following the revolutionary developments in Russia. "The uprising has begun," he wrote. "Force against force... Moscow and the South, the Caucasus and Poland are ready to join the proletariat of St. Petersburg. The slogan of the workers has become: 'Death or Freedom!'."[7] On January 12, 1905 he wrote: "The general strike is spreading to the provinces... The workers are demonstrating in Lodz, an uprising is being prepared in Warsaw."[8]

The revolutionary wave in Warsaw and other industrial centres was rising. At the end of January, Dzerzhinsky informed the Committee of the SDKP and L Abroad about the general strike in Warsaw. Specifically, he wrote that the proletariat was ready for the struggle, that smaller factories and workshops were joining larger ones, and that transport workers had gone on strike too. "The behaviour of the police indicates that the troops will follow tomorrow."

Dzerzhinsky was the soul of the proletarian movement in Warsaw and the leader of Party work. Adolf Warski wrote later: "In the tide of the forces of the revolution, against this constantly growing field of action, Josef lived to the fullest: he was in his element, this was his life, seething, full, rich in the joys of Party successes and in the growing movement." He seemed to forget what it was to be tired. He walked from one factory to another to talk to workers, give advice, and encourage them to be staunch and courageous in the fight against tsarism. He controlled all contacts, secret addresses, finances, and the keys for decoding cypher messages. The revolutionary wave was sweeping across the other industrial centres of the Kingdom of Poland; the movement was gaining momentum. On January 22, 1905, Dzerzhinsky arrived in Lodz, where he got in touch with the Party committee and with the central agitators' group operating there. He saw with satisfaction that Party influence on the workers was growing.

Nearly every issue of the 'Bolshevik newspaper Forward, printed in Switzerland, featured articles about the general strikes in Warsaw and in Lodz, the working-class movement in the Dabrowa coal-mining basin, Katowice, Kalisz, and other towns.

Lenin was informed about the movement that had been launched in Poland as a sign of solidarity with the workers of St. Petersburg, and himself wrote a piece about the events in Warsaw and Lodz for the Forward. This and other articles which Lenin began to write after the first days of the revolution were designed to focus the attention on the struggle of the Polish proletariat, which, headed by the SocialDemocratic Party, was advancing the same demands as those inscribed on the red flags of Russia's workers.

Demonstrations, political strikes, and armed outbursts of the workers required that the Party exercise some sort of control over their struggle. Dzerzhinsky worked hard to consolidate local Party committees which were to lead the mass action of the people. He visited Party organisations, gave them useful tips on conducting agitation and propaganda, and urged them to involve more young people into the movement. He drew up a plan of Party work in the provinces and carefully studied the conditions of workers.

Jakub Hanecki, a member of the Party Main Board who was with Dzerzhinsky in Warsaw, later wrote: "It is difficult to imagine the formidable, inexhaustible energy which he put into his work. Night rest was mostly non-existent for him. He sometimes had to be forced to eat. He worked 18- 20 hours a day. Today he would be in Warsaw, tomorrow in Lodz, the day after in Czestochowa, in the Dabrowa area, Lithuania. He organised and built up local committees, spoke at workers meetings, wrote leaflets." Each minute the threat of arrest hung over him.

Dzerzhinsky's letters reveal how hard he was working. Many end with the words: "I must finish—it is already four in the morning, and tomorrow—well, today really—I've got to be up at eight."

Dzerzhinsky helped set up new party committees, recruited new cadres, and did much to train and educate professional revolutionaries. In one of his letters he wrote about the establishment of a Russian Social-Democratic group consisting, as he put it, of "competent and energetic people". He defined their objectives as follows: "political self-education, acquisition of practical work skills, agitation and organisational work among the Russian workers and the intelligentsia, material and technical aid". He fell back on this group when the need arose for people to conduct propaganda work in the army in Russian.

He was pleased when local Party branches were successful in organising strikes, took up relevant revolutionary slogans, and displayed initiative, independence, and vigour.

He underscored the importance of the ideological education of Party personnel, expansion of the group of activists, agitators and propaganda workers, and their adequate training. He assisted committee members in setting up study groups of agitators in the same trade, which, together with teaching Marxist theory, discussed current political issues. In Warsaw, the most active section was that of the metalworkers. Its members formed Social-Democratic branches at factories and held meetings of their representatives. In this work Dzerzhinsky was guided by Lenin's advice—to turn each factory into a stronghold of the proletarian party. Such groups also included masons, shoemakers, saddlers, carpenters.

Well-trained people were required to guide and organise the work of these groups. "With this end in view," wrote Dzerzhinsky to colleagues abroad, "we must find for each of these groups a propaganda worker from among the intelligentsia (who would accumulate some experience of Party work there and would later be able to become a leader)." At Dzerzhinsky's suggestion, Party bodies concentrated more closely on work with the more conscientious workers and intellectuals and encouraged them to join the

Social-Democratic Party. The revolution of 1905-07 made a major contribution to the training of Zosia

Muszkat (in future, wife of Dzerzhinsky), Edward Prochniak, Stanislaw Bobinski, and Stefania

Przedecka, who later became prominent members of the Polish, Russian and international working-class movement.

Dzerzhinsky carefully and patiently selected and trained people for organisational and political work among the masses, and made sure that the Party activists had access to information.

He himself often spoke at classes of workers' groups at the factories of Warsaw, Lodz, Czestochowa, the Dabrowa coal-mining basin and at meetings and other gatherings. "It was rewarding to see how the people gain confidence," wrote Dzerzhinsky of one of his meetings with workers, "to watch them begin to acquire courage and faith in their strength when I started talking to them about the great goals set by the working class, the unity of the proletariat of different nationalities and states, the workers' social- democratic party, and about the freedom and political rights that they need just as they need air or bread."

The workers were attracted by the ease and simplicity of Dzerzhinsky's manner and his reputation as a brave and steadfast fighter for the proletarian cause. His example helped persuade many to become Party activists.

In the first days of the revolution, when the social vigour of the working people was rapidly growing, there was a shortage of propaganda literature. "The general strike," wrote Dzerzhinsky to his friends abroad, "has shown that we must start mass political agitation, which is quite impossible given the number of leaflets I receive here. I am convinced that we must launch local production in all towns; we are working hard to carry this out, and, I hope, with some success."

After two underground printing presses were opened in Warsaw and Lodz, Dzerzhinsky requested the Party leadership abroad to send over leaflets written in code or in invisible ink for printing at the local presses.

He also stressed the need for the people to quickly receive the leaflets. In his letter of March 30, 1905, he wrote: "The May Day leaflet must be distributed as early as the first half of April. Let us have the manuscript."

Preparation for the celebration of May Day in Warsaw began well in advance. In mid- April 1905, a special commission and detachments of armed workers were set up. "The banners are ready," wrote

Dzerzhinsky. "So are the speakers and the detachments of armed workers. The May Day commission is in charge of that." The leaflet issued by the Main Board of the Social- Democratic Party "May 1! To all workers in the town and the country" was printed and distributed in good time, so the workers had a chance to read it and prepare for the celebration. Other May Day literature was also received by the committees in time.

On May 1, Warsaw workers staged a work stoppage and went out into the streets to take part in meetings and demonstrations. Preparing for the decisive battle against the autocracy and bourgeoisie, the Polish proletariat launched its most significant mass action led by Dzerzhinsky, Hanecki and Warski.

The demonstration of the Warsaw workers lasted two hours. They marched bearing red banners and flags, sang revolutionary songs and chanted the slogans "Long live the general May Day strike!", "Long live the eight-hour working day! Long live socialism!", "Down with war!", "Down with the autocracy!"

When the demonstrators reached the Jerusalem Alleys, a pistol shot sounded, then the firing began. Tsarist troops shot at workers, women and children. Dzerzhinsky was among the demonstrators and saw the dead and wounded fall. Sofia Dzerzhinskaya wrote later: "Mindless of the danger, Josef helped carry away the wounded, hid them from the police and had the most severely wounded men taken to hospitals."

The day after the shooting Dzerzhinsky summoned the Warsaw committee of the Party. A strike of protest against the shooting of the demonstrators was scheduled for May 4.

On May 2, the Warsaw committee published a leaflet under the heading "Long live the revolution!", and on May 4, an organised strike was held. Factories, workshops, offices, theatres and shops stopped work.

The events of May 1-4 in Warsaw revealed the maturity of the Polish proletariat and the strength of the Social- Democratic Party.

48

They ultimately led to an armed uprising in Lodz, which took place in June 1905.

The uprising of Lodz workers evoked a response throughout Russia. Dzerzhinsky and other Party members immediately printed a series of leaflets urging the workers to launch a general strike of solidarity with the workers of Lodz.

However, the Lodz committee of the Social-Democratic Party was caught unawares by the sweep of events, and failed to live up to its role as the organiser of the strike or to supply the insurgents with weapons. This demonstrated that the Polish Social-Democrats had underestimated the need to guide the movement politically and organisationally, and that their technical training was inadequate.

The lessons of the armed uprising in Lodz helped Dzerzhinsky to finally evolve a Leninist view of the function of the proletarian party in revolution as the organiser, leader and educator of the masses. Always in the thick of the revolutionary struggle, Dzerzhinsky greatly helped the Social-Democratic committees master all of its forms.

The Warsaw Committee of the Social-Democratic Party designated July 17, 1905, as the date of an interregional Party conference. Around noon, participants began to arrive to Dembe Velke station by the Warsaw train whence they made their way to a nearby forest where the conference was to be held. The police had received information that members of the Warsaw committee would be among those present, and sent troops and its men to the site of the conference where they surrounded the participants.

Dzerzhinsky, who was already there, commanded in a strong voice: "Comrades! Give me anything illegal you've got with you. I've nothing to lose in case of arrest." The list of captured documents included the Bolsheviks' newspaper Proletary (The Proletarian). Soon, the Warsaw police department found out that the prisoner who called himself Jan Krzeczkowski was in fact Felix Dzerzhinsky who had escaped from exile. Also arrested were Wincenty Matuszewski, A. Krajewski and some other leaders of the SocialDemocratic Party. For the third time in his life, Dzerzhinsky was taken to prison.

In the meantime, the Bolsheviks were mustering forces for conducting mass political strikes and an armed uprising. The strike that began in Moscow on October 6, 1905 rapidly spread to Russia's industrial centres and became general. Frightened by the mounting scope of the revolution, the tsarist government agreed to make concessions hoping to save the autocracy. On October 17, the tsar issued a manifesto which promised freedom of assembly, freedom of speech and some other rights, which, however, the authorities had no intention of observing. Under pressure from the revolutionary movement, the tsar declared an amnesty, and on November 2 Dzerzhinsky walked out of the prison gates into the streets of

Warsaw. The strike was still on in the city. Neither the transport nor hansom cabs were running. Henryk

Walecki, who was released at the same time as Dzerzhinsky, wrote that as the two were walking, Dzerzhinsky kept repeating: "Do not trust their constitutions, do not entertain illusions, do not come out of the underground."

Together with other released Party members, Dzerzhinsky arrived at the conference held by the Warsaw committee of the Social-Democratic Party in connection with the revolutionary fervour which continued to mount in view of the October strike which had spread throughout Russia. ("The ovation that greeted them can easily be imagined," wrote A. Krajewski. Jakub Goldenberg, who was chairing the conference, immediately passed his functions over to Dzerzhinsky.

Yu. Krasny had always vividly recalled one, very important part of Dzerzhinsky's speech at the conference: 'The time has come to take up arms and act with arms in our hands. The word arms, or armed struggle, filled the entire speech, and it still rings in my ears."

Dzerzhinsky advocated the proletarian forms of the revolutionary struggle that Lenin had developed. He believed that the ultimate goal should be to overthrow the autocracy and establish a democratic republic by force of arms.

Dzerzhinsky frequently went further than his Party comrades outlining the goals of revolution. On a number of occasions he was known to criticise the leaflets and manuscripts brought in from abroad as not filling the needs of the moment. He thought not only the content important but the tone and clarity, did not want the literature to sound didactive. Dzerzhinsky's experience—and he had an excellent knowledge of the make-up, needs, working conditions and life of the working people—convinced him that the men had to have clearly defined political goals. The past struggle revealed how best to encourage workers' action by the printed word, to make the most efficient use of printed material. "We must publish this by all means," he wrote abroad about the programme pamphlet. "All points of our programme must be supplied with an explanation of the historical process which will lead up to socialism, and an explanation of the concept of class and class character, political party, dictatorship, attitude to other parties, and the tactics of our party."

Dzerzhinsky stressed the importance of oral and printed propaganda to liven up the strike movement, and repeatedly requested Rosa Luxemburg and other Party members abroad to send more literature, particularly popular leaflets intended for peasants, intelligentsia and the army. He was aware that Party slogans make a stronger impact when they are addressed to workers in a particular trade or profession. "Each group, each trade will have professional agitators," wrote Dzerzhinsky. He believed that the Party's propaganda should reach workers of all nationalities living on the territory of the Kingdom of Poland.

The Social-Democratic Party had not advanced any agrarian programme, and its branches in the Kingdom of Poland had no clear-cut instructions as to work among the peasants. However, following the events of January 1905, mass peasants' movement began to unfold. On February 13, 1905, Dzerzhinsky asked Rosa Luxemburg to write and publish a manifesto intended for peasants. It was at his suggestion that the Main Board of the Social-Democratic Party issued "A Word to Our Brothers the Peasants" and "To the Countryfolk!" urging the peasants to join the struggle of the workers against the autocracy. True, the Main Board had in mind mostly hired agricultural labourers, more or less ignored the poorer peasants, and completely disregarded the middle peasants.

Dzerzhinsky personally persuaded the local Party branches to extend their activities to rural areas and try to exercise leadership over the peasant movement. Speaking at the fifth Congress of the SDKP and L in June 1906 he stated that socialist ideas had reached the countryside, but that "a sound organisation of agricultural labourers is still nonexistent", although the situation indicated that the Party should start mass agitation among the peasants so as to win them over to the side of the proletariat.

Dzerzhinsky was also concerned with reaching the troops. Revolutionary events and the SocialDemocratic propaganda work had stirred up unrest among the garrisons stationed in Poland. The Bolsheviks considered conducting and agitation in the army and involving the troops in the revolutionary campaign a major objective in the overall struggle against the autocracy. On the territory of the Kingdom of Poland this work was conducted by the Revolutionary Military Organisation (RMO) of the RSDLP which had been set up back in 1904 and closely cooperated with the SDKP and L.

Dzerzhinsky was in fact the organiser and leader of revolutionary-military work among the troops, and was responsible for the contacts between the SDKP and L and the RMO of the RSDLP. He reported to the Party branch abroad that the Southern Committee of the SDKP and L was doing a great deal of work in the army, and had "revolutionised entire regiments". Finally, in the summer of 1905, the SDKP and L and the RSDLP agreed on conducting joint work in the tsarist troops stationed on the territory of the Kingdom of Poland. Dzerzhinsky's efforts were one of the factors that had made this possible.

Party work in the army was gaining in scope and was closely linked with the overall activities of the SDKP and L. Dzerzhinsky had become convinced as had Lenin before him, that the army would play an important part in any armed uprising. At a regional Party conference held in November 1905 he remarked: "Our present work in the army should aim to organise the soldiers for an armed uprising."

The conference was convened in Warsaw while the revolution continued to seethe. Taking part were Felix Dzerzhinsky, Julian Marchlewski, Adolf Warski, Jan Tyszka, Zdzislaw Leder, Josef Unszlicht, Jakub Hanecki, Bronislaw Wesolowski. The Polish Social-Democrats discussed the current situation and the tasks of the Party, the trade unions, the attitude to the peasant movement, and work in the army. The conference members were critical of the tsar's October 17 Manifesto and warned the workers and peasants not to take it at face value but to continue their campaign to overthrow the existing system.

Dzerzhinsky reported on Party work among the troops, stressing the need to step up propaganda and agitation. The conference adopted a number of decisions aimed at uniting the Polish and Russian revolutionary movement to overthrow the autocracy, eliminate the bourgeois landowner class, establish a democratic republic, attain autonomy for Poland, and convene an all-Russia constituent assembly. The conference was an important event that promoted the mass revolutionary movement in Poland.

Dzerzhinsky was convinced that for propaganda work among the various strata of the Polish population and other nationalities to be effective, adequate information should be provided about events underway in other parts of the Russian Empire. This would make it possible to compare the achievements scored in different parts of the country and learn by each other's experience. Dzerzhinsky had a great need for Russian literature: nearly each letter to the Main Board contained requests for it.

The Polish Social-Democrats had tried to help the Polish workers realise that their interests were identical with those of Russian workers, and that only through their joint effort could success be achieved. The front ranks of the Russian and Polish proletariat were ready to unite in a single party, and the SocialDemocracy of the Kingdom of Poland and Lithuania had even drawn up the terms of such a merger.

Dzerzhinsky, Warski and Hanecki were to represent the Party at the Fourth (Unity) RSDLP Congress held in April 1906 in Stockholm. There, Dzerzhinsky first met Lenin, who was to become his life-long friend, teacher and associate.

The organisational unity of the two parties that the congress managed to attain had major political significance for drawing the Polish and the Russian proletariat closer together. The traditional union between the two parties was formalised by forming a single social-democratic Marxist party.

In a speech welcoming this event, Lenin stated that it would serve as the most reliable guarantee for future success and the consolidation of an indestructible union.

In June 1906, soon after the Fourth (Unity) Congress of the RSDLP, the Fifth Congress of the SDKP and L was held. The report of the Main Board to the congress was delivered by Dzerzhinsky. This was an important document both politically and historically, for it contained reliable and exhaustive information about the state of the Polish working-class movement in the first year of the revolution, the advancement of the Polish proletariat's revolutionary involvement, the function of Polish Social-Democrats as leaders of the movement, and the growing solidarity between the Polish and the Russian working class.

Dzerzhinsky advocated a dialectical approach to forms of action which were to be modified depending on the course of events. His ideas on the mass political strike as an effective form of the proletarian struggle echoed Lenin's views. He believed that large-scale political popular actions, such as the May Day demonstrations in Warsaw and Lodz, were "but a step away from mass armed action— an armed uprising".

The Polish proletariat welcomed the merger of the two parties. Its significance for the working-class struggle was vividly described by Dzerzhinsky: "The principle that in the Russian state only one party of the working class should exist, and the establishment by both sides of the fact that both organisations adhere to a purely class point of view based on proletarian socialism—these prerequisites were sufficient for our Party to strongly strive towards unification with the Russian Social-Democratic Labour Party." The congress approved the report of the Main Board of the Social-Democracy of the Kingdom of Poland and Lithuania, adopted the new Party Rules drafted by Dzerzhinsky, and voiced its gratitude for his indefatigable work.

The position of the Polish Social-Democrats promoted the consolidation of the general anti-Menshevik front and cooperation of a large group of Polish revolutionaries with Lenin, with Bolsheviks. Further contacts between the SDKP and L and the RSDLP were to be maintained by representatives of the Main Board in the Central Organ (CO) and the Central Committee (CC) of the Bolshevik Party, which was provided for by the terms of the merger of the two parties and the organisational rules adopted by the Fourth (Unity) Congress of the RSDLP. One of the representatives of the Polish Social-Democratic Party in the CO was Dzerzhinsky. On August 7, 1906, he arrived in St. Petersburg, where Lenin was residing at the time. Lenin did a great deal of work heading the RSDLP Central Committee, the legal Bolshevik newspaper Novaya Zhizn (New Life), and guiding the entire revolutionary work of the Bolsheviks.

Dzerzhinsky arrived in the city at the time when the controversy between the Bolsheviks and the Mensheviks on major theoretical and practical issues was at its sharpest. From the beginning, he unhesitatingly took the side of the Bolshevik members of the Central Committee. He spoke at Central Committee meetings defending the Bolsheviks' stand, forwarded Bolshevik literature to the committees of the Social-Democracy of the Kingdom of Poland and Lithuania, established and maintained contacts between the leaders of the Polish Social-Democrats and the editorial boards of the Bolshevik press. From that time onwards, Dzerzhinsky's work was nationwide.

His correspondence with Warsaw makes it clear that he enjoyed the complete confidence of the Bolshevik leaders, was informed in detail of their plans, and that persistent efforts were made to more actively involve the Polish Social-Democrats in the Bolshevik press.

The decision of the Warsaw Social-Democratic Party committee of the SDKP and L on the need to convene another RSDLP congress, which Dzerzhinsky forwarded to the Proletary newspaper, was of considerable importance to Lenin. The conflict between the majority of the Party and the Menshevik Central Committee was mounting. Dzerzhinsky's support of the Bolsheviks was influential. "The Bolsheviks will raise the issue tomorrow, and I will support them," he wrote to Warsaw. His letters conveyed the tense atmosphere at the Central Committee meetings which discussed the question of convening an extraordinary congress. "It even came to an open quarrel," he wrote, "as I lost my temper and cursed them (the Mensheviks. – Auth.) for their opportunism." He was with the Bolsheviks on all issues. "As you see, I fight and submit proposals," he wrote in a letter to the Main Board. "The Bolsheviks say that my presence here is useful, that as a result of this struggle the Central Committee tends to reckon with us more, and that my 'fury' has made the Mensheviks lose some of their self- confidence."

While in St. Petersburg, Dzerzhinsky attended Bolshevik meetings and talked with Lenin and his followers. He was instrumental in smuggling Lenin's works and other Bolshevik literature into Poland. Lenin and other Bolsheviks increased Dzerzhinsky's awareness of the significance of Lenin's ideas for the revolutionary struggle of both the Polish and the Russian proletariat.

In November 1906, the Second (First All-Russia) RSDLP Conference was held in Tammerfors.

Dzerzhinsky was one of the delegates of the Social-Democracy of the Kingdom of Poland and Lithuania. All Polish Social-Democrats unconditionally sided with the Bolsheviks, but the majority voted for the Menshevik resolution permitting alliances with the liberal bourgeoisie. To oppose it, Lenin entered the so-called "Minority Opinion",[9] i.e., a Bolshevik platform to which Dzerzhinsky and other representatives of the Social-Democracy of the Kingdom of Poland and Lithuania ascribed.

Straight from the Tammerfors Conference Dzerzhinsky headed back to Warsaw, where the Polish SocialDemocrats had launched a large-scale propaganda campaign under Bolshevik slogans.

In December 1906 Dzerzhinsky visited Lodz, where factory owners had declared a lock-out and threw thousands of workers out into the street without any means of sustenance. Dzerzhinsky compiled a report on the lock-out at the Lodz factories and the condition of the working class in that major industrial centre.

Upon returning to Warsaw, Dzerzhinsky went to a secret address which the police had been surveilling for three days. Dzerzhinsky and some other Party activists were arrested and taken to the city hall where they were put into a cramped and dirty cell.

Dzerzhinsky was not in the best of health, but he could not remain idle in the circumstances. He arranged for the wardens to bring him a brush and some water. "A few hours later," wrote one of Dzerzhinsky's fellow-prisoners, "everything in the cell—the floor, the doors, the walls, the window—was scrubbed clean. Dzerzhinsky worked with such abandon, as if it were the most important Party task."

Dzerzhinsky was detained at the city hall for three weeks and then transferred to a prison to await trial. The cells were six steps long and three steps wide. For Dzerzhinsky, who was suffering from a lung disease, the conditions were particularly hard, but he was as animated as ever. First he was elected head of the Social-Democratic group of prisoners, and then set up a school where, depending on their educational level, prisoners could take classes ranging from elementary reading to the theory of Marxism.

Dzerzhinsky, who was jokingly nicknamed "inspector" by his friends, did his best to help the prisoners make the best possible use of their time in prison—to improve the political knowledge they would need to continue their struggle against the autocracy.

At the time of Dzerzhinsky's imprisonment, the Social-Democracy of the Kingdom of Poland and Lithuania was preparing to take part in the Fifth RSDLP Congress. Local Party committees were holding conferences to elect delegates to the congress, which was scheduled for May 1907 and was to be held in London.

The confrontation with the Mensheviks was as sharp as ever. The resolute support rendered by the Polish Social-Democrats to the

Bolsheviks helped to reveal the opportunistic character of the Mensheviks' platform. On all major issues, the Polish delegates at the congress sided with the Bolsheviks.[10]

In his absence, Dzerzhinsky (he was still in prison) was elected to the RSDLP Central Committee. Three days after the congress closed, he was released on bail thanks to the efforts of his relatives and friends.

Now he lived under even stricter police surveillance. Having spent some time at his brother s countryhouse and in somewhat better health, he again became wholly engrossed in Party work. * * *

Notes

[1]A part of Poland which was incorporated into the Russian Empire following Poland's third partition between Austria, Prussia and Russia in the late eighteenth century.

[2]The Bund, the General Jewish Workers' Union of Lithuania, Poland and Russia, was set up in 1897.

[3]Clara Zetkin (1857-1933)-a prominent figure of the German and the international working-class movement.

[4]SRs (Socialist-Revolutionaries)-the largest petty-bourgeois party in Russia between 1901 and 1923; prior to the October 1917 Revolution it operated underground.

[5]The first issue appeared in November 1902, the last—in July/August 1918. The first editors of the paper were Adolf Warski, Julian Marchlewski, and Jan Tyszka.

[6]Since the Second RSDLP Congress requested that two and not three delegates be sent, Dzerzhinsky was not present at it.

[7]V. I. Lenin, "Revolution in Russia", Collected Works, Vol. 8, 1974, p. 71.

[8]V. I. Lenin, "The Beginning of the Revolution in Russia", Collected Works, Vol. 8, 1974, p. 98.

[9]See: V. I. Lenin, "Minority Opinion Entered at the All-Russia Conference of the RSDLP. On Behalf of the Social-Democratic Delegates of Poland, the Latvian Territory, St. Petersburg, Moscow, the Central Industrial Region and the Volga Area", Collected Works, Vol. 41, 1969, p. 188.

[10]   See: V. I. Lenin, "The Fifth Congress of the Russian Social- Democratic Labour Party", Collected Works, Vol. 12, 1962, p. 469.

Chapter Three

THE YEARS OF REACTION AND THE NEW REVOLUTIONARY UPSURGE. PRISON AND EXILE (1907-February 1917)

The First Russian Revolution was suppressed, and, beginning in 1907, political reaction set in.

Thousands of workers and peasants were shot or hanged on sentences passed by court martials or by punitive detachments without trial. In 1909, the prisons held 170,000 people. Repressions were particularly severe when it came to Bolshevik groups. The legal workers' press was banned.

In the Kingdom of Poland, reaction was worse than elsewhere. Martial law was introduced throughout the country, and court martials routinely meted out harsh sentences.

The SDKP and L was doing its best to expose the ruthlessness of the autocracy and bolster confidence in a new revolutionary upsurge.

Dzerzhinsky plunged into work with renewed vigour. Above all, he took pains to liven up the activities of the Warsaw Social-Democratic organisation. He also toured many industrial centres, restoring disrupted Party contacts and establishing new secret addresses, and supervising the .printing and distribution of underground literature, newspapers and leaflets. As always, he was especially concerned with recruiting and educating propaganda workers.

In the autumn of 1907, Dzerzhinsky made several trips to Lodz. There, as in the other towns of the

Kingdom of Poland, harsh repressions were in full swing. As a sign of protest, the workers went on strike. At Dzerzhinsky's suggestion, the Main Board sent materials about the events in Lodz not only to the underground Polish press but also to foreign newspapers in hopes of "provoking meetings of protest throughout Europe".

Later, Dzerzhinsky's wife wrote about his vigorous activities during that time, the willpower and courage he demonstrated, and his ability to inspire faith in the ultimate victory of the revolution:

"I came to know him better in the beginning of 1908. That was a very hard period of the blackest reaction. The Party organisation was almost entirely smashed, the prisons were overcrowded. The vacillating elements turned away from the Party. In Warsaw, only about 5 or 6 Party activists were left. We met seldom, and with difficulty. The people were often late. Work was slack.

"But then 'Jozef made an appearance,... and the Party organisation was galvanised into immediate action. Everyone looked rejuvenated, filled with new energy. People were no longer late. Flats for the activists' meetings appeared as if by miracle. Party discipline was re-established without a word from 'Juzef. He inspired us all by his enthusiasm, his faith in an early new upsurge of the revolution."

On April 3, 1908, Dzerzhinsky was arrested again and put into the No. 10 Block of the Warsaw citadel. This was his fifth arrest, and he spent 16 months in prison. As before, the police failed to make him utter a single word about the Party organisation or his contacts.

His moral courage and revolutionary optimism are reflected in his prison diary. "Life would not be worth living," wrote Dzerzhinsky in his diary in May 1908, "if mankind had not been guided by the star of socialism, the star of the future."

Twice, in January and in April 1909, the Warsaw court sentenced Dzerzhinsky to life exile in Siberia and deprivation of all civil status rights for escaping from exile and "participation in a criminal association" (i.e., work in the underground Social-Democracy of the Kingdom of Poland and Lithuania).

On August 31 he was deported, and in mid-September brought to Krasnoyarsk. A few days later, he was told of the decision concerning his future domicile: the remote village of Belskoye in the taiga, 300 km from Krasnoyarsk.

On September 24, 1909, Dzerzhinsky arrived at Belskoye, but did not stay there long. The police and the clergy "discerned in his behaviour manifestation of arrogance and the wish to make trouble", and did their best to get rid of him. In early October 1909, he was transferred to a still more distant spot, the village of Sukhovo, and from there, a month later, to the village of Taseyevo. Dzerzhinsky took a room in the house of the local blacksmith, a former exile, Anton Krogulsky (in some documents, Rogulsky), who had participated in the Polish uprising of 1863. There he was to remain as an "eternal exile" until his death.

On November 13, 1909, Dzerzhinsky escaped from Taseyevo. The secrecy of his escape was such that a search for him began only three months later, by which time he was thousands of kilometres away from Taseyevo, on the Italian island of Capri. The Main Board of the SDKP and L had sent him there to take treatment.

Having spent nearly two years in prison and in exile, Dzerzhinsky needed time to find his bearings in the situation prevailing in the country and the Party. While on Capri, he read Social-Democratic publications for the years 1908 and 1909, and Party documents forwarded to him by friends in the Party Main Board.

On return from Capri, Dzerzhinsky travelled to Berne, Zurich and Berlin on Party business, and gradually came to realise that the best thing would be for him to move secretly to St. Petersburg in order to keep the Main Board informed of the situation in the RSDLP and maintain constant ties with the Central Committee Russian Bureau.

However, the Party leadership suggested that he return to Krakow, where he arrived in March 1910 to take up the job of secretary and treasurer of the SDKP and L Main Board. Once in Krakow, he acquainted himself with the state of affairs in the Party branches of the Kingdom of Poland. It was far from encouraging. There were not enough people and printed material, and the people sent from abroad were often apprehended. In the absence of timely information and specific instructions from the Main Board, many underground groups were "stewing in their own juice" and were not competent enough to head the mounting revolutionary movement. The immediate task was to build up the underground organisations ideologically and politically. While in Krakow, Dzerzhinsky had to re-establish contacts, render assistance to Party groups, maintain ties with the Main Board and the Party Bureau of Foreign Groups, keep in touch with the Krakow printing press which dealt with Party publications and do the proofreading. His job as Party treasurer consumed a great deal of time and effort, and he was also responsible for storing and transporting Party literature to the Kingdom of Poland, supplying underground activists with documents, looking for new addresses to which the Party correspondence could be sent, and keeping the Party archives in order.

In August 1910, he reported on the political situation and the tasks of the Party at the regional conference of the Social-Democratic Party held in Krakow. His report was based on Lenin's ideas on the need to strengthen the organisational and political work of the Party at the time of the growing revolutionary movement, and to continue to level daily just criticism against the bourgeois and petty- bourgeois parties. Dzerzhinsky called on the Party to step up its propaganda activities among the working-class members of the left wing of the Polish Socialist Party and win them over to the position of the Social-Democratic Party.

The work of the Krakow Branch of the Party grew markedly livelier. In late May 1910, it established a self- education club for Krakow and Galician workers. The first talk, about the history of the class struggle in France, was given by Dzerzhinsky.

Despite his enormous work load, Dzerzhinsky found time to further his own education. A systematic method of studying scientific literature that he had evolved back at the beginning of his revolutionary career was proving most helpful. In Krakow, Dzerzhinsky made a thorough study of Marx's and Engels's philosophical works, including The Poverty of Philosophy, Anti-Dühring, Ludwig Feuerbach and the End of Classical German Philosophy, Lenin's Materialism and Empirio-Criticism, works by Kant, Mach and some other bourgeois philosophers. In addition, he went back to his study of the theory of rent and other categories of the

Marxist political economy which first he had begun in Wilno and Kowno and continued in his Vyatka exile.

The Krakow police kept Dzerzhinsky under secret surveillance and sometimes summoned him for questioning.

Dzerzhinsky was very concerned about the state of affairs in the RSDLP, where the controversy between the Bolsheviks on the one hand and the Mensheviks and other opportunist groups on the other was mounting. As a member of the RSDLP Central Committee, he took a lively interest in intra-party issues. In February 1911, he wrote to Tyszka: "As concerns the policies of the CO [Central Organ],[1] I subscribe to them to the extent of my knowledge of these matters; I even go further, for I agree with Lenin's policy. You know what my position is."

To bolster the work of underground Party organisations, in May 1911 Dzerzhinsky made trips to Warsaw, Lodz and other towns of the Kingdom of Poland, where he lent a hand in the distribution of underground literature, held several Party meetings, and ascertained the situation for himself.

Between May 28 and June 4, 1911, Dzerzhinsky and Tyszka took part in the conference held by the eight members of the RSDLP Central Committee residing abroad. At Lenin's suggestion it was convened in Paris and considered "the issue of the restoration of the Central Committee in connection with the overall position of the Party". The report was delivered by Lenin.

The conference also discussed the question of preparing a general Party conference. A commission was set up to deal with this matter.

At the conference, Dzerzhinsky spoke out in defence of Lenin's stand. On May 27, on the eve of the conference, he wrote from Paris that he had had meetings with Lenin, that the Bolsheviks regarded the present Central Committee as "a stinking corpse", and that the central Party bodies should be purged of traitors who must not remain Party members.

On May 29, the second day of the conference's work, Lenin and Dzerzhinsky exchanged notes on the question under discussion. It is clear from Lenin's note, which he called "a treaty between Lenin and

Juzef", that Dzerzhinsky supported expelling the Mensheviks from the Party. "This has to be done", he stated firmly.

After the conference, he returned to Krakow, but still maintained contact with the Bolshevik Centre in Paris. In one of his letters of July 1 1911 he wrote that Krakow was a more convenient spot than Paris for directing the RSDLP practical work in Russia, and reported on the opportunity to ensure a safe crossing of the border for Party activists.

"For many reasons," he wrote, "it is most inconvenient to conduct practical work from Paris... If here (in Krakow.—Auth.) someone should undertake it, it would be easy to arrange a crossing." Lenin had probably taken this letter into account when deciding to move from Paris to Krakow in the summer of 1912.

In mid-November 1911 Dzerzhinsky left for Brussels on Party business. On his return trip, he spent a few days in Paris, and then proceeded to Berlin, where he stayed until the end of December.

In January 1912, the Sixth All-Russia Conference of the RSDLP chaired by Lenin was held in Prague. It defined the tactics of the Party in view of a new revolutionary wave in Russia. Having analysed the political situation in the country, the conference stated that the overthrow of the autocracy and seizure of power by the proletariat in alliance with the peasantry was still the objective of a democratic overturn in

Russia.

The conference elected a Central Committee comprised of seven members and headed by Lenin.

Dzerzhinsky was deeply troubled by the fact that the Social-Democracy of the Kingdom of Poland and

Lithuania had sent no representatives to the Prague Conference. He voiced his concern in a letter to the Main Board, and in March 1912 asked for a "report on Lenin's conference". In that letter, Dzerzhinsky tried to persuade the Main Board to allow him to leave Krakow and settle somewhere in the Kingdom of Poland.

Finally, permission was granted. Prior to leaving for Warsaw on March 22, 1912, Dzerzhinsky wrote and forwarded to the Main Board "A Letter to My Comrades", which was to be published in case of his arrest. "Out of the last 14 years of my life," he wrote, "I have spent six in prison and one in exile. I should not be sorry to DC exiled again if this would help the Party cast off the alien elements which penetrated it during the rising of the revolutionary wave and are now sponging of it."

Back in Warsaw, Dzerzhinsky was very busy. He held Party and workers' meetings throughout the city, taught workers' groups, searched for new addresses where underground literature could be kept, and had it smuggled to Polish towns.

The revolutionary movement continued to rise. The events of April 4, 1912[2] acted as a powerful impetus. Learning of the incident, Dzerzhinsky addressed a letter to the Main Board asking that an appeal be issued and then sent to him. At his suggestion, the appeal urged the Polish workers to respond to the events on the Lena by determined action. In May 1912, 25,000 people in Warsaw and 10,000 in Czestochowa staged a strike in response to the appeal of the SDKP and L.

Dzerzhinsky received valuable assistance in his work from Sofia (Zosia) Dzerzhinskaya (nee Muszkat), a professional revolutionary and member of the SDKP and L. The two met in 1905 when both were involved in underground work in Warsaw. Sofia was a propaganda worker and a member of first the district and then the city (Warsaw) Committee of the SDKP and L. She often took part in Party congresses. In 1906 she was arrested and put into the Warsaw prison, where Dzerzhinsky was also being detained at the time. Having served her sentence, Sofia continued underground work in a number of Polish towns. In 1909 she was arrested for the second time in Warsaw, and three months later was deported abroad. She settled in Krakow where she again met Dzerzhinsky, who had returned from his Siberian exile. The two worked together to put the Party work in order, establish secret correspondence with Party committees and copy manuscripts of essays and other materials for the Czerwony Sztandar that were sent in from Berlin (where the Party Main Board had its headquarters). Sofia would forward these materials to Warsaw, where the newspaper was printed at an underground press. The work was of great importance for the Party and required a great deal of patience and care. Sofia was active in the Krakow branch of the SDKP and L, where she was engaged mostly in building up the Party's foreign contacts.

Felix Dzerzhinsky and Sofia Muszkat fell in love and were married in August 1910. But their happiness was soon disrupted. In November 1910 Sofia was sent by the Party to do underground work in Warsaw, and in late December she was arrested.

In June 1911, while still in prison, Sofia gave birth to a son and named him Jan. The baby remained with her in the prison cell for the first eight months of his life. The tsarist court sentenced her to the deprivation of all civil status rights and life exile in Eastern Siberia. The child, very weak and sickly, was placed in a private nursery. Later, Sofia's uncle, Marian Muszkat, a medical doctor, took the child under his care, and the boy recovered.

In the autumn of 1912 Sofia escaped from exile and safely made her way to Krakow, where she hoped to join her husband. But upon reaching the Russian-Austrian border, she learned that Dzerzhinsky had been arrested for the sixth time a few days before, on September 1, 1912, while he was in the midst, of some important Party work.

The report drawn up by the police department on September 26 cited "incriminating" evidence against

Dzerzhinsky. It stated that he had set up and headed a new Warsaw committee acknowledged by the Main Board, and "at the same time engaged in Party work there, staged strikes, and issued proclamations to the workers concerning current events in workers' and political life. During six months he had resided in Warsaw, Dzerzhinsky had made trips to Lodz and also went to Krakow to make reports to the Main Board on the results of his work". It was obvious that the police had collected extensive information about Dzerzhinsky's activities.

Soon after his arrest, the Main Board featured his letter written on March 22, 1912, in the Party press, supplying it with the following foreword:

"Each of you knows him. Out of the 34 years of his life, he has spent six years in prison and more than one year in exile. He joined the movement at the age of 17 and worked in Warsaw for 12 years. Everywhere he was in the front ranks, where the work was hardest, the responsibility the greatest, the dangers the worst. An organiser, agitator and Party leader, he was ready at any time to do anything to promote the cause, from the pettiest, most trivial technical matters to jobs requiring the broadest knowledge of political thought. Showing iron strength and fiery enthusiasm, he worked to restore Party organisations smashed by the enemy or disintegrating through slipshod work... He laid at the altar of the Party his youth, his health, and his private life."

The investigation into Dzerzhinsky's activities lasted almost two years, during which time he was kept at the No. 10 Block of the Warsaw Citadel. His court trial was held on April 29, 1914; Dzerzhinsky was sentenced to three years of hard labour for his escape from Siberian exile. His participation in the underground Party activities was still being investigated.

In July 1914, in connection with the start of the First World War, 502 prisoners, Dzerzhinsky among them, were transferred to a prison in the town of Orel in Russia. He remained there until April 21, 1915, and was then taken to Orel central prison.

Kept in the same cell with Dzerzhinsky were mostly young weavers from Lodz. Dzerzhinsky had always found it easy to mix with workers. He divided them into two groups and started teaching them Polish and Polish literature. In the evenings,' lying on their bunks, the young men listened to Dzerzhinsky talk about political topics and recite passages from the classic writers of Polish literature—Adam Mickiewicz, Juliusz Slowacki, Henryk Sienkiewicz, Marja Konopnicka and Eliza Orzeszkowa.

While in Orel prison, Dzerzhinsky carried on a never- ending campaign against the Mensheviks and the Bund. He was also exhorting the prisoners to fight for better conditions and against the arbitrary rule of the authorities.

68

Dzerzhinsky did not even suspect that his fate was a matter of grave concern for Lenin, Nadezhda

Krupskaya, Lenin's wife and also a professional revolutionary, and other members of the Union for the

Assistance to Political Prisoners, which had established its headquarters first in Krakow and later in Switzerland. Correspondence between Sergiusz Bagocki, the Union chairman, and Nadezhda Krupskaya and Sofia Dzerzhinskaya for the year 1915 shows that Krupskaya was aware that Dzerzhinsky had no money and therefore requested that he be given material assistance.

In late March 1916 Dzerzhinsky was transferred to Moscow, first to the Taganka and then Butyrka prison. In May of the same year, he was sentenced to six years' hard labour for his revolutionary activities in 1910-12, "excluding the three years served under the sentence of the Warsaw regional court passed on April 29, 1914".

After the new sentence had been passed, the Moscow court approximately calculated the sentence to be served beginning in May 1916 to be concluded only in May 1919.

Whether he was a prisoner or a free man, Dzerzhinsky never lost his faith in the inevitability of another Russian revolution in the near future. A worker and Social- Democrat, Mlinarski, who was Dzerzhinsky's fellow-prisoner in Orel and was kept in the next cell in the Taganka prison, wrote that even in prison Dzerzhinsky used to say that better days would be here soon. "Tsarism will have a price to pay for the war," he said.

"It might be that if the war lasts another year, the workers and peasants clad in soldiers' uniforms will wipe out the autocracy; a revolution will take place, and we shall go home. Of course we shall return not to sit out the difficult times but to fight against the old world and build a new happy life for all these working people."

Dzerzhinsky was released from the Butyrka prison by Moscow workers on March 1,

1917. He was not yet 40, and had given 22 years to the revolutionary movement.

Notes

[1]The Central Organ was at that time the Sotsial-Demokrat newspaper. Lenin was on its editorial board and in fact headed its publication.

[2]On April 4, 1912, troops shot down a peaceful march of strikers at the gold mines near the River Lena in Siberia.

Chapter Four

FIGHTING FOR THE VICTORY OF THE SOCIALIST REVOLUTION (MARCH-OCTOBER 1917)

As a result of the bourgeois February Revolution of 1917, the autocracy was overthrown, and a peculiar political situation evolved in the country. There were two governments, two dictatorships: the bourgeois

Provisional Government was the vehicle of bourgeois dictatorship, while the Soviets of Workers' and Soldiers' Deputies represented the revolutionary-democratic dictatorship of the proletariat and the peasantry.

The Bolshevik Party, which was no longer obliged to remain underground, had to tackle new tasks stemming from the transition to the socialist stage of the revolution. These were defined by Lenin in the very first days of the revolution in his "Letters from Afar" and some other works.

After his release from prison, Dzerzhinsky spent some time in Moscow. He was ill and worn out but in high spirits. He was not in the habit of concentrating on his personal life or his illness, and plunged into revolutionary work straight away. In the evening of March 1, 1917, he was already speaking at the second sitting of the Moscow Soviet of Workers' Deputies, where he was brought still wearing prison clothes. Dzerzhinsky hailed the victory of the Russian revolution and congratulated the revolutionary workers and soldiers who had overthrown the autocracy.

The meeting adopted important decisions designed to promote the revolution. The Soviet requested the workers employed in the services to resume work. The rest of the factories were to continue the strike in order to consolidate the victory of the revolution. District workers' committees were being set up, and soldiers' representation was introduced. The soldiers were to form the Moscow Soviet of Soldiers' Deputies.

Dzerzhinsky also spoke at a workers' and soldiers' meeting held in Skobelev (now Soviet) Square. His sister J. Dzerzhinskaya, who was living in Moscow at the time, wrote later: "On that day, he spoke many times before Moscow workers and got back home to me only at night, still wearing prison clothes. At that time I was living with my daughter in Krivoy Alley. Felix made his home with us.

"His friends were always in and out of the flat. From the Polish Committee (for assistance to the refugees—Auth.) I brought coats and suits for my brother and his friends. Our room was very damp and dark and Felix, my daughter and I moved to another room at 5 Uspensky Alley."

On assignment from the Moscow Committee, he spoke almost daily at workers' and soldiers' meetings all over Moscow, explaining to his audiences the reactionary nature of the Provisional Government's, Mensheviks' and SRs' policies, and calling on the people to join the campaign for peace and the withdrawal of the country from the imperialist war.

Dzerzhinsky thought it very important to work in the Polish community (in the war years, about 3 million Poles were living on Russian territory). Most of the Poles were soldiers who had been recruited by the tsarist army in the first days of the war, railway and industrial workers evacuated from the Kingdom of Poland, refugees, and prisoners whom the revolution had set free. This motley assembly of people comprised quite a few members of the SDKP and L, the PSP and other Polish political parties, including those of the bourgeoisie.

Bourgeois and pseudo-socialist parties were making a great effort to persuade Polish workers and soldiers not to 'interfere into Russian affairs". At the same time, they urged the Poles to form national detachments to be used against the revolution and for the restoration of the Polish bourgeois state.

Dzerzhinsky and the other Polish revolutionaries who had arrived in Petrograd and Moscow from prison, exile and through emigration were faced with the need to organise the Polish Social-Democrats residing in Russia along Bolshevik principles and launch a determined propaganda campaign to win Polish workers and soldiers over to the side of the revolution.

On March 3, 1917, the first, organisational meeting of the SDKP and L members was held in Moscow. About 50 people met and unanimously adopted a resolution which confirmed the community of interests of the Polish and Russian proletariat and called on Polish workers to extend support to the revolution in Russia.

The SDKP and L group assisted by the Moscow Party Committee began an active organisational and political campaign among the Polish workers evacuated to Moscow. Dzerzhinsky was a driving force behind the new tactics. Nearly every day he could be seen at workers' meetings. On March 5, the group held a Polish meeting, at which Dzerzhinsky proposed adopting a resolution which stated that the Polish and Russian workers were striving towards the same goals. The resolution was adopted by a 700 to 5 vote majority. On March 12, a proletarian demonstration organised by the Moscow Party Committee was held in the city. Taking part in it alongside with Russian workers and soldiers were about 6,000 Poles who carried banners of the SDKP and L and the PSP.

The hard work and tension became too much for Dzerzhinsky, and he fell ill in mid-March. He wrote about his condition to his wife, who at that time was in Switzerland with their son Jan.

"For several days now I have been taking it easy almost in the countryside, in Sokolniki, for the impressions and frenzy of the first days of freedom and the revolution proved too strong, and my nerves, weakened as they are by all those years of prison silence, failed to stand up to the burden placed on them. I fell slightly ill, but now, after a few days in bed, the fever is completely gone and I am feeling quite well. The doctor hasn't found anything alarming either, so I shall probably be back in the thick of things in a week at most.

"I'm using the time to fill in the gaps in my knowledge [of the political and Party situation] and put my thoughts in some sort of order... I am totally engrossed in the work."

On March 26, 1917, Dzerzhinsky chaired the conference of the Moscow group of the SDKP and L, which confirmed the decision adopted on March 3 and unanimously approved the resolution on the unity of action with the Bolshevik Party and the advisability of joining it.

The address issued by the conference, "To All Russian Workers", read: "We Polish workers united under the banner of social-democracy address you so that all the world may hear what you already know: we are with you, comrades. We are with you now as we were with you before, throughout the time of our suffering and our glorious struggle of 1905. Our joint effort and our sacrifices have not been in vain. We, the people and the soldiers have dealt a powerful blow to the autocracy, which has fallen for good. The executioner of the working class and all peoples inhabiting Russia is no more."

Carrying out the orders of the Moscow Party Committee, Dzerzhinsky did a great deal of work among the evacuated Polish railwaymen, who formed a separate workers' group (branch). Dzerzhinsky often attended its meetings, as well as general assemblies of railway workers, talked to the men about the goals of the working class and its Party in the revolution, and helped draw up resolutions.

In late March-early April 1917, the Executive Committee of the Moscow Soviet of Workers' Deputies was re-elected at the suggestion of the Moscow Party Committee. Dzerzhinsky was among nine Bolsheviks on a list of candidates to the Moscow Soviet Executive Committee, and was elected at the plenary meeting of the Moscow Soviet held on April 11.

The leadership of the Bolshevik Party, including Dzerzhinsky, stressed the importance of the work among the soldiers of the Moscow garrison, which numbered about 50,000 men. Dzerzhinsky was active in the Military Bureau of the RSDLP (B) Moscow Committee.

In April, the Moscow Committee formed a special commission, headed by Dzerzhinsky, which was entrusted with restoring Bolshevik organisations in the army, and to start creating the Red Guards. Dzerzhinsky tackled the new task in his usual vigorous manner. Soon, a large-scale propaganda campaign was under way in the army. Soldiers' groups or sections were set up in a number of units of the

Moscow garrison which worked in cooperation with district Party organisations. At factories, workers began to form the first Red Guards detachments and detachments of armed workers consisting of Party members.

The garrison had quite a number of Polish soldiers; the most active were united into a group under the Moscow Committee Military Bureau. Dzerzhinsky often attended and spoke at the meetings of Polish soldiers. It is interesting to read a short report which he wrote in Polish, probably for the Polish section of the Moscow Party Committee. It is an account of a meeting (held not earlier than April 17) of Polish soldiers employed at the Moscow heavy artillery workshops. "About 40 people in all were present," reads the report. "The subjects under discussion were the war and the International... The assembled men requested that we regularly send our people to tell them about the situation and settle organisational matters. The meetings will convene on Sunday mornings." The report stressed that there was a fairly large number of Social-Democrats among the soldiers.

Dzerzhinsky's prestige and popularity in the Moscow Party organisation continued to grow. He was directly involved in the work of city Party conferences and meetings and helped draw up resolutions. The first city conference held in April 1917 elected him its deputy chairman.

The conference ended in a demonstration of delegates and the workers and soldiers who had joined them to mark the fifth anniversary of the events on the river Lena. Meetings were held at which Dzerzhinsky, Ivan Skvortsov-Stepanov and other leaders of the Moscow Bolsheviks spoke about the need to form a united revolutionary front of workers and soldiers.

On April 3, Lenin returned to Petrograd from exile. Thousands of workers, soldiers and sailors assembled in the square at the Finland Railway Station to greet him. Standing on an armoured car, Lenin made a speech—the first for many years—voicing his appreciation of the feat performed by the workers and soldiers "who had succeeded not only in liberating Russia from tsarist despotism, but in starting a social revolution on an international scale...".[1]

On April 4, Lenin spoke before the Central Committee, the Petrograd Committee and the Bolshevik delegates of the All-Russia Conference of Soviets of Workers' and Soldiers' Deputies. His report was entitled "The Tasks of the Proletariat in the Present Revolution", or the April Theses, which supplied answers to the questions posed by the revolution: the transition from the democratic to the socialist stage, the attitude of the proletariat and its Party to the war and the bourgeois Provisional Government, the republic of Soviets, the ways of gaining a majority in them, the urgent changes to be introduced in town and the countryside, the tasks of the Party in the new historical situation, and the establishment of the Third, Communist International.

In April, Moscow hosted three Party conferences to deal with the questions stemming from Lenin's April Theses. Dzerzhinsky was present at all of them. The Second City Conference elected him a delegate to the Moscow Regional and Seventh All-Russia Party conferences.

The latter was held in Petrograd in April 1917. Apart from Dzerzhinsky, Polish Social- Democrats Stanislaw Budzynski, Julian Leszczynski and Josef Unszlicht took part in the conference.

The conference discussed and adopted decisions on major political and organisational issues. Lenin spoke about 30 times: he delivered reports on the main items on the agenda, was very active in the debate, and drew up almost all draft resolutions. He supplied answers to all the principal questions posed by the war, peace and revolution, carried further and specified the points he made in the April Theses.

Universal approval was extended to Lenin's resolution on the current situation, which approved his idea that socialism was capable of winning in one individual country, i.e., Russia.

The resolution on the agrarian question which Lenin proposed provided for the confiscation of landed estates and nationalisation of all land in the country.

Dzerzhinsky, who spoke in the debate on the national question, held the erroneous opinion that the principle of self-determination for every nation was incompatible with internationalism, and that this principle would play into the hands of bourgeois nationalists and separatists, and as far as Poland was concerned, would bolster the campaign of Polish nationalists and chauvinists.

Lenin, who had profound respect for Dzerzhinsky, tried to convince him not only at the meetings but in private talks during the breaks that his views were unsound and should be revised. Lenin appreciated the Polish Social-Democrats' internationalist stand and the striving for an alliance with the proletarians of all countries, but contended that to promote internationalism, one does "not have to repeat the same words. What you have to do is to stress, in Russia, the freedom of secession for oppressed nations and, in Poland, their freedom to unite. Freedom to unite implies freedom to secede. We Russians must emphasise freedom to secede, while the Poles must emphasise freedom to unite."[2]

Lenin's efforts were not in vain. His draft resolution on the national question was adopted by a majority vote.

Later, after the October Revolution, Dzerzhinsky criticised the erroneous views of Polish and Lithuanian

Social-Democrats and his own initial ideas on the national and certain other questions. He stressed that Lenin's proposal was the only way for the working people of Poland to succeed in building an independent socialist state.

The April Conference proposed electing Dzerzhinsky as a member of the Central Committee, but he requested that his candidature be withdrawn due to his bad health, and his request was granted.

The conference elected a new Central Committee headed by Lenin, which acted as a legal collective Party organ.

Having returned to Moscow from the conference, Dzerzhinsky and other Party leaders began work to carry out its decisions. Preparations for the socialist revolution were proceeding. The Moscow City Conference held in May 1917 approved Lenin's course towards a socialist revolution and outlined what had to be done to further build up the Party.

Thanks to the thorough and persistent campaign of Moscow Bolsheviks, the slogan "All Power to the Soviets!" was growing more and more popular, and Dzerzhinsky was one of the people who had helped promote it. But in May his health sharply deteriorated, and the Moscow Party Committee decided to send him to Orenburg Region to drink kount'is (fermented mare's milk), which was thought to be an effective TB cure.

In June 1917, a Central Executive Committee of the groups of the Social-Democracy of the Kingdom of

Poland and Lithuania in Russia was set up in Petrograd. Its members were Stanislaw Bobinski, Stanislaw

Budzynski, Felix Dzerzhinsky, Julian Leszczynski, Josef Unszlicht, Edward Prochniak, and Jakub Fenigstein (Dolecki). Candidate members of the Central Executive Committee were Stefania Przedecka, Samuel Lazowert, Bronislaw Wesolowski, and Mieczyslaw Warszawski (Bronski).

The Committee was to coordinate the work of all SDKP and L groups in Russia, keep in touch with the Social-Democratic Party in Poland, represent it in the SDKP and L and prepare and convene conferences of the groups in Russia. It was also to supervise the publication of the printed organ, the Trybuna newspaper, which began to circulate in Petrograd on May 27, 1917, and enjoyed the support of the Bolshevik Party Central Committee.

Dzerzhinsky returned to Moscow in early July. By that time, the situation and the alignment of class forces in Russia had changed dramatically.

After 'he July shooting of demonstrations of workers and soldiers in Petrograd, the SRs and Mensheviks had voluntarily surrendered power to the bourgeoisie. The dual power was no longer in effect. The peaceful stage of the revolution was over; counter-revolution assumed the offensive.

On July 5, military cadets raided the headquarters of Pravda; its publication was banned along with that of Trybuna. The Trybuna staff

was arrested, and on July 7 the government issued an order for Lenin's
 arrest.

In light of the July events the Bolshevik Party was faced with new tasks: to explain to the people what had happened and to work out a new tactics which would be effective under the changed circumstances.

On July 10, Lenin wrote "The Political Situation", which stated, in part, that, aided and abetted by the Mensheviks and SRs, counter-revolutionary elements had seized state power. "The aim of the insurrection," he wrote, "can only be to transfer power to the proletariat, supported by the poor peasants, with a view to putting our Party programme into effect."[3]

He suggested, in view of the changed situation, that the slogan "All Power to the Soviets!" should be temporarily withdrawn, for it was effective only as long as the revolution developed peacefully and had lost its validity after the July events.[4] Now Lenin called on the Bolsheviks to regroup and employ both legal and underground forms of work. His views on the more important issues of the revolution and its new tactics formed the basis of the decisions adopted by the Sixth RSDLP(B) Congress held in Petrograd from July 26 to August 3, 1917. Party conferences of more than 20 major Party organisations were held prior to the congress.

Dzerzhinsky represented the Moscow city organisation at the congress. Lenin was unable to personally attend, but his presence was felt. The Central Committee Secretariat supplied the delegates with Lenin's work "On Slogans". One of the first questions discussed at the congress was whether Lenin should make an appearance at a counterrevolutionary court trial. Grigory (Sergo) Orjonikidze, who was the principal speaker on the question, was against it.

Dzerzhinsky, who spoke first after Orjonikidze's opening remarks, also opposed Lenin's appearance at a trial. ' I shall be concise," he said. "The comrade who spoke before me has voiced my viewpoint... We must give a definite answer to the recriminations of the bourgeois press, which seeks to drive a wedge into our ranks... We must make it clear to our comrades that we do not trust the Provisional Government or the bourgeoisie, and that we shall not surrender Lenin."

The congress unanimously decided that Lenin must not appear at a trial, and voiced protest against police persecution of the leader of the revolutionary proletariat and claimed its solidarity with Lenin and the other Bolsheviks working underground or languishing in prison.

On all the major issues, Dzerzhinsky shared the Leninist viewpoint; he unhesitatingly supported an armed uprising. He was elected to the Central Committee and sent to Petrograd.

Lenin continued to direct the preparations for the uprising from underground. He was living not far from

Petrograd, in Razliv, where he was secretly visited by (Sergo) Orjonikidze, Joseph Stalin, Felix

Dzerzhinsky, and Yakov Sverdlov. They informed Lenin of the situation in Petrograd and received advice and instructions from him.

Dzerzhinsky was soon totally engrossed in the work of the Central Committee and Petrograd Party

Committee and the Petrograd Soviet of Workers' and Soldiers' Deputies. On August 5, 1917, the Central Committee plenary meeting elected him to the "narrow" CC consisting of 11 people, and the next day he was made a member or the CC Secretariat, which was in charge of all organisational Party work.

Having seized state power during the July events, the bourgeoisie, aided by the Mensheviks and SRs, was preparing to establish a military dictatorship. General Kornilov, who had the support of imperialist quarters in Britain, France and the USA, was to be made dictator.

On August 25, General Kornilov moved the 3rd Cavalry Corps commanded by the monarchist General Krymov from the front to Petrograd. Responding to the appeal of the Bolshevik Party, workers and soldiers of Petrograd took up arms against Kornilov's rebellion.

Together with the other Central Committee members, Dzerzhinsky helped arm the workers, form Red

Guard units, and prepare them for combat. He was a member of the Petrograd Committee of Popular Struggle Against Counter-Revolution, which helped to mobilise and arm the workers who had risen against the rebels.

Kornilov made an attempt to enlist the services of the Polish officers who centred around the so-called Supreme Polish Military Committee in Petrograd. One of the goals of the Committee, which was headed by members of the bourgeois National- Democratic Party, was to combat "Bolshevism and defeatist propaganda in the army".

On September 2, the Polish Trybuna newspaper published Dzerzhinsky's article "The Polish Allies of Kornilov", which revealed that the Polish counter-revolutionary officers were involved in the Kornilov plot. On September 5, it was reprinted in the Russian Bolshevik Rabochy Put (Workers' Path) newspaper.

"The Polish counter-revolution," wrote Dzerzhinsky, "is not a myth, it is a reality with which not only the Polish but the Russian revolutionary democratic circles must reckon."

The efforts to suppress the counter-revolutionary rebellion brought the Party and the working people even closer together; the Bolsheviks were coming to dominate in the Soviets. In late August-early September 1917, both the Petrograd and the Moscow Soviets adopted Bolshevik resolutions on the issue of state power. The slogan "All Power to the Soviets!" was resurrected, but now it implied an armed uprising against the Provisional Government and the establishment of proletarian dictatorship.

Acting on Lenin's directions, the Party concentrated on preparing for an armed uprising.

In the meantime, the revolutionary crisis was ripening. The situation required that Lenin return to the capital. On October 3, the Central Committee voted for Lenin's return from Finland to Petrograd in order to "make constant and close contacts possible". On October 7, Lenin secretly arrived in Petrograd and began personally to supervise preparations for the uprising.

Dzerzhinsky and the other Central Committee members were now accountable directly to him. They visited Lenin at his secret flat, informed him of the mood prevailing among the workers, the garrison soldiers and sailors, and received instructions from him.

On October 10, Dzerzhinsky was present at the historic meeting of the Central Committee at which Lenin made a report on the current situation. His in-depth analysis of the domestic and international situation showed that an armed uprising was imminent, and could very well end in total success. All practical Party work, he stated, must be geared towards the uprising. The Central Committee adopted Lenin's resolution by a vote of ten to two. The resolution read: "Recognising that an armed uprising is inevitable and quite ripe, the Central Committee suggests that all Party organisations be guided by this, and that all practical matters be discussed and resolved from this stand."

At the same meeting, Dzerzhinsky proposed that a Politbureau be formed to exercise political leadership over the preparations for the uprising. It was to comprise seven people and be headed by Lenin.

During this time, Dzerzhinsky and other prominent Party members frequently spoke at factories urging the workers to join the organisational and technical work involved in preparations for the uprising.

On October 12, a Revolutionary Military Committee (RMC) was set up at the Petrograd Soviet of
Workers' and Soldiers' Deputies on an order from the Party Central Committee. As one of its members, Dzerzhinsky was entrusted with ensuring the reliable protection of Smolny, the headquarters of the revolution, and with maintaining contacts with the city suburbs.

The decisive events were already close at hand. On October 16, Dzerzhinsky was present at the extended Central Committee meeting at which Lenin delivered a report on the tasks to be tackled by the Party in preparation for the uprising. "The position," said Lenin, "was clear—either Kornilov's dictatorship or the dictatorship of the proletariat and the poorer strata of the peasantry... From a political analysis of the class struggle in Russia and in Europe there emerged the necessity to pursue the most determined and most active policy, which could be only armed uprising."[5]

Dzerzhinsky took part in the debates following the report. He criticised those who vacillated when it came to setting the date of the uprising, claiming that it was not yet ripe nor well enough prepared technically.

The Central Committee meeting elected the Revolutionary Military Centre to exercise leadership over the uprising. The members were Yakov Sverdlov, Joseph Stalin, Andrei Bubnov, Moissei Uritsky and Felix Dzerzhinsky. The Centre was incorporated in the Revolutionary Military Committee (RMC) and became its Party core.

Soon after the extended Central Committee meeting, Smolny hosted an assembly of the Petrograd Party activists— about a hundred representatives of larger enterprises and army units. On behalf of the Central Committee, Dzerzhinsky made a report on the preparatory work to be done by the Petrograd Bolsheviks before the uprising. He commented on Lenin's resolutions of October 10 and 16, and called on Party activists to promote them in all possible ways. The assembly unanimously voted to begin the uprising immediately.

The Central and Petrograd committees were thoroughly checking the city Party organisations' readiness for the uprising and the strength of their links with workers, the soldiers of the Petrograd garrison and the sailors in the Baltic fleet.

Beginning with October 20, twenty-four hour guard duty was introduced at the RMC, and regular contacts were maintained with the district Soviets, army units and battleships. The RMC Members of the Revolutionary Military Centre were busy for almost 24 hours a day and nearly forgot what sleep and rest meant. They received workers, soldiers, sailors, Party members, commanders of Red Guard detachments, Bolsheviks who arrived from Moscow, the Ural area, Siberia, the Ukraine, Byelorussia and the fighting fronts, listened to what they had to say, gave advice and directions, and kept in touch with factories and army units.

RMC commissars, who were handpicked and instructed by Dzerzhinsky and Sverdlov, helped to attain a state of combat readiness in the troops and on battleships, and supervised and controlled the factories' production and distribution of goods, especially military materiel.

A tremendous amount of work fell to the lot of the Central Committee headed by Lenin. The CC meetings discussed reports on the developments at the fighting fronts, the convening of a congress of Soviets, the alignment of forces and reports of the MRC and its Party Centre, and gave detailed consideration to everything that was likely to be required for a successful armed uprising.

In the decisive weeks and days just before the uprising, ties between the Central Committee and local Party branches were strengthened. The latter were given instructions and assistance through letters and personally by Bolshevik propaganda workers. Leaders of local Party branches and activists from among the workers, soldiers and peasants came to Petrograd whenever necessary.

They were also doing a great deal of work required for successfully carrying out the Bolsheviks' organisational, propaganda, military and technical plans. The Central Committee sent its representatives to the provinces to direct the uprising.

The RSDLP(B) Central Committee acted as the headquarters of the revolution and worked along the principles of collective leadership. In the three months preceding the October Revolution it held over 30 meetings.

On October 22, at the suggestion of the Central Committee, the Bolsheviks held the Day of the Petrograd Soviet, an inspection of the revolutionary forces before the decisive attack. Dzerzhinsky spoke at workers' meetings in a number of city districts.

The Party was also working to bring up to mark the armed forces of the revolution, the Red Guard detachments, which by October 22 numbered over 20,000 men. On that day, the first Petrograd conference of Red Guards was held, at which about 100 people, mostly Bolsheviks, assembled. Guided by Lenin's advice and directions, the city Bolsheviks had managed to organise and train a competent body of men capable of prompt action.

84

The Day of the Petrograd Soviet and the Red Guards' conference declared seizure of power by the Bolsheviks as top priority.

On the morning of October 24, an extraordinary meeting of the Central Committee took place.

Dzerzhinsky was among those present, while Lenin was still working underground. The first CC decision obliged all members not to leave Smolny without the special permission of the Central Committee.

On October 24, the Petrograd RSDLP(B) Committee passed a decision to immediately overthrow the

Provisional Government and transfer state power over to the Soviets of Workers' and Soldiers' Deputies both in the centre and the provinces. The first unit of soldiers and Red Guards that was to seize the enemy strongholds marched off from Smolny on the morning of October 24 under Dzerzhinsky's command. By night, the soldiers had captured the Central Telegraph.

Soon after the seizure of the telegraph, Lenin instructed the RMC to promptly advise the Bolshevik organisations in other towns and regions that the armed uprising was under way. Closely following the progress of events, he urged the RMC to lose no time storming the Winter Palace and placing the Provisional Government under arrest.

On October 24, Lenin left his secret flat, arrived at Smolny and assumed the immediate leadership of the uprising, which was rapidly gaining momentum. By the morning of October 25, all premises housing government bodies, with the exception of the Winter Palace, and all major strongholds were in the hands of the insurgents.

That same day, under the guidance of the Bolshevik Party Central Committee, Petrograd workers, soldiers and sailors carried out the plan Lenin had mapped out for an armed uprising and overthrew the Provisional Government. The RMC made public Lenin's appeal "To the Citizens of Russia!", which stated in part: "The Provisional Government has been deposed. State power has passed into the hands of the organ of the Petrograd Soviet of Workers' and Soldiers' Deputies—the Revolutionary Military Committee, which heads the Petrograd proletariat and the garrison."[6]

On the night of October 25, the Second Congress of Soviets opened in Petrograd. It adopted Lenin's address "To Workers, Peasants and Soldiers!" announcing that the uprising had been victorious.

On the night of October 25, the storming of the Winter Palace began and lasted for several hours. At 2

a.m. on October 26, the last stronghold of counter-revolution fell. The members of the Provisional Government were taken into custody.

On October 26 Lenin spoke at the Second Congress of Soviets on the issues of peace and land. The congress approved his decrees on peace and on land, and formed the first worker and peasant government, the Council of People's Commissars headed by Lenin.

Dzerzhinsky was a delegate at that historic congress. Speaking on behalf of the Polish proletariat on the subject of Lenin's report on peace, he said: "The Polish proletariat has always fought side by side with the Russian proletariat. The Decree (on peace.—Auth.) has been enthusiastically welcomed by the SocialDemocrats of Poland and Lithuania.

We know that the only force capable of emancipating the world is the proletariat which is fighting for socialism. When socialism triumphs, capitalism will be smashed and national oppression will be abolished."

The congress elected Dzerzhinsky to the All-Russia Central Executive Committee.[7] Notes

[1]V. I. Lenin, "Speech in the Finland Station Square to Workers, Soldiers and Sailors, April 3 (16), 1917", Collected Works, Vol., 41, 1969, p. 399.

[2]V. I. Lenin, "The Seventh (April) All-Russia Conference of the R.S.D.L.P.(B.)," Collected Works, Vol. 24, 1974, p. 298.

[3]V. I. Lenin, "The Political Situation", Collected Works, Vol. 25, 1964, p. 180.

[4]Ibid., p. 179.

[5]V. I. Lenin, "Meeting of the Central Committee of the R.S.D.L.P.(B.), October 16 (29), 1917", Collected Works, Vol. 26, 1964, pp. 191-92.

[6]V. I. Lenin, Collected Works, Vol. 26, 1964, p. 236.

[7]The supreme legislative, administrative and controlling body of state authority in Soviet Russia in 1917-37.

Chapter Five

PROTECTING THE REVOLUTION

The success of the October Revolution opened up a period of drastic change in all aspects of social life. Needless to say, this work provoked fierce opposition on the part of the overthrown classes and their stooges, Mensheviks and SRs. Egged on by international imperialist quarters and supported by them, they spared no effort and scorned no methods, including armed action, to smash Soviet power and restore the bourgeois system. The country was faced with a task of paramount importance: to defend what the revolution had accomplished. In this campaign, Dzerzhinsky played a truly outstanding part. The years after the revolution were probably the most important in his life. He became one of Lenin's closest associates in the work to organise the defence of the revolution and to build socialism.

After the October events, Dzerzhinsky continued work on the Petrograd Revolutionary Military Committee. Late in the month, it was placed directly under the All-Russia Central Executive Committee and its functions had substantially expanded. Specifically, it was to fight counter- revolutionary activities, maintain public order in the country, pull down the old state apparatus and build a new one. The RMC was in charge of supplying food to towns and the army, distributing weapons and money, requisitioning buildings, vehicles and surplus goods in the greatest demand from the bourgeoisie, and conducting propaganda.

Dzerzhinsky was one of the leading figures in the RMC. He took part in nearly all of its plenary meetings, proving himself to be a steady champion of the Bolshevik line on all issues. He was elected to the RMC headquarters and later to its executive commission. At its meetings, Dzerzhinsky often spoke before worker and soldier delegates to explain the events underway in the country and expose the lies and slander of the bourgeois press against the Bolsheviks.

In the complicated situation that prevailed in the first days after the Revolution, Dzerzhinsky was Lenin's staunchest supporter and dealt firmly with counterrevolutionaries and defeatists inside the Party.

After helping to suppress the revolt masterminded by Kerensky and General Krasnov, Dzerzhinsky worked to break up the Petrograd City Duma, a major counterrevolutionary centre.

A serious threat to the existence of the young Soviet state was posed by the bourgeois press, which was spreading lies about the Bolsheviks and inciting counter-revolutionary elements to unleash a civil war. On October 27, the Council of People's Commissars passed a decree on the press which banned all publications trying to stir up opposition or insubordination to the government, sow discontent or provoke criminal acts. The Revolutionary Military Committee immediately began to introduce the decree. A number of mandates, including those on the confiscation of counter- revolutionary publications and the closing down of the printing presses and offices of bourgeois newspapers, were signed by Dzerzhinsky. As member of the RMC, and from mid- November a member of the People's Commissariat for International Affairs Collegium, Dzerzhinsky headed the campaign against sabotage which threatened to disrupt the building of the Soviet state, introduce chaos into the country's political and economic life, and provoke dissatisfaction with the new authorities. The RMC declared the saboteurs enemies of the people who were liable to arrest. On November 14, the RMC arrested a group of office workers under the former Ministry for State Charitable Institutions. On Dzerzhinsky's order the saboteurs were released only after they had submitted the keys and documents to the Soviet authorities. On November 23, Dzerzhinsky signed a warrant for the arrest of a group of State Bank employees who refused to work under the new system.

Dzerzhinsky's duties in the Revolutionary Military Committee were many. He organised and supervised the guarding of wine cellars and the requisitioning of goods from profiteers, and sanctioned meetings and assemblies; he helped organise the defence of the country's state borders, was in charge of dispatching armaments and propaganda literature to the provinces and supplying army units and offices with food, clothes and fuel; he instituted the search for valuables stolen from the Winter Palace, saw to the opening of a cheap canteen for lower-ranking office personnel, provided maimed war veterans with artificial limbs, and did much more.

In the second half of November, Dzerzhinsky made an important contribution to the restructuring of

Petrograd militia, which had been set up under the Provisional Government. After the October

Revolution, its top-ranking personnel refused to work under the RMC and chose to engage in sabotage. Dzerzhinsky sanctioned the arrest of its chief. However, the organisation also incorporated a body of men who were willing to cooperate with the new authorities. About 6,000 militiamen declared they were ready to work under the RMC; only 600 refused. This made it possible to use the old militia for maintaining public law and order up to the time when a new, revolutionary militia could be established.

Dzerzhinsky's work in the Revolutionary Military Committee was not confined to Petrograd and its outskirts. He gave valuable assistance to local Party bodies and Soviets righting to consolidate the Soviet system and combat counter-revolutionary activities.

As the Soviet state apparatus became better organised, it became apparent that in many spheres the functions of the RMC and the People's Commissariats began to overlap. On November 25, the Council of People's Commissars decided to take some of the work load from the RMC and handed over some of its functions to pertinent bodies. It stated that the RMC should concern itself mainly with combating counter-revolutionary activities. On November 21, Dzerzhinsky had suggested that a commission of five for the struggle against counter-revolution be set up within the Revolutionary Military Committee.

On December 5, the RMC adopted a resolution on the cancellation of all its departments and the handing over of materials to the appropriate sections of the All- Russia Central Executive Committee (CEC), the Council of People's Commissars, and the Petrograd City and district Soviets. The abolition of the RMC concluded one of the most important stages in Dzerzhinsky's work to establish and build up the Soviet state and defend the achievements of the October Revolution.

In early December 1917, the political situation in the country deteriorated further. The counterrevolutionary elements stepped up their activities, civil war flared up in the country's outlying regions, sabotage continued to grow, and the campaign of lies and slander launched by the bourgeois, SR and Menshevik press was as vicious as ever. The situation was particularly grave in Petrograd, where the personnel of former ministries, the State Bank, the treasury and the City Council had been on strike for over a month. The pensions and grants to widows, orphans and war invalids had been stopped. At some factories, the workers were no longer receiving wages. The saboteurs disrupted the distribution of fuel thus posing a very real threat to the future operation of the industry. The Union of the State Office Personnel Associations decided to go on a nation-wide political strike.

In the capital, matters were further aggravated by a rising wave of pogroms and robberies. Groups of bandits incited by counter-revolutionaries broke into and smashed wine cellars, shops and drugstores and supplied alcohol to the garrison soldiers. The Committee for the Struggle Against the Pogroms set up by the Petrograd Soviet on December 2 uncovered an organisation which printed and distributed appeals for the overthrow of Soviet power. Also discovered were caches of weapons, secret flats and correspondence between counter-revolutionary groups. The Soviet state was indeed severely threatened.

On December 6, 1917, the Council of People's Commissars discussed the pending strike of office workers. Dzerzhinsky was instructed to set up a commission for finding ways of preventing the strike. On December 7, Lenin sent him a note stating that urgent measures must be taken in order to suppress the counter-revolutionaries and saboteurs.

That very day, Dzerzhinsky reported to the Council of People's Commissars on the membership, structure, objectives and rights of such a commission. "Its purpose," he remarked, "is (1) to cut short and foil all counter- revolutionary efforts and sabotage activities throughout Russia, no matter from where they may proceed.

"2) To turn over to the Revolutionary Tribunal all saboteurs and counterrevolutionaries, and to develop methods of combating them.

"3) The commission will conduct only a preliminary investigation, to the extent required by effective counteraction".

The commission, Dzerzhinsky proceeded to say, should concentrate above all on combating the antiSoviet press, eliminating sabotage, and suppressing the criminal activities of counter-revolutionary elements. It should be granted the right to confiscate property, evict criminals from their lodgings, take away their food coupons, publish lists of the counter-revolutionaries' names, etc.

After listening to Dzerzhinsky's report, the Council of People's Commissars decided: "To call the commission the All-Russia Extraordinary Commission at the Council of People's Commissars to Combat Counter-revolution and Sabotage, and to approve its establishment." Dzerzhinsky was appointed chairman.

The next day, which was December 8, the All-Russia Extraordinary Commission (Vecheka) meeting elected its presidium consisting of five people and headed by Dzerzhinsky. The organisational structure of the commission was soon evolved, too. It incorporated departments on combating counter-revolution, sabotage and profiteering, as well as the organisational department which was to keep in touch with the local Soviet bodies and help them combat internal enemies. The core of the Commission was formed by veteran Bolsheviks and professional revolutionaries Jams Peters, Ivan Ksenofontov, Dmitry Yevseyev, Vassily Fomhrand Stepan Shchukin.

The formation of the All-Russia Extraordinary Commission signified the emergence of state security bodies of a new, socialist type which protected the achievements of the revolution, the vital interests of the working class, the peasantry, and all toiling people.

After the Council of People's Commissars approved the membership of the All-Russia Extraordinary Commission, Dzerzhinsky .devoted himself to building up its efficiency. One of his first steps was to recruit competent and reliable personnel. Dzerzhinsky believed that the men should come predominantly from the working class, be staunch supporters of the Soviet system, and to be moral and incorruptible. He appealed to the RSDLP(B) Central Committee, the Petrograd Soviet and the Red Guards headquarters to recommend unquestionably honest men "aware of their great mission as revolutionaries, who cannot be bribed or succumb to the corrupting influence of gold". The staff of the Extraordinary Commission was recruited quite quickly.

Dzerzhinsky coordinated the work of all departments, channelling their efforts to achieve a common goal. He was a figure of tremendous authority, and in addition to his significant political experience, loyalty to the ideals of the revolution, scrupulous honesty and considerate attitude to others, he was a superb organiser. Quickly perceiving the special talents of each man, he competently appointed them, making sure that they were aware of the significance of the work with which they had been entrusted.

Dzerzhinsky justly believed that the success of the Vecheka in the fight against the opponents of Soviet power would, to a large extent, depend on popular support. He stressed that the workers, soldiers and peasants should be given a good idea of the activities of the Commission and be appealed to for help in case of need.

The documents of the Soviet government, which Dzerzhinsky helped draw up, clearly defined the competence and rights of the All-Russia Extraordinary Commission, and its relationship with other state bodies. They confirmed the Vecheka's direct subordination and accountability to the Council of People's Commissars and its right to institute a search for counter-revolutionary elements and take the necessary steps to curtail criminal activities, and defined the procedure by which its staff was to be recruited.

Dzerzhinsky not only exercised general leadership over the Vecheka's work but was personally involved in many of its operations against counter-revolutionaries, saboteurs and profiteers. He was present at searches and arrests, investigated quite a number of cases, and did shift duty at the All-Russia Extraordinary

Commission's presidium. We possess numerous notes taken by Dzerzhinsky during his shift duty recording the information submitted by citizens of Petrograd about the criminal activities of enemies of the Soviet system.

Dzerzhinsky was a believer in prompt action. Cheka men would be dispatched to make a search and an arrest, and some infiltrated anti-Soviet organisations and eventually blew them up.

The Extraordinary Commission was instrumental in eliminating sabotage in Petrograd. On December 22, a search was conducted in the building where the Union of the State Office Personnel Associations, a nest of saboteurs, had its headquarters. Cheka men found mimeographed bulletins of the central strike committee, subscription sheets, and visiting cards and notebooks. Dzerzhinsky personally studied the papers and questioned the arrested men, worked to discover the financial sources for the running of the organisation, and the degree of the members' personal involvement in its activities and their political views. He then drew up a detailed plan for further investigation, and a list of the organisers and most active participants in sabotage activities. On December 30, 1917, they were arrested by the Vecheka.

It was found that the Union and the strike committee operating under it were a major centre of sabotage not only in Petrograd but throughout the country. They received money from Russian and foreign capitalists and banks. The Commission uncovered strike committees functioning at ministries and offices.

In the course of the investigation the Commission destroyed the strike committee apparatus and isolated its leaders from rank-and-file members. The men who gave a written promise no longer to engage in sabotage were released.

In the late 1917-early 1918 the Commission was informed of the existence in the city of anti-Soviet centres which recruited and shipped officers to the River Don area where they joined the White Cossack units.[1] The Extraordinary Commission was to uncover and destroy these centres. Dzerzhinsky personally helped put an end to the Organisation for the Struggle Against Bolshevism and the Recruiting of Troops for Kaledin, Everything for the Homeland, The White Cross, The Black Dot, The Alliance for the Assistance to Invalid Officers, The Military League and a number of other groups.

In late February 1918, when German troops were advancing towards Petrograd, Soviet power was threatened. Counter-revolutionary elements became active once more. White Guards units, which had contacts with German imperialist circles, were preparing a rebellion in Petrograd. The city was teeming with criminals who terrorised the population. On February 21, at Lenin's suggestion, the Council of People's Commissars passed the decree "The Socialist Fatherland Is in Danger!" which contained a plan for mobilising all available forces in order to rebuff the enemy. The last, eighth point of the Decree granted the revolutionary bodies, including the Vecheka, extraordinary powers in the campaign against hooliganism, enemy agents, profiteers, counter-revolutionary agitators and German spies. On Dzerzhinsky's proposal, the Extraordinary Commission issued a statement informing the citizens that no mercy would be shown towards the enemies of the Soviet system.

As the Germans advanced towards Petrograd, Dzerzhinsky channelled the efforts of his staff into fighting gangsterism. In late February-early March the Vecheka uncovered and disbanded several gangs, whose leaders were severely punished. Gradually, the wave of terror in Petrograd began to roll back, and revolutionary order was re-established.

The Cheka was also involved in combating profiteering. As was reported in the CEC Izvestia newspaper, the efforts of Dzerzhinsky's Commission to check speculation in gold were "crowned with brilliant success after a very short time". Alongside with gold, large amounts of consumer goods and foodstuffs were confiscated.

Work on the Extraordinary Commission consumed a great deal of Dzerzhinsky's time and energy, and yet he remained active in other fields as well. He was regularly present at the RSDLP(B) Central Committee meetings, which at that time were devoted mostly to the withdrawal of the Soviet Republic from the imperialist war. In the course of peace talks, Germany and its allies demanded that the Soviet Government permit the German troops to remain in Poland, the Ukraine, Byelorussia and the Baltic area. The alternative to these humiliating terms would be a revolutionary war against German imperialism, which Soviet Russia was simply unable to wage. The old army had almost entirely fallen apart, while a new, Red Army was only being formed. The workers and peasants were longing for peace; continuation of the war would have doomed the revolution. Lenin was convinced that to save the Soviet Republic, a peace treaty with Germany had to be signed immediately whatever its terms. But not everyone in the Central Committee was of the same opinion. Dzerzhinsky, too, adopted a different stand, believing that a peace treaty would strengthen German imperialism and offer no guarantee against further ultimatums. "Signing this peace treaty, we snail save nothing," he said.

The peace talks held in Brest were interrupted. On February 18, 1918, the German army assumed the offensive and began to advance deeper into the country.

On February 23, Germany submitted another, harsher ultimatum whose terms called for slicing off the Baltic area and part of Byelorussia from Soviet Russia, forcing the Soviet Government to recognise the bourgeois Central Rada of the Ukraine, demobilise the army, and pay a huge indemnity. At the Central Committee meeting which convened on that same day, Lenin demanded that these terms be accepted.

Thanks to his determination, the Central Committee agreed to accept immediately the German ultimatum. Dzerzhinsky abstained from voting.

On March 3, 1918, the peace treaty with Germany was signed in Brest. The Extraordinary Seventh Congress of the RCP(B)[2] held a few days later approved this step. On March 8, the congress elected a new Central Committee, with Dzerzhinsky as one of its members.

At around that time, the Soviet Government moved from Petrograd to Moscow, and so did the Extraordinary Commission. The bulk of the cases under investigation was handed over to the newlyestablished Petrograd Extraordinary Commission headed by Moissei Uritsky.

The situation in Moscow, as elsewhere in the country, was extremely complicated. The exploiter classes which had suffered a defeat in open combat now engaged in underground subversive activities. In the spring of 1918, a number of large paramilitary secret organisations sprang up, including The Union for the Defence of the Motherland and Freedom, The Right Centre and The Union of Resurrection, which set themselves the goal of overthrowing the Soviet system. They received financial assistance from abroad.

Profiteers, bribe-takers, hooligans and gangsters posed a serious threat to the Soviet Republic. They disrupted state discipline and public order and introduced chaos into the life of society. In many cities and towns, anarchist gangs captured buildings, raided offices, and robbed the people. The bourgeois, SR and Menshevik press continued to disseminate slander against the policies of the Communist Party and the Soviet Government. The need to suppress these activities was even more urgent than in the first months after the October Revolution.

The Extraordinary Commission Collegium issued a decree on the immediate establishment of local Chekas to combat counter-revolution, profiteering, abuse of official position and the subversive activities of the press. In April 1918, the Chekas were formed in Kaluga, Astrakhan and many other towns.

On May 11, the All-Russia Central Executive Committee Presidium banned the newspapers which were sowing panic among the people and provoking dissatisfaction with the Soviet system. These newspapers were to be fined and their editors arrested. In view of its urgency, the execution of this decision was entrusted to the Extraordinary Commission.

Dzerzhinsky organised and reinforced the armed units at the disposal of the Vecheka and saw to it that their personnel were well-trained.

As the Commission's functions gained in scope, it became essential to further build up its staff. On May 18, Dzerzhinsky raised this issue at the RCP(B) Central Committee meeting, which considered his report and decided to appoint prominent Soviet statesmen and Party functionaries Martyn Lacis and Varvara

Yakovleva to responsible positions in the Extraordinary Commission. In addition, the Central Executive Committee, the Moscow RCP(B) Committee and district Party committees were required to send Communists to work there.

Seeking to reinforce the ranks of his organisation with ideologically mature and dedicated people, Dzerzhinsky stressed the need for enhancing political awareness. Speaking at the Collegium meetings, he repeated time and again that only those who were prepared to sacrifice all for the cause of the revolution, had a well-developed sense of duty and were willing to follow orders of their superiors promptly were fit for work at the Cheka. He also requested that those who were not prepared to assume full responsibility for their work and who had not always performed their duties well be asked to leave. On April 26, at the Collegium meeting, he talked about the need to purge the Commission.

Dzerzhinsky insisted that the Cheka's staff should never overstep the boundaries of law, and that those people placed under arrest should be treated with courtesy. When he learned that one of his men hit the person he was questioning, he personally investigated the matter. He wrote on the cover of the examination record: "The commission has investigated the matter and has decided to severely reprimand the guilty party, and in the future, to institute court proceedings against anyone who so much as lays a finger on a detainee." Dzerzhinsky considered it impermissible to use provocation and taught his staff to act before a crime that would entail arrests and other repressive acts took place. In his words, the principal goal of the Cheka was "to prevent crime, which, of course, might not produce impressive results but is actually much more productive".

Dzerzhinsky urged the Cheka's personnel to expand and strengthen ties with the working people, for he considered this a necessary condition for efficient work.

In the spring of 1918, acting on Dzerzhinsky's plan, the Extraordinary Commission broke up a number of anarchist groups in Moscow. In the small hours of the morning of April 12, the units of the Moscow garrison and Cheka detachments surrounded the buildings occupied by anarchists. About 600 people were arrested, most of whom were not convinced anarchists but burglars and gangsters.

Soon, the same sort of operation was carried out in Petrograd, Saratov, Voronezh, and other towns and cities. The elimination of anarchist groups helped consolidate Soviet power and strengthened the security of the people.

Another series of blows was dealt against profiteers. In March and April, Dzerzhinsky investigated a number of cases of illegal sales of spirits to owners of Moscow's tearooms and dining halls. The persons guilty of the speculation were deported from Moscow, and their property confiscated. A major operation was conducted against the Russian Union for the Commerce and Industry to Advance the Domestic and Foreign Exchange of Goods, which was headed by big factory-owners in Moscow who had sold from tens of thousands to hundreds of thousands of poods[3] of articles to Moscow profiteers and intermediaries. Under a Vecheka decree, the Union's property was confiscated. Soon, the Soviet Government nationalised the companies associated with it.

The Cheka uncovered criminal contacts between Russian profiteers and employees of the German embassy. German diplomats and representatives of trade firms were buying up stock and other securities of factories to be nationalised at extremely low prices. Under the terms of the Treaty of Brest-Litovsk (the old name of Brest), they could present them to the Soviet Government to be reimbursed in gold at face value. However, the Cheka, which had previously sentenced a number of big-time profiteers to death for high treason and illegal transactions involving sales of stock, prevented this speculation.

The Cheka was also in charge of cases involving abuse of official position. Under Dzerzhinsky's immediate guidance, it uncovered and investigated a great number of cases of embezzlements, bribetaking, extortion, and counterfeiting.

Another of its functions was to combat the counter-revolutionary press. In May and June, it terminated the activities of Vperyod (Forward), Rodina (Motherland), Zemlya i Volya (Land and Freedom), Narodnoye Slovo (People's World), and Novosti Dnya (Daily News), SR and Menshevik publications issued in Moscow and Petrograd, which slandered the Soviet Government's foreign and domestic policies. A number of similar publications, as well as "non-partisan" gutter sheets, were closed down in other towns, too.

The Cheka waged a successful campaign against counterrevolutionary activities. In late March, it uncovered and suppressed the Landowners' Union, which maintained contacts with the White Guard generals Kornilov and Kaledin. In April, it concluded its investigation into the activities of a counterrevolutionary group which numbered among its members the American citizen W. A. Barri, ex-officers of the White Army, and Countess Lanskaya. The group failed in its attempt to create a storm unit which it hoped to move it to the Don area, with the men disguised as Red Guards. The Barri organisation had a great deal of money at its disposal which was used to render "material assistance" to the volunteers and supply them with food and clothing. This case was handed over to the Moscow Revolutionary Tribunal for further investigation.

In May 1918, Dzerzhinsky's Commission was successful in uncovering the counterrevolutionary Union for the Defence of the Motherland and Freedom. The first information about its existence came from a worker of the Moscow Kauchuk Factory, who reported that one of the nearby private clinics was visited by suspicious-looking men who posed as patients but who, judging from their bearing, were probably officers.

At about the same time, the commander of the Lettish regiment reported to Vecheka Deputy Chairman Janis Peters that a nurse at the Iverskaya Hospital had told him about an armed uprising under preparation in Moscow. She herself had learned about it from a military cadet she knew. Dzerzhinsky ordered that the hospital, the private clinic, and the military cadet be kept under surveillance.

In the early hours of the morning of May 29, a group of men headed by Peters surrounded the house where the conspirators had assembled and arrested the lot. The search produced the seal and documents of the Union for the Defence of the Motherland and Freedom, scraps of a torn-up letter, half of a visiting card torn along a zigzag line, and address and telephone books. Other members of the Union were arrested, too.

Together with Martyn Lacis, Dzerzhinsky began to question the men and study the documents confiscated during the search. The investigation revealed that the Union was a large and efficiently operated secret military organisation which numbered about 5,000 counter-revolutionaries and had branches in a number of cities. The conspirators had found ways to infiltrate Soviet government bodies, army units, and military organisations. The main objective of the Union was to overthrow the Soviet system, establish a military dictatorship headed by Boris Savinkov, an SR leader, and re-enter the war against Germany.

It was no easy task to destroy the Union. It was necessary to master the art of uncovering the activities of sophisticated secret counter-revolutionary organisations which used codes and passwords and had an intricate structure. Dzerzhinsky's investigation set an example for all his staff to follow. Even the most impatient commissars and investigating officers," wrote Janis Peters, "learned from him how insignificant scraps of paper could be valuable leads in uncovering counter-revolutionary plots."

The White Guards were not the only group plotting against the Soviet state; SRs and Mensheviks were also waging their own vigorous campaigns. In the spring and summer of 1918, right-wing SRs and Mensheviks launched a large-scale propaganda campaign, hoping to incite the people to take up arms against the Soviet government and help set up "a general democratic" government.

They were involved in the revolt in Yaroslavl staged by the Union for the Defence of the Motherland and Freedom, and provoked anti-Soviet actions in Kostroma, Saratov, Volsk, Tambov and a number of other cities. They tried to instigate strikes among factory workers and to trigger kulak[4] revolts in the countryside.

On May 23, 1918, the Council of People's Commissars enjoined the Vecheka to step up its campaign against the hostile activities of counter-revolutionary parties. Rightwing SR and Menshevik leaders were put under surveillance. On June 13, the Extraordinary Commission was informed that an SR and Menshevik conference was to be convened in a certain club-house to devise a plan for anti-Soviet struggle. To disguise its purpose, the conference organisers referred to it as "An Extraordinary Assembly of Representatives of Moscow's Factories and Workshops". Right-wing SRs and Mensheviks from Petrograd, Tula, Bryansk and Penza were expected to attend the conference. On the same day, the Cheka arrested the participants at the counter- revolutionary gathering and confiscated a large number of antiSoviet documents, including the "Appeal to the Workers of Moscow", "Instruction of the Delegation to Moscow Workers", "Instruction to Petrograd Workers", and draft resolutions of the conference which urged the workers to overthrow the Soviet government. There was evidence indicating that the counterrevolutionaries had requested the allies to send a landing force and open an anti-German front on the territory of Russia, and had slandered the Bolshevik Party and its leaders. Dzerzhinsky was personally involved in the investigation of this affair.

Most of Dzerzhinsky's time and effort went into the struggle against anarchism, gangsterism and abuse of office, and uncovering the schemes hatched by White Guards, SRs and Mensheviks. He was rarely at home, spending days and nights at the Cheka. A narrow iron bed covered with an army blanket stood in his office behind a screen, and he often slept there at night. "I'm in the very fire of the struggle," he wrote to his wife on May 27, 1918. "It is the life of a soldier who can have no rest, for our home must be saved. There is no time to think about one's nearest and dearest, or about oneself. The work and the struggle are hell."

Dzerzhinsky's goal was to turn the Cheka into an efficient body that would serve the proletarian state, the punishing sword of the revolution. "Our task," he said in an interview with a Novaya Zhizn (New Life) reporter, "is to combat the enemies of Soviet power and the new system of life. Such enemies are both our political opponents and all the gangsters, swindlers, profiteers and other criminals who are undermining the foundations of the socialist system. With respect to them, we are merciless."

However, left-wing SRs made it difficult to introduce effective methods of struggle against the enemies of the country. Using the right or veto, they prevented the passage of the Vecheka resolutions to severely punish the most active members of The Union for the Defence of the Motherland and Freedom.

Left-wing SRs undermined the Bolshevik Party's activities not only at the Cheka. At that time, they were preparing a revolt in Moscow, which was to be instigated by the assassination of the German Ambassador Wilhelm Mirbach. One of the Cheka detachments commanded by left-wing SR D. Popov was planned to act as the principal strike force. In late June-early July Popov sent nearly all men loyal to the Soviet Government to the front and replaced them with demoralised Black Sea Fleet sailors and anarchists.

On July 6, 1918, left-wing SRs Blyumkin and Andreyev, who had been provided with a false Cheka mandate, entered the German Embassy and killed Mirbach. The assassination of this high-ranking official placed Soviet-German relations in great jeopardy and threatened a renewal of war. Simultaneously, leftwing SRs launched a revolt against the Soviet Government and attempted to seize major, strategically important buildings and locations in Moscow.

When the news reached Dzerzhinsky, he took steps to ascertain whether the assassination was

Blyumkin's private decision or a plot devised by the left-wing SR Party. Mindless of the danger involved, he, accompanied by three Cheka men went straight to the rebels' headquarters, where they were arrested by the SRs. Dzerzhinsky did not show any fear and sharply berated the traitors. He tried to explain to the deceived men what they had been made party to.

The news that the Vecheka Chairman was being detained by the SRs provoked strong indignation and anxiety among the people. Everyone realised that his life was in grave danger. Meetings were held at factories where the workers demanded that Dzerzhinsky and the other captured Bolsheviks be set free at once.

Lenin was greatly concerned when he learned about what had happened. "It would be wrong to say that Lenin turned pale—he turned virtually white," wrote Vladimir Bonch-Bruyevich afterwards. "He looked like this when he was angry or much shaken by dangerous unforeseen circumstances."

On July 7, the revolt was suppressed. When the Soviet troops began firing at SR headquarters, the leaders of the revolt fled ignominiously. Dzerzhinsky and the other Bolsheviks were set free. Dzerzhinsky was shattered by the leftwing SRs' treachery. He could not forgive himself for not having foreseen their intentions earlier. He submitted a request to the Council of People's Commissars asking to be released from his duties as Chairman of the Vecheka and from any employment there, for he was one of the main witnesses for the Mirbach assassination case. The Council of People's Commissars granted his request, but ordered him to remain on the new Vecheka Collegium. Janis Peters was temporarily appointed the Vecheka Chairman.

Notes

[1]At that time, an anti-Soviet revolt of wealthy Cossacks headed by Ataman (Cossack chieftain)
Kaledin flared up in the Don region.

[2]The Congress renamed the Russian Social-Democratic Labour Party (Bolsheviks) into the Russian Communist Party (Bolsheviks), or the RCP(B).

[3]Pood equals 16 kg.

[4]Kulaks – Russian term (literally "fist") for the rural bourgeoisie which emerged as a result of the social differentiation of the peasantry.

Chapter Six

WORK AS THE VECHEKA CHAIRMAN DURING THE CIVIL WAR AND FOREIGN ARMED INTERVENTION

In the summer of 1918 the international and domestic situation of the Soviet Republic sharply deteriorated. Most of its territory was occupied by the interventionists and the White Guards, with Soviet power surviving only in Central Russia. However, even in that region the situation was precarious. White Guards, SRs and Mensheviks were staging one revolt after another and managed to temporarily seize power in a number of cities. Vast regions were swept over by kulak rebellions. Stirring up the dissatisfaction of a large, part of the middle peasantry with the government's strict food policy, the kulaks tried to provoke opposition to the Soviet system. The more reactionary part of the clergy was also antagonistic.

Foreign intelligence services also stepped up their activities. British, French and US diplomats were involved in conspiracies aimed at toppling Soviet power. They financed and sponsored such military organisations as The National Centre, The Union of the Restoration, and others. In some of the towns on the Volga, branches of the Union for the Defence of the Motherland and Freedom were still active.

The Communist Party and the Soviet Government launched a campaign to more resolutely combat the interventionists and domestic counter-revolution. The Vecheka was to take more effective steps to stop criminal counterrevolutionary activities. Dzerzhinsky remained its actual head, although for a month and a half after the revolt of July 6 he did not officially hold the position of chairman. On August 22, 1918, he was re-appointed by the Council of People's Commissars.

Dzerzhinsky's efforts were channelled into reshaping the work of the Vecheka and the local

Extraordinary Commissions to make it more efficient. Left-wing SRs were removed from them all. In Moscow, Vologda, Saratov, and Novgorod, Cheka bodies uncovered White Guard centres recruiting officers and helping them to make their way to the interventionists' armies. Simultaneously, the Cheka struck against counter-revolutionary groups which were preparing revolts in the Volga area, the Northwest and in the central regions. In many cases, the Chekas were able to trace contacts between British, French, American and German diplomats and domestic counter-revolutionary organisations.

Dzerzhinsky spent much time in the actual investigation of cases. He visited prisons and talked to suspects in an effort to ascertain the circumstances of their arrest and their degree of guilt. In a number of cases, he suggested that the department for the struggle against counter-revolution should release persons against whom there was insufficient evidence.

As before, Dzerzhinsky did not spare himself. "My dear," he wrote to his wife in August 1918, "forgive me for not having written for so long. In my thoughts I am with you, but I m so pressed for time! All the time I'm like a soldier going into combat, and perhaps for the last time."

On August 30, the Chairman of the Petrograd Extraordinary Commission, Moissei Uritsky, was assassinated by an SR. On Lenin's order, Dzerzhinsky immediately left for Petrograd to look into the matter. There, even more terrible news was waiting for him: an attempt had been made on Lenin's life, and his state was critical.

The news that Lenin had been wounded provoked a storm of indignation in the country. The Central Executive Committee declared the republic a military camp. On September 5, having heard Dzerzhinsky's report on the work of the Cheka, the Council of People's Commissars passed a resolution on red terror as a temporary extraordinary measure of the proletarian state's self-defence, a response to white terror. As Dzerzhinsky put it, this step was "nothing but an expression of the will of the poorest peasantry and the proletariat—to check all attempts at a revolt, and to win".[1] The Cheka was responsible for the implementation of the resolution.

After the assassination attempt on Lenin, the Cheka launched even more determined action against counter-revolutionary elements. In the early morning of September 1, its men arrested the leader of "the ambassadors' plot", British diplomat Robert Lockhart, and the members of the spy organisation he headed. The Cheka was first informed of the organisation's existence and its links with the White Guards back in May. Two Cheka men, J. Buikis and Janis Sprogis, were instructed to infiltrate one of the groups connected with the British intelligence disguised as officers opposed to the Soviet system. The two men were soon accepted as bona fide members of the group. Lockhart instructed Buikis, who was using the alias of Smidhens, to introduce him to the commanding officer of the Lettish unit guarding the Kremlin. Dzerzhinsky's plan called for a rendezvous between Lockhart and commander of the artillery Eduard Berzin, who was introduced to Lockhart as a nationalist and enemy of Soviet power. The plotters gave him 1.2 million roubles with which to bribe the Lettish units to arrest the leaders of the state, including Lenin himself. Berzin assured Lockhart that he was in complete agreement with this plan, and passed the money over to the Vecheka.

The operation against the plotters was scheduled for September, but the events of August 30 made prompt action essential.

At about the same time, a group of conspirators, who met secretly at the British Embassy, was broken up in Petrograd. About 40 conspirators, including several White Guards, were arrested. A search of the premises yielded arms and correspondence with Russian counter-revolutionaries.

The elimination of Lockhart's group meant that the attempts of the Entente to stage a coup d'état in Soviet Russia had failed.

The truly heroic struggle of the Cheka and local Extraordinary Commissions against counter-revolution demoralised the class enemies and strengthened the security of the Socialist Republic. True, a number of mistakes were made in the process. Some innocent persons were arrested; searches, especially in the provinces, were sometimes made without adhering to the rules of procedure, and the investigation of cases was at times too prolonged. A shortage of experienced personnel exacerbated the situation.

On October 28, 1918, the All-Russia Central Executive Committee adopted the Statute on the All-Russia and Local Extraordinary Commissions. The former was recognised as the central organ for coordinating the activities of local commissions and carrying out a planned campaign against counter-revolution, profiteering and abuse of office in the territory of the Russian Federation; its direct accountability to the Council of People's Commissars was confirmed. The local Extraordinary Commissions, the Statute read, were to have the legal status of the other departments of Executive Committees of the Soviets. The Soviets were also to appoint and recall the personnel of the extraordinary commissions, while their chairmen were to be elected by the executive committees of the Soviets and to be approved by the AllRussia Extraordinary Commission. The All-Russia Central Executive Committee confirmed the dual accountability of the local Extraordinary Commissions.

Dzerzhinsky's viewpoint had been taken into account when the draft Statute on the Extraordinary Commissions was being drawn up.

In early October, 1918, Dzerzhinsky left for Switzerland to see his family, and get some rest. His wife Sofia and son Jacek, who had emigrated from Russia before the First World War, lived in Bern. Dzerzhinsky had not seen his wife for eight years, and knew his son, who was born in prison, only from photographs. Dzerzhinsky spent part of his leave in Bern with his family, and part in Lugano, by the lake.

In late October, he left for Soviet Russia via Germany, where a revolution was in progress, stopping over in Berlin.

Dzerzhinsky returned to Moscow a few days before the first anniversary of the October Revolution. On the day of the anniversary, the Cheka personnel had a rally and a concert at their club. During the meeting Lenin surprised those present by making an appearance. He was welcomed with warm applause. In his speech, he referred to the Cheka as a defender of the socialist state, stressed the need to apply strong measures against the resisting exploiter classes, and outlined the standards set for Cheka personnel. He spoke about his appreciation of the effort made by Cheka men to suppress the enemies of the revolution, and said that their mistakes were rooted in the proletariat's insufficient experience in managing state affairs. He critically referred to those intellectuals who failed or did not wish to give an objective assessment of the Cheka's activities, but instead harped on individual faults in its work and slandered the organisation. "The important thing for us," he said, "is that the Cheka is directly exercising the dictatorship of the proletariat, and in that respect its services are invaluable. There is no way of emancipating the people except by forcibly suppressing the exploiters. That is what the Cheka is doing, and therein lies its service to the proletariat."[2]

Lenin's speech helped many Cheka personnel to form a correct idea of the Party political line in the struggle against counter-revolution and boosted the men's morale.

By late autumn, the direction of the Cheka's activities had changed substantially. The victories of the Red Army over the White Czechs and White Guards, stronger positions of proletarian dictatorship, the defeat of Germany in the war, abrogation of the Treaty of Brest-Litovsk, and the upsurge of the revolutionary movement in the West all combined to compel petty-bourgeois democratic quarters to begin to accept Soviet power. For this reason, Lenin altered the tactics of the proletariat with respect to the middle peasants, pointing to the need to form an alliance with them instead or just keeping them neutral. The new situation required that the Cheka bodies show more flexibility and subtle differentiation.

In late November 1918 the Second All-Russia Conference of Extraordinary Commissions was held. In the opening speech, Dzerzhinsky stated that the Vecheka must display maximum revolutionary energy and political maturity and operate on a more planned and systematic basis.

The conference adopted resolutions on the current situation, revolts in the countryside and organisational issues, and worked out measures to combat the White Guards and kulaks. It recognised the expediency of setting up transport departments at the All-Russia and local Chekas for work on railways and water and motor routes. The conference urged the Chekas to act in close collaboration with all Soviet bodies, help them to fulfil their functions, and to act strictly within the law.

After the conference, Dzerzhinsky took part in the work of the Council of Workers' and Peasants'

Defence Commission which had been inspecting the Cheka's activities and met to discuss the results. On December 3, Lenin, who was the Commission's chairman, made a number of important suggestions on tightening Party control over the Cheka bodies and placing more stress on legality in their work. He considered it essential that the Chekas be headed by people who had been Party members for no less than two years and proposed that the People's Commissariats and Party and trade-union bodies be allowed to take on probation persons arrested by Extraordinary Commissions, and that the People's Commissariats and RCP(B) Committees be given the right to take part in the investigation. He also proposed that the Vecheka expand its department handling complaints and requests to speed up investigations, and that harsher punishment for slanderous reports be introduced.

Dzerzhinsky and the other members of the Defence Council's Commission supported Lenin's suggestions, which formed the basis for the Defence Council's resolution of December 11, 1918, "On the Arrest Procedure of Soviet Office and Factory Workers by the All-Russia Extraordinary Commission".

In December, the Moscow Cheka was set up by the Moscow Soviet of Workers', Peasants' and the Red Army Deputies. Dzerzhinsky, who was appointed its chairman, defined its structure, purpose and objectives, and helped recruit the staff.

In the spring and summer of 1919, the country went through yet another critical period. The Red Army was desperately fighting against White Guards and White Poles, who were being trained and armed by the Entente. Spy and secret counter-revolutionary organisations within the country, which generally had contacts with foreign intelligence services, were becoming more active. The enemies of Soviet power staged revolts, strikes and subversive acts. A number of military experts at the fighting fronts went over to the side of the enemy. Criminal gangs operated in towns, and bands of deserters roamed the countryside. Under the extremely harsh conditions of war, famine and economic dislocation, appropriation of public property, profiteering, bribe-taking, embezzlements posed a very grave threat.

The Menshevik and SR parties, which in the winter of 1918-19 chose not to engage in armed action against the Soviet Republic, were now in the same camp as the White Guard counter-revolutionary elements. Not only had they stepped up anti-Soviet propaganda among the people but also instigated strikes at war industry factories and revolts in the army at the time of the fiercest battles against the White armies. Left-wing SRs and anarchists were still hostile and prepared to go to any lengths to undermine Soviet power, the proletarian dictatorship. The stubborn resistance put up by the class enemies made it imperative to introduce harsher punitive measures and strict order and discipline on the home front.

Dzerzhinsky was extremely involved with work to unify the Soviet home front. In the spring and summer of 1919, he often requested the Party Central Committee and the Soviet Government to sanction stricter measures towards strengthening the country's security. On March 14, in accordance with the decision of the Vecheka Presidium, he made a report "On the Gravity of the Current Situation" to the Party Central Committee meeting. He suggested that martial law be introduced in the areas where counterrevolutionary revolts were flaring up. The Central Committee supported this proposal. The Cheka was instructed to increase its efforts to suppress the subversive activities of the counter-revolutionary elements, specifically, SRs and Mensheviks.

On April 13, Dzerzhinsky reported to the Party Central Committee meeting on the steps taken by the Cheka to tighten the protection of the Kremlin and the security of government offices. Dzerzhinsky also reported on the measures taken by the Cheka to put an end to the subversive activities of the right-wing SRs and Mensheviks.

In late May, after the Red Army had suffered one defeat after another, counter-revolutionary groups and organisations in Moscow launched a fresh campaign. Panic mongers spread rumours throughout the city and anti-Soviet propaganda was conducted in the streets. On May 28, at Dzerzhinsky's suggestion, a joint All-Russia and Moscow Extraordinary Commissions' meeting was held at which the Moscow Committee of the RCP(B) and the People's Commissariat for Internal Affairs (NKVD) were also represented. Dzerzhinsky, who was the first speaker, stressed the urgent need to form a flexible and rather small organisation capable of supervising the work of all bodies engaged in direct action against the enemies of the revolution.

After a debate on Dzerzhinsky's report, the meeting decided to set up, under the Moscow Extraordinary Commission, an operative headquarters which would include representatives of that body and of the special and transport departments of the All- Russia Extraordinary Commission. The new organisation was to be headed by Janis Peters, member of the All-Russia Extraordinary Commission Collegium.

On May 31, 1919, Lenin and Dzerzhinsky issued the "Beware of Spies!" appeal which urged the people to show greater vigilance and to try to uncover and catch spies and White Guard plotters. Special measures were to be introduced concerning transport and the army. "All class- conscious workers and peasants must rise up in defence of Soviet power and must fight the spies and whiteguard traitors. Let every man be on the watch and in regular contact, organised on military lines, with the committees of the Party, with the Extraordinary Commission and with the most trusted and experienced comrades among the Soviet officials."[3]

In the spring and summer of 1919, Dzerzhinsky carried out a number of special assignments of the Defence Council promoting the security of the Soviet Republic.

On April 1, Lenin sent a telephone message to the Vecheka calling attention to the enemies' enhanced subversive activities, and enjoining it "to take the most urgent measures to suppress every attempt to cause explosions, to wreck railways and to foment strikes".[4]

Acting on these instructions, on April 3 Dzerzhinsky issued an order to all Extraordinary Commissions to put the grain depots, railway installations and lines and all strategic buildings under guard.

The persons caught in the act of subversion were to be dealt with severely, while the people agitating against Soviet power be handed over to the Revolutionary Tribunal.

In the summer and autumn of that same year, the Defence Council appointed Dzerzhinsky to a number of commissions engaged in drawing up draft resolutions on the introduction of martial law on the railways and measures against deserters, allocating manpower for the building of defence installations on the Southern Front, guard duty at depots, shops and war industry enterprises, taking step against counterrevolutionary elements in the army, and the confiscating of articles of military clothing and equipment from the population.

Working on his numerous assignments of the Party Central Committee and the Defence Council to strengthen the home front, Dzerzhinsky was also engaged in work to enhance the competence and efficiency of the Cheka bodies, improve their structure, reinforce them by recruiting reliable, loyal and trusted Communists, and promote the men's ideological and political awareness. In the spring of 1919 he supervised the reorganisation of the Cheka transport departments, which eventually led to the strengthening of the security of the Soviet transport system. Steps were also taken to consolidate the special departments both organisationally and politically.

On August 18, the Party Central Committee recommended Dzerzhinsky for the post of head of the Vecheka Special Department. On August 27, the Revolutionary Military

Council confirmed his appointment; at the same time, Dzerzhinsky stayed on as Chairman of the AllRussia Extraordinary Commission, and the People's Commissariat for Internal Affairs.

The mounting resistance of the overthrown exploiter classes necessitated more Cheka personnel to cover more territory. In the meantime, in late 1918-early 1919, many Cheka men were transferred to Party and local government bodies in the regions that had been liberated from German occupation—the Ukraine, Latvia, Lithuania, Estonia, and Byelorussia. On March 13, Dzerzhinsky forwarded a letter to the Party Central Committee pointing out the difficulties facing many Chekas after the most experienced men had left. On behalf of the All-Russia Extraordinary Commission, he requested the Central Committee to instruct the Party organisations to allow the men who had the necessary work experience in the Chekas to remain in their jobs, stating that, "Chekas need the most responsible and the most dedicated comrades".

The request was considered on March 14 and granted.

Throughout that year, Dzerzhinsky made several more requests for assistance in manning the Cheka apparatus. Acting on these requests, the Central Committee passed a number of resolutions on reinforcing the personnel of Chekas and special departments. In December, it forwarded a letter to local Party committees instructing them to immediately find and send to Chekas "the largest number possible of steadfast men who can be counted upon to display a responsible attitude and fill important positions there". The Central Committee reminded the local Party bodies that Cheka men were not to be called up without their superiors' consent and until adequate replacements were found. Party committees were enjoined to be especially careful when recruiting men for Chekas, and Communists of Chekas—to be more involved in the work of local Party bodies.

The support and assistance of the Central Committee and local Party organisations plus Dzerzhinsky's persistence made it possible for Cheka bodies to form a reliable core of loyal and experienced Communists. In early 1920, Dzerzhinsky wrote that, "for the most part, the staff are veteran revolutionaries who have passed through the hard school of the tsarist autocracy and tsarist reprisals". More than half of Cheka's personnel were Party members. All responsible positions in Chekas and special departments were filled by Communists.

Dzerzhinsky considered the training of Cheka personnel to be especially important. Back in the autumn of 1918, a three-week course was started at the All-Russia Extraordinary Commission which trained investigating officers, intelligence men and Cheka instructors and organisational staff. In December 1919 Dzerzhinsky requested that the Party Central Committee send 200 Communists to help organise a twomonth course. On December 26, the Central Committee instructed local Party committees to send the men, taking care to stress that the choice of candidates required particular consideration. "All of them," the letter read, "must be of scrupulous honesty and unquestionable loyalty to the cause of the proletarian revolution, they must be its staunch champions, and be fully literate." Hundreds of Communists who received the necessary political and professional training were afterwards employed at Chekas and special departments.

The steps taken by Dzerzhinsky, with the assistance of the Party Central Committee and local Party committees, substantially enhanced the Cheka efficiency. The personnel gained a better understanding of their duties, were made more competent, and developed stronger links with the people. Chekas were now ready to deal crushing blows against White Guard centres.

The most important operation of the All-Russia Extraordinary Commission in 1919 was the elimination of the counter-revolutionary organisation The National Centre with branches in Petrograd, Siberia, the

Urals and Kuban. It had close contacts with the paramilitary secret organisation known as the

Headquarters of the Volunteer Army of the Moscow Region. The Headquarters had a considerable armed force consisting of instructors and cadets from three military colleges, armoured cars and artillery. The National Centre obtained and sent to White Guard Generals Denikin and Kolchak important information concerning the position of Red Army units and their armaments. Supported by Headquarters of the Volunteer Army of the Moscow Region, it planned to launch a revolt to overthrow Soviet power in Moscow in the first half of September.

In July and August, the All-Russia Extraordinary Commission Special Department eliminated the Petrograd branch of the National Centre. A great number of documents were confiscated, some of which allowed the Cheka to trace the origins of the plot to the secret centre in Moscow. At about the same time, the Special Department received information about the existence of the Volunteer Army of the Moscow Region Headquarters and the revolt that was being prepared.

On August 22, Deputy Chairman of the Cheka Special Department Ivan Pavlunovsky sent Lenin a report on the operation against the National Centre informing him that "the arrests would be made on the arrival of Comrade Dzerzhinsky".[5] After reading the report, Lenin sent a message to Dzerzhinsky: "This note, i.e., the operation, must be given special attention. Make as many arrests as quickly as possible."

Returning from Petrograd, Dzerzhinsky assumed control of the operation, which began in the early morning of August 29. In a stack of firewood behind a house, Cheka men round a tin box containing documents which revealed the strategic plans of the Soviet command, the position and armaments of Red Army units, and a letter to the Denikin "government" on the preparations for a counter-revolutionary revolt. The search, which lasted throughout the night, yielded a list of names and telephone numbers of the organisation members concealed in a marble press-papier. That morning the papers were brought to Dzerzhinsky. "His face, which was haggard with lack of sleep and incredibly hard work, lit up at once, he scanned the list and said confidently: 'Now we've got them all!'," wrote Fyodor Fomin, a participant in the operation. That day, many of the conspirators were arrested.

In the first half of September, the Cheka was finally ready to abolish the Headquarters of the Volunteer

Army of the Moscow Region. On September 18, Cheka men, assisted by Red Guards and Moscow Bolsheviks, seized the Headquarters and disarmed the military colleges that were the principal force behind the revolt. Arrests were made on September 19 and 20 as well. The operation over, Dzerzhinsky assembled the men and gave them a detailed account of the character, objectives and purpose of the crushed organisation, and analysed the actions or participants in the operation. On September 21, he reported to the Party Central Committee on the elimination of the National Centre and the Headquarters of the Volunteer Army of the Moscow Region.

On September 24, at the Moscow City Conference of the RCP(B), Dzerzhinsky spoke about the uncovering of the White Guard conspiracy, describing in some detail the plotters' objectives, the armed force at their disposal, plans for the revolt, and the course of the operation.

"Our campaign against conspiracy," he said by way of conclusion, will be successful only if the Cheka meets with daily support on the part of each Communist."

The enemies of the revolution were, however, still active. On September 25, terrorists exploded a bomb at a meeting of the Moscow RCP(B) Committee. Twelve men, including Moscow Committee Secretary Vladimir Zagorsky, were killed.

Dzerzhinsky was in direct control of the investigation, which revealed that the explosion had been staged by an anarchist group. Questioning one of the arrested men, Dzerzhinsky learned that another terrorist act was being prepared by the anarchists and found out the address of the criminals' headquarters. The group was eliminated in early November.

Soon afterwards, Dzerzhinsky received important information from the Special Department of the

Seventh Army and the Petrograd Cheka that a major spy organisation connected with White Guard General Yudenich and British intelligence had been uncovered. It was headed by Paul Dukes, a British subject, who had fled from Russia some time before. The conspirators communicated information about the Red Army to Yudenich and prepared on his behalf an operational plan for an offensive against Petrograd. They had knocked together units to take part in the revolt, and even formed their own "government". Paul Dukes' organisation also had contacts with a French and other spy groups.

Dzerzhinsky left for Petrograd. Under his direction, the staff of the Special Department and the Petrograd Cheka arrested the spies and conspirators in November 1919. Dzerzhinsky was personally involved in the investigation and was present at the meeting of the

Petrograd Cheka Collegium, which passed sentences on 'the participants in the White Guard plot.

Upon his return to Moscow, he reported to the Vecheka on the operation to uncover and eliminate the spy organisation in Petrograd. Events unfolded in this way. A Red Army man noticed that a girl walking ahead or him had dropped a parcel. He picked it up and called out to her, but she started to run. The man thought this suspicious, ran after the girl and brought her to the Petrograd Cheka. The parcel contained plans of military installations and other secret information. It turned out that the detained girl was the daughter of the head of the French spy group in Petrograd, who was subsequently arrested. At a questioning session he arrogantly declared:

"You've caught me by pure chance, only because my daughter lost her nerve."

"You are mistaken," replied Dzerzhinsky. "If the people did not support us, if each worker and each Red

Army man did not realise that the struggle against the enemies of the revolution is the duty not only of the Cheka but of the whole nation—the loss of the parcel would not have led to the uncovering of your organisation. Your daughter dropped it accidentally, but it was no accident that the Red Army man noticed it, detained your daughter and brought her here. This is where the source of our strength lies."

In late 1919-early 1920, the Cheka uncovered the organisation known as the Tactical Centre, a nationwide union of major anti-Soviet groups and associations—the Council of Public Figures, the National Centre, and the Union for the Resurrection of Russia. The Tactical Centre's objective was to restore Russia's "state integrity", convene a "national assembly", and restore private property. Kolchak was earmarked for the role 01 supreme ruler of the Russian state. The Tactical Centre maintained contacts with the Headquarters of the Volunteer Army of the Moscow Region through the leaders of the National Centre.

These secret White Guard centres were eventually destroyed, thus wrecking the plans of domestic counter- revolution and foreign intelligence services.

In the autumn of 1919, the Cheka was instructed by the RCP(B) Central Committee and the Defence Council to concentrate its efforts on overcoming economic dislocation. Speculation in food and consumer goods greatly hindered the country's economic revival. Speculators managed to get jobs at the organisations entrusted with the distribution of goods and at storehouses and engineered thefts, frequently on a large scale. The articles were then sold at black markets. Speculation involved bribe taking, embezzlement and other abuses of official position.

On September 17, at a meeting of the Narrow Council of People's Commissars Dzerzhinsky proposed a draft decree on stepping up the campaign against speculation, which was approved by the assembly. Soon afterwards, on October 21, the Council of People's Commissars passed a decree which relegated >all cases of large-scale speculation in foodstuffs and registered goods, as well as all cases of abuse of official position by persons found guilty of theft, counterfeiting, violating the procedure of issuing orders, speculation and bribe-taking to the newly established Vecheka Special Revolutionary Tribunal.

At the first session of the Tribunal, which he chaired, Dzerzhinsky said that for the revolution to attain final victory, the people had not only to win the battles waged at the fronts but to master the economic apparatus, which still contained specialists loyal to the bourgeoisie, persons pursuing their own selfish ends and other people who wanted to see Soviet power overthrown. Defining the responsibilities of the Tribunal, Dzerzhinsky stated: "We do not at all seek to destroy everyone who used to be a capitalist; on the contrary, we should like to enlist their services, but we also say: 'Be honest, do not introduce disorder into our ranks, and you will be given the same rights as all the rest of the working people.' But woe to those who wish to return the past: we shall destroy them mercilessly as our class enemies."

The Special Revolutionary Tribunal made an important contribution to the struggle against speculation and appropriation of socialist property.

In the autumn of 1919, the Party Central Committee and the Soviet Government instructed the Vecheka to render aid to Party and Soviet bodies in their work to overcome the fuel crisis. The situation was so grave that the Central Committee addressed a letter written by Lenin to all Party organisations which read: "The fuel crisis must be overcome at all costs, otherwise it will be impossible to solve the food problem, or the general economic problem."[6]

This issue was considered several times at meetings of the Vecheka Collegium and Presidium which were chaired by Dzerzhinsky. A number of steps were mapped out providing for the participation of Cheka personnel in this campaign.

The transport Extraordinary Commissions registered the available fuel, helped to fish out floated timber, and load the firewood. They instituted proceedings against those who abused their position in the field of procurement, transportation and distribution of fuel, and those citizens who shirked compulsory work. Thanks to the steps taken by the Party bodies, Soviets and Extraordinary Commissions, the fuel crisis was eventually overcome.

The Vecheka personnel also helped in combating epidemics, which flared up and rapidly spread as a result of widespread famine and the absence of medicines, soap and sanitary conditions. On November 8, the Defence Council formed a Special All-Russia Commission on Improving the Sanitary Conditions in the Republic, whose members included Lenin and Dzerzhinsky. Chekas were to incorporate persons responsible for sanitary matters and form a mobile sanitary commission.

On November 15, Dzerzhinsky and Nikolai Semashko, the People's Commissar for Health, issued a decree "On Steps to Combat Disorder in the Sanitary Field", which stated that this work would be a major Cheka function. Chekas were to inspect the sanitary state of the barracks, hospitals, educational establishments, railway stations, evacuation centres and troops trains, and to extend assistance to the health-care bodies in the setting up of sanitary cordons.

In late 1919 Dzerzhinsky was involved in preparations for the First Congress of Special Departments. At that time, new forms of subversive activities began to be directed against the Red Army, and more efficient measures had to be introduced to enhance the security of the Soviet armed forces.

The First Congress opened on December 22. Its work was directed by Dzerzhinsky and Ivan Pavlunovsky, Deputy Chairman of the Vecheka Special Department. The delegates noted that counterrevolutionaries were trying to take under control the central administrative bodies of the Red Army, the central military establishments and general staffs. The congress termed this form of subversive activities "technical counterrevolution".

Dzerzhinsky made a long speech to the congress in which he reviewed the history of the Special Departments and proposed that the Party Central Committee send to the Special Departments the most loyal and experienced Communists, and called on Cheka men to step up their campaign against "technical counter-revolution" in the Red Army.

In late 1919-early 1920, the Red Army was winning decisive victories in the Civil War and was thrusting east in pursuit of Kolchak's army. On the Southern Front, the Army routed Denikin's troops, pushing them back towards the Azov and the Black Sea. Yudenich was thrown back from Petrograd.

The improved military and political situation allowed the Soviet state to relax its punitive policies. At the

Eighth All-Russia Conference of the RCP(B), Lenin stated that the material welfare of skilled specialists from the old (tsarist) regime should be improved, and that rough treatment and unjustified repressions of the intelligentsia and petty- bourgeois strata would not be tolerated.

Guided by Lenin's instructions, on December 17, 1919, Dzerzhinsky issued an order on the strict observance of revolutionary legality by all Cheka bodies. Skilled specialists were to be arrested only where there was irrefutable proof of their involvement in White Guard groups or participation in speculation and sabotage. It was forbidden to arrest citizens for petty crimes or on the basis of unverified information concerning their criminal activities.

On January 17, 1920, the All-Russia Central Executive Committee and the Council of People's Commissars passed a decree abolishing capital punishment as a sentence passed by the Vecheka or its bodies, or by the Revolutionary Tribunals. In light of the fact that the Civil War was not yet over, and that the threat of another foreign invasion was by no means over, this document proved once again the humane nature of the socialist state. Lenin said the decree was one of the major measures of Soviet home policy. He especially noted that it had been initiated by Dzerzhinsky.

This step had been made possible not only by the successes of the Red Army but also by the suppression of counter-revolutionary activities on the home front by the Cheka. In recognition of Dzerzhinsky's substantial contribution to the victory over counter-revolution, on January 24, 1920, the All-Russia Central Executive Committee decorated him with the Order of the Red Banner, stating that as Chairman of the All-Russia Extraordinary Commission he "displayed major organisational abilities, indefatigable energy and level-headedness, placing the interests of the working class over any other considerations' and feelings. Dzerzhinsky's work guaranteed stability at the home front, and enabled the Red Army to perform its combat duties confidently."

After the Civil War was ended, the people concentrated on combating economic dislocation. The country was in a very difficult position. The majority of factories stood idle due to a shortage of fuel and raw materials; many mines and pits had been flooded. The people were going through a period of terrible hardship and privation.

The transition to peaceful constructive work made it necessary for Cheka bodies to modify their tactics and objectives. These matters were discussed at the Fourth All- Russia Conference of Extraordinary Commissions convened in February 1920.

Dzerzhinsky stated in the opening speech that the fight against counter-revolution, profiteering and abuse of official position had entered a new stage. The counterrevolutionary elements at the fronts and within the country had been broken up but not totally eliminated, and the remaining groups were sure to start looking for new methods of struggle against Soviet power. Dzerzhinsky urged Cheka men to lose none of their vigilance in uncovering and checking the subversive activities of the enemies who had managed to attain positions in the bodies responsible for the procurement and distribution of food and the transport system.

At the conference's final meeting held on February 6, Lenin reported that although the principal counter- revolutionary elements had been routed, fresh attempts at revolts and terrorist acts were very likely. He also said that Cheka bodies must remain on the alert and maintain combat readiness, and called on the men to take an active part in overcoming economic dislocation, especially on the transport system.

Dzerzhinsky did a great deal to involve Cheka bodies in the work to normalise the transport situation. In February, March and April, the bulk of decrees and orders of the Cheka concerned transport. Cheka personnel ensured the maintenance of strict labour discipline among the railroad workers, investigated all accidents, helped prepare for the opening of the navigation season on water routes. In response to an appeal of the Party, Cheka bodies dispatched nearly all their men with experience as engine-drivers, fitters, turners and stokers to work on transport.

Dzerzhinsky was especially concerned with Cheka bodies in the army. On April 7, he and Menzhinsky, Deputy Chairman of the Vecheka Special Department, signed a decree on reinforcing the staffs of the army's special departments. This was of paramount importance in view of the looming war against the White Poles.

In the second half of February 1920, Dzerzhinsky was placed in charge of putting down a counterrevolutionary revolt staged by kulaks, bourgeois nationalists, White Guards and SRs in the north of the Bashkir Republic. The revolt was suppressed during the spring, but the situation in the republic remained grave, for the local nationalists continued to plot for the Bashkir Republic's secession from Soviet Russia. Dzerzhinsky stated as much at the RCP(B) Central Committee Plenary Meeting held on April 5, which decided to appoint him to the commission working on a draft decree on the state system of the Bashkir Republic. On April 8, the Central Committee approved the main provisions of the document drawn up by the commission on the Bashkir question, and passed them over to the Central Committee Politbureau for final revision. The new draft decree specified the status of Bashkiria as an autonomous Soviet socialist republic incorporated in the RSFSR. The Bashkir Cheka was merged with the All-Russia Cheka and assimilated into its organisational structure. This promoted the interests of both Russians and Bashkirs, strengthened the relations between them and enhanced the efficiency of the campaign against the enemies of Soviet power. The principles underlying the relations between the Bashkir and the All-Russia Extraordinary Commissions provided the foundation of the latter's relations with the Chekas of the other autonomous republics within the RSFSR.

On April 5, the RCP(B) Central Committee adopted a decision to send Dzerzhinsky to the Ukraine to help introduce universal compulsory labour. However, two weeks later it became clear that his job would prove more extensive. It appeared that a war with bourgeois and landowner Poland was imminent. At the urging of the USA, Britain and France, Poland refused to sign a peace treaty with the Russian Federation, the Ukrainian and Byelorussian Soviet Socialist Republics and was marshalling troops in preparation for an attack on the Soviet republics. Moreover, the Ukraine was being victimised by bands of the bourgeois nationalist Petlyura and anarchist Makhno. They terrorised the population, assassinated Soviet officials, plundered state storehouses, staged subversive acts on railways, and damaged telephone and telegraph wires. Should hostilities against the White Poles resume, the activities of these bands would be likely seriously to undermine the distribution of armaments, ammunition and food to the Red Army. The Army rear had to be reinforced without delay.

On April 20, the Central Committee Politbureau decided to set an earlier date for Dzerzhinsky's departure for the Ukraine, and on April 26, the day after Poland attacked Soviet Russia, he was instructed to take urgent and effective steps to check gangsterism.

Dzerzhinsky arrived in Kharkov on May 5, 1920, and plunged into work straight away. In May, June and the first half of July, he was present and spoke at nearly all Politbureau meetings of the Central

Committee of the Communist Party of the Ukraine, and submitted a number of practical proposals on the questions under discussion.

He had to deal with a wide range of issues, such as moving workers into flats once occupied by the bourgeoisie, organising the distribution of food to children and the general public, helping to hold a week of assistance to sick and wounded Red Army men, inspecting the activities of military organisations, purging the militia and the criminal investigation department, guarding the trains, combating profiteering and many other matters. He generously shared his tremendous experience of Party and state work with local authorities, helped improve the Ukraine's state apparatus and reinforce the Red Army rear.

As was expected, Dzerzhinsky did a great deal to raise the efficiency of work of Cheka bodies, and to expand their links with the All-Russia Extraordinary Commission. He stressed the need to step up activities in the countryside in order to better suppress gangsterism, and insisted on better food supplies for the Cheka staff. "I am tempted by the thought, he wrote, "to stay here longer, and not on a temporary engagement. Having settled down here and supported by the RCP(B) Central Committee, I could in the course of two or three months help the Cheka grow stronger... If you agree, get the approval of the CC. I'm not cut out to be a casual worker."

While in the Ukraine, Dzerzhinsky kept in daily touch with the All-Russia Cheka. He wrote and sent telegrams to Deputy Chairman Ksenofontov inquiring about the state of affairs and giving advice on various matters.

In mid-July, 1920 Dzerzhinsky returned to Moscow to take part in the RCP(B) Central Committee plenary meeting, which decided to send him to the Western Front.

The CC Organisational Bureau, in collaboration with Dzerzhinsky, appointed a new Collegium of the Vecheka, which was approved by the Council of People's Commissars on July 29. He also obtained the approval of the Party Committee for measures he planned to introduce to make the work of the Collegium more efficient, i.e., reinforcing the principles of one-man leadership in Vecheka departments and also drastically reducing the sphere of operation of the principle of collegiality. He considered it necessary to give the Vecheka the status of a military organisation.

While working at the Western Front, Dzerzhinsky received information forwarded by Vecheka Secretary Venyamin Gerson about all cases of major importance investigated there, and sometimes asked for documents on which the Vecheka wished to have his opinion. He frequently called the Vecheka on the hot line and sent telegraphic messages. He concentrated on reinforcing the special departments of the armies engaged on the Western Front, and gave repeated warnings about the enhanced danger of foreign intelligence agents penetrating into Soviet territory. Dzerzhinsky suggested that responsible commandants be appointed to all border stations, and special units be assigned to guarding the border. On August 15, he sent Lenin a telegram that read: "It is necessary to remember the existence of an open German border."

Dzerzhinsky strictly instructed the special departments to show consideration for local dwellers. In his telegram to Vyacheslav Menzhinsky dispatched on August 11, he requested that all special departments of the Western Front be instructed to step up the campaign against the persons guilty of criminal actions against the population, and recommended that Polish citizens not be deported to the deep rear if suspicion of espionage activities on their part did not arise.

In early September, Dzerzhinsky travelled to Moscow on some business for the Polish Bureau of the Central Committee and chaired the Vecheka Collegium meeting held on September 6. On September 20, the Party Central Committee plenary meeting found it expedient to demobilise Dzerzhinsky and recall him for work at the Vecheka after a restructure.

A few days earlier, on September 17, the Council of Labour and Defence (CLD) gave the Cheka staff the status of active Red Army servicemen. The decree, signed by Lenin, formalised the status of the AllRussia Extraordinary Commission as a military organisation. All Central Executive Committee decrees and resolutions pertaining to army discipline were now compulsory for the Chekas. Their staff was given the same rights as the Red Army men concerning food and consumer goods supplies.

On September 24, Dzerzhinsky issued an order, based on the CLD decree, prescribing strict military centralisation of the Cheka bodies, personal responsibility of the staff for their work, army order, precision and promptness when acting on assignments from the centre. "Cheka work," the order read, in part, "is henceforth regarded as fulfilling a combat assignment under the conditions of open hostilities on the domestic front."

In October, the CLD appointed Dzerzhinsky Chairman of the Committee for the Defence of Moscow and the Moscow Military District for the purpose of coordinating the efforts of Cheka and military bodies. At that time, the All-Russia Extraordinary Commission was advised about a White Guard putsch being planned in Moscow. The rebels hoped that they would be able to incite Red Army men, exhausted as they were by the war and economic difficulties, to rise up against Soviet power. They were also rehearsing terrorist acts against Communist Party and Soviet Government leaders.

However, the Cheka and the Defence Committee were able to prevent the White Guard putsch in Moscow.

In the autumn of 1920, Dzerzhinsky directed the campaign of Cheka bodies and the Interior Guard Forces units against the secret centres headed by Petlyura. He also kept an eye on the activities of Makhno's men. In the early morning of November 26, Ukrainian Cheka personnel arrested the most active anarchists in Kharkov, Kiev, Poltava and some other cities. On Dzerzhinsky's order, the criminals were sent to Moscow. At the same time, Red Army and the Interior Guard Forces dealt a decisive blow against Makhno bands. The Makhno movement ceased to exist as an organised force of the Ukrainian kulaks.

At that time Dzerzhinsky also headed the commission investigating the assassination in Petrograd of a number of CC members and activists of the Communist Party of Finland.

On November 24, Dzerzhinsky issued a decree on thoroughly checking the reports discrediting Soviet citizens. "Not infrequently," the decree read, "the authors of such reports cannot be trusted, and are motivated to send in a report by the desire to get even, to undermine the authority of certain official, and sometimes even remove him for the sake of their own careers." To avoid bringing in unfounded charges against a group of office employees and individual citizens, each report was to be carefully considered and kept secret until further investigation should reveal whether court proceedings were indicated. "If such investigation proves the report groundless," the decree stated, "written with a view to get even, etc., charges should be brought against the author of the report for false accusation and undermining the authority of Soviet power."

During the war against bourgeois-landowner Poland and White Guard General Wrangel, the All-Russia Extraordinary Commission headed by Dzerzhinsky managed to preserve order on the home front. The Cheka uncovered a number of White Guard organisations which had contacts with Wrangel's and the Entente's intelligence services. The Headquarters for the Salvation of Russia which was preparing an uprising on the Don was broken up in Rostov. In Kuban, Cheka men caught quite a number of Wrangel's spies who had managed to get jobs as office workers. Several major counterrevolutionary centres were eliminated in the Ukraine, Siberia, and the Caucasus.

Dzerzhinsky made an invaluable personal contribution to the successful fight of the Vecheka against the enemies of the new system. His work as the All-Russia Extraordinary Commission Chairman revealed once again his profound faith in the cause of communism and determination to combat everything that stood in the way of its victory. He tried to make the Cheka a reliable assistant for the Party in its campaign against the counter-revolution. "The Cheka," he said, "must be a Central Committee body; otherwise it will become harmful, will degenerate into a secret police or counterrevolutionary organ."

Dzerzhinsky stressed the importance of strengthening the Cheka's links with the people, winning their support in the fight against the enemies of the revolution, and never overstepping the boundaries of the revolutionary law. This, he believed, was one of the sources of the strength of Cheka bodies, and a guarantee of their success.

The Cheka's personnel, he held, must take care to leave no crime undetected and unpunished, and at the same time must strictly observe the laws of the socialist state and be guided by them in all situations. "This is necessary," wrote Dzerzhinsky in one of the decrees, "to avoid mistakes and not to turn into offenders against Soviet power, whose interests we are called upon to protect." He warned his men that severe punishment would be meted out to those who failed to act on the orders, decrees and resolutions of state bodies and the Cheka, or who had not carried them out to the letter.

The example he himself set did much to promote Cheka men's political consciousness, fearlessness in confronting the enemy, discipline based on understanding of the revolutionary duty, initiative, modesty, and consideration of others. "An insensitive man is unfit for work in the Cheka," Dzerzhinsky would say.

Thanks to his unquestioning and boundless loyalty to the ideals of communism, his understanding of Party duty and great ability as an organiser, Dzerzhinsky was able to ensure the smooth and efficient functioning of the Cheka and turn it into a truly formidable body which provided reliable protection of revolutionary gains from hostile elements.

Notes

[1] Mass red terror was stopped in early November 1918.

[2]V. I. Lenin, "Speech at a Rally and Concert for the All-Russia Extraordinary

Commission Staff, November 7, 1918", Collected Works, Vol. 28, 1974, p. 170.

[3]V. I. Lenin, Collected Works, Vol. 29, 1977, p. 403.

[4]V. I. Lenin, Collected Works, Vol. 29, p. 254.

[5]Dzerzhinsky was in Petrograd at that time.

[6]V. I. Lenin, "The Fight to Overcome the Fuel Crisis", Collected Works, Vol. 30, 1977, p. 140.

Chapter Seven

AT THE PEOPLE'S COMMISSARIAT FOR INTERNAL AFFAIRS

In October 1917, the Second All-Russia Congress of Soviets proclaimed the Council of People's Commissars headed by Lenin the highest body of state authority of the Soviet Republic. One of its members was the People's Commissar for Internal Affairs.

Everywhere in the country, Communists supervised the organisation of new bodies of Soviet state authority and administration. The All-Russia Central Executive Committee and the Council of People's Commissars instructed the People's Commissariat for Internal Affairs (NKVD) to take an active part in forming the Soviet state apparatus, coordinate the work of the various Soviet government bodies, ensure protection of revolutionary law and order, and suppress sabotage on the part of office workers.

On November 17, 1917, the Council of People's Commissars had appointed Grigory Petrovsky People's Commissar for Internal Affairs. Among the members of the Commissariat's Collegium were Dzerzhinsky and Uritsky.

Dzerzhinsky was put in charge of the most urgent task, providing the population with food. This sector was being badly sabotaged: some office workers deliberately altered accounts, concealed foodstuffs and refused to act on orders from the Soviet Government. It was deemed a matter of top priority to put a halt to the campaign launched by the employees of the former Food Ministry, who refused to recognise the powers of the new People's Commissar for Food and to hand over the Ministry's archives, documents and business correspondence. On November 27, Dzerzhinsky signed three warrants for the removal of documents.

The energetic measures introduced by the People's Commissariat for Internal Affairs and the

Revolutionary Military Committee to stem sabotage activities, plus large-scale propaganda work among the office workers and removal of anti-Soviet elements had made it possible for the People's Commissariat for Food to begin functioning more smoothly.

The relations between the People's Commissariat for Internal Affairs and the Vecheka were defined in the Statute on the Vecheka approved by the All-Russia Central Executive Committee on October 28, 1918. It stated that the Chairman of the All-Russia Cheka automatically became a member of the Collegium of the People's Commissariat for Internal Affairs, and that the Commissariat delegated its representatives to the Vecheka.

On November 14, 1918, the Collegium held a session at which People's Commissar for Internal Affairs Petrovsky and All-Russia Cheka Chairman Dzerzhinsky were present. Petrovsky made a report "On Coordinating the Activities of the Vecheka and the NKVD".

Petrovsky remained first in command for almost eighteen months, and throughout that time, Dzerzhinsky was his reliable and energetic associate. After the restoration of Soviet power in the Ukraine, Petrovsky was sent to that republic at the request of the Ukrainian Government and on Lenin's recommendation. After Petrovsky discontinued his duties as the People's Commissar for Internal Affairs, the RCP(B)

Central Committee and the Soviet Government decided to merge the leadership of the Vecheka and the NKVD. On March 30, 1919, the All-Russia Central Executive Committee appointed Chairman of the Vecheka Dzerzhinsky the RSFSR People's Commissar for Internal Affairs. The merger served to build up both these bodies and made it possible to concentrate efforts on consolidating revolutionary law and order and combating counter-revolutionary elements inside the country.

Dzerzhinsky made it a point to promote businesslike and friendly relations between the Vecheka and NKVD bodies. The joint efforts of the two organisations ensured their smooth and efficient cooperation. A great deal had been accomplished in establishing and maintaining public and state security in the provinces. The militia and criminal investigation departments were reinforced by Cheka personnel. Some

Cheka functions involved in combating speculation and abuse of official position were handed over to them, while the Vecheka concentrated more on fighting counterrevolutionary activities.

When in 1922 the State Political Department (GPU) was formed within the NKVD, the latter's functions were expanded. Dzerzhinsky, the People's Commissar for Internal Affairs, was also appointed the GPU Chairman.

During this time the entire state apparatus was being overhauled, and the NKVD was not left out. Dzerzhinsky emphasised the necessity of introducing scientific labour organisation to make work more efficient and flexible and to find optimal forms of relationship between the bodies of state and public security. He believed that this should be a continuing process. Among other things, he instructed his assistants to find ways to reduce the personnel.

Since the Soviet Republic was fighting domestic as well as foreign enemies, both equally dangerous, Dzerzhinsky considered it a matter of top priority to set up special interior forces.

On March 30, 1919, the Collegium of the All-Russia Extraordinary Commission which he chaired heard a report made by Konstantin Valobuyev, Chief of Staff, Vecheka Forces, and instructed him to draw up a draft decree of the Defence Council of the establishment of a unified body to direct the armed struggle against counter-revolution.

At a meeting of the Defence Council of May 19, 1919, Dzerzhinsky raised the question of uniting all the interior forces. On May 28, the Council of Workers' and Peasants' Defence passed a resolution "On Auxiliary Forces", which was edited and signed by Lenin. Acting on this resolution, on July 21, 1919,

Dzerzhinsky, as People's Commissar for Internal Affairs, approved the structure and composition of the Interior Guard Forces. They were to incorporate brigades, regiments, battalions, squadrons, batteries and crews and serve a variety of purposes. The territory of the republic was divided into eleven sectors in accordance with the number of military districts existing at the time. The troops in each sector were headed by a headquarters and a Military Council was formed to exercise leadership over them. On December 31, 1919, the Revolutionary Military Council of the Republic granted the troops' headquarters

the status of general staff of a front. The troops headquarters was by the Military Council with Dzerzhinsky in charge.

Dzerzhinsky was well aware of the objectives set before the Interior Guard Forces. Towards the end of the Civil War, one of their primary tasks was to fight gangsterism and guard strategically important installations and enterprises. At about the same time, another function was added to their list of duties— to protect national property from encroachments by enemies of Soviet power. This necessitated new steps towards strengthening the Interior Guard Forces. The resolution issued by the Labour and Defence Council on September 1, 1920 and signed by Lenin effected a merger of the NKVD interior Guard Forces with guard troops. A single system of interior service was thus evolved, the Interior Service Forces under the RSFSR People's Commissariat, for Internal Affairs.

On November 24, 1920, the Labour and Defence Council vested the Vecheka Special Department with full responsibility for protecting the state borders. In this connection, the Interior Service Forces were called upon to man the special departments.

A number of units were despatched to staff border stations and posts. They were accountable to the

Vecheka special departments in the provinces, and received assignments from the Special Department of the Vecheka through their commanding officers.

As both the People's Commissar for Internal Affairs and the Vecheka Chairman, Dzerzhinsky secured smooth cooperation between the Vecheka special departments in charge of guarding the country's borders and the Interior Service Forces under the NKVD.

Thus, it was to a large extent through Dzerzhinsky's efforts that towards the end of the Civil War and foreign invasion, all interior troops belonged to the same department and could thus be placed in key sectors. Also, forces and equipment could be efficiently manoeuvred, distributed and re-located when the need arose.

As Chairman of the Military Council of Interior Forces, Dzerzhinsky required that his men live up to the standards established for the Red Army. He also set high standards for political commissars among the personnel, and invariably demanded that the decrees issued by the Soviet Government be unquestionably supported and implemented everywhere.

On February 28, 1920 Dzerzhinsky signed a resolution on introducing one-man leadership in the Interior

Guard Forces. The resolution also established that in those units where the commanding officer was a Communist, the post of political commissar was to be replaced by that of second-in-command in charge of political affairs. Both officers would be responsible for political work among the troops.

The competent guidance of the Party Central Committee and Lenin himself had made it possible to quickly build up the Interior Forces and enhance their combat capacity. Dzerzhinsky made a great contribution to this work. By the summer of 1920, 16.7 per cent of their personnel were Communists, which for that time was a very high figure indeed, and some battalions and companies were made up almost entirely of Communists.

Despite the great load of work, the continuing struggle against counter-revolutionary activities and the numerous assignments of the government and the Red Army command, the men in the Interior Forces worked to improve their military education. Dzerzhinsky placed great importance on drilling, mastering the weaponry, studying manuals, and being constantly on the alert. He made a great contribution to the advancement of Party and political work in the troops, and raised the level of training and education of the personnel. Dzerzhinsky believed that these goals could best be achieved if all the men attended classes, the less educated were assisted in trainee units, and special training sessions were conducted with political instructors and commanding officers who were Party members. Dzerzhinsky highly valued the educational work conducted by Party and Komsomol bodies, political reports at servicemen's general meetings, and individual talks with the men to explain the essence and purpose of Party policies and international affairs.

A great effort was made to eradicate illiteracy among the personnel. While in early 1919, one-third of the men could neither read nor write, by the end of 1920, only one man in ten was still illiterate.

More and more units built their own cultural facilities, and their work improved gradually. Battalions put out leaflets and handwritten journals on a regular basis. Officers and men took an active part in the campaigns launched to assist the front and help restore the economy.

On the basis of a decision passed by the Party Central Committee and under Dzerzhinsky's direct guidance, a plan of educational work was developed for Cheka units, especially for political instructors, Communists and commanding officers, who were required to have a detailed knowledge of the functioning of the bodies and units of state and public security.

Dzerzhinsky believed that each unit should become the training ground for future ideologically mature and skilled specialists who would be able to make a substantial contribution to the fight against "the still undefeated counter- revolution and attempts to use economic tricks to undermine our re-emerging industry and the Soviet economy as a whole".

The political education of the men in the Interior Guard Forces was the focus of the First All-Russia

Conference of Army Commissars and Heads of Political Secretariats. It noted that each day the Interior Forces were acting on combat assignments from the Party and the Government, and called on each man to improve his skill, work conscientiously, acquire a good understanding of the policy of the Communist Party, and study the forms and methods of the counter-revolutionary elements' subversive activities.

As commander-in-chief of the Interior Forces, Dzerzhinsky did a great deal to ensure that the most valuable experience was spread and used by the entire force, and that the revolutionary and combat traditions were carefully preserved and developed further. On

November 27, 1920, he issued an order which obliged all commanding officers of units and formations to prepare reviews of their three-years' service "to the cause of the defence of the October Revolution and consolidation of Soviet power".

In another order for the troops, Dzerzhinsky stated that the history of the units which had taken part in the suppression of counter-revolutionary actions staged by the Russian and foreign bourgeoisie and the heroic struggle of the first Cheka men was of great significance in the education of the young servicemen. He suggested that "commanding officers immediately begin to write down a history of their units".

Training the personnel of the Interior Forces in the revolutionary traditions laid down by their predecessors, Dzerzhinsky stressed the need for all commanders and Red Army men to keep in close touch with the people, use the support of public organisations, observe strictly socialist law, and do their best to develop initiative, competence and courage.

The Interior Forces under the NKVD and the Vecheka fought against counterrevolutionary activities inside the country and also made a major contribution to the ultimate victory of the Red Army over the foreign interventionists and White Guards. Moreover, they sometimes directly participated in the fighting at the fronts. Between March and June or 1919, 42,000 officers and men from the Interior Forces had been sent to the fighting fronts. According to far from complete data, over 150 servicemen in these forces were decorated with the highest award of the time, the Order of the Red Banner, for conspicuous valour and heroism displayed at the front.

Together with his activities as head of the Interior Forces, Dzerzhinsky was personally involved in the implementation of Lenin's plan for the establishment and strengthening of the workers' and peasants' militia (Soviet police). In October 1917, the NKVD issued a decree on the establishment of the workers' militia, which was cabled to all Soviets.

Local Soviets formed an armed Red Guard or workers' militia units. They had complete freedom when choosing these units' organisational forms and structure. The majority of the Soviets preferred to establish permanent militia units with their personnel recommended by public organisations.

The establishment of a fundamentally new type of militia was no easy task. But the Soviets received the help of the NKVD. Dzerzhinsky, as a member of the NKVD Collegium and later the Vecheka Chairman, was directly involved in working out the organisational patterns and the manning, training and operative use of the militia. Dzerzhinsky took direct part in working put the legal status of the Soviet worker-andpeasant militia.

Since his appointment as the People's Commissar for Internal Affairs, the organisation and training of the militia was his primary concern. Above all, he sought to establish the militia as a paramilitary organisation. On April 3, 1919, the Council of People's Commissars' decree "On the Soviet Workers' and Peasants' Militia", which was signed by Lenin, was made public. It introduced compulsory military training and military discipline in all militia units. The militia and criminal investigation department personnel who were liable to be drafted into the Red Army stayed at their posts, and their work was considered a form of military service. Militia units operating in the regions where fighting was in progress could be sent to the fighting front along with the Red Army personnel.

Dzerzhinsky made frequent trips to the provinces to become personally acquainted with the work of local militia bodies and took steps to strengthen them. He was intolerant of parochialism, divisive activities and a formalistic attitude to the organisation of administrative bodies.

He also made an important contribution to the establishment of militia units at rail- and waterways and enterprises, and endorsed the regulations concerning their functions and relationship with the Interior Forces and departmental guard units.

With the introduction of the New Economic Policy (NEP)[1], which was initiated by the Tenth RCP(B) Congress, in March 1921, the bodies of state and public security had to be adapted to the new economic conditions and new goals. Dzerzhinsky realised that this would require an efficient and smoothly functioning administrative apparatus of the militia.

To enhance the militia's performance and improve the material conditions of its personnel, the Labour and Defence Council passed a number of important resolutions by Dzerzhinsky. On February 7, 1921, the responsibility of supplying militia men with clothing was passed over to the Main Military Economic Department. Steps were taken to make the supplies of weaponry, ammunition, uniforms and foodstuffs more adequate.

Dzerzhinsky was concerned with promoting competent and efficient management of militia bodies both in the centre and in the provinces. His goal was to place well-trained, ideologically mature and hardworking men in positions of responsibility. He insisted on the careful selection of high-ranking personnel to ensure that each person at the top was dedicated and reliable. He also demanded that- the militia establish stronger ties with the Vecheka and the Interior Forces under the People's Commissariat for Internal Affairs.

At Dzerzhinsky's request, on October 24, 1921, the All-Russia Central Executive Committee issued a decree which obliged the local Executive Committees to display greater care in selecting candidates for high posts in the militia, and made all dismissals and transfers of such personnel subject to the approval of the Militia Department of the Republic.

High standards were set for the ideological and theoretical training of the militia, for its men were required to be not merely as technical instruments in the hands of the Soviet Government, but conscious and active promoters of its policy. The militia corps was to be reinforced with skilled personnel trained in law, political affairs, and special subjects. Particular attention was focussed on the need to raise the standards of ideological and educational work of the militia political secretariats.

By decision of the Party and the Government, the militia was purged of unreliable and slipshod workers, and a network of schools and courses was set up to train and upgrade the skills of the personnel. Party and Komsomol organisations were to look for people whose

140

training and character could make them suitable for work in the militia.

The measures taken by Dzerzhinsky and other prominent Party members to carry through Lenin's ideas concerning the system of protection of law and order were later incorporated in the Statute on the Service in the Workers' and Peasants' Militia, which was drawn up with Dzerzhinsky's help.

The NKVD was also responsible for the functioning of corrective-labour institutions. The basic principles of their work were defined by Lenin and the Communist Party, with an emphasis on the features that made them different from the methods of coercion used by the ruling classes in capitalist society. The legal section of the Second Party Programme,, which the Eighth Congress of the RCP(B) adopted in 1919, was drafted by Lenin. The congress approved the major provisions on Soviet courts, the Soviet punitive corrective-labour policy, and the corrective-labour law. The .Programme emphasised the educational role of socialist legislation: "In the field of punishment, the courts organised along these lines have already led to a drastic change in the nature of punishment, passing down a large number of suspended sentences, introducing public reprimand as a punitive measure, substituting imprisonment with compulsory labour without deprivation of freedom, replacing prisons by corrective institutions and making it possible to use fellow- workers' or comrades' court."

Dzerzhinsky was a vigorous promoter of the policy of the state and the Party in the field of crime suppression and corrective-labour punishment. His authority as Chairman of the Vecheka and the People's Commissar for Internal Affairs was invariably used to make sure that an innocent person was not illegally arrested or prosecuted.

From the first days of the existence of the Soviet state, Dzerzhinsky was involved in overhauling the old punitive system used by tsarism and introducing a new corrective-labour policy. He made an invaluable contribution to implementing Lenin's principles of the punitive and corrective-labour policy.

At Dzerzhinsky's initiative, the Soviet Government persistently worked to find optimal forms of organisation of revolutionary tribunals, seeking to ensure their smoother functioning. In the harsh years of the Civil War, their primary purpose was to promptly and accurately strike against the enemies of the revolution. At Lenin's suggestion, Dzerzhinsky spoke on this subject at the All-Russia Central Executive

Committee meeting of February 17, 1919, which discussed the question of the reorganisation of tribunals.

"Practice... has shown," he said, "that in order to combat crime successfully, a trial and punishment should follow as quickly as possible after the crime."

The task was to protect the interests of the overwhelming majority of the population from encroachments by a handful of counter-revolutionaries. Another side of the problem was the need to force Soviet offices and organisations assume more responsibility for their duties, if necessary, by introducing "punishment for negligence, slipshod work, tardiness, etc." These suggestions, made by Dzerzhinsky, were approved by the Central Executive Committee session.

After the New Economic Policy was put into effect, the questions of punitive and corrective-labour policy acquired an even sharper edge. On January 13, 1921, Dzerzhinsky chaired special commission meeting devoted to these issues. A decision was reached to form commissions at trade unions in the centre and in the provinces. "While having none of the functions of a court of justice," reported Dzerzhinsky to the RCP(B) Central Committee, these commissions should set themselves the goal of reconsidering the cases of the accused of proletarian and peasant origin, as well as involving broad proletarian masses in the struggle against crime in the proletarian stratum."

The principal trends in the punitive and corrective-labour policy of the Soviet state, as Dzerzhinsky noted more than once, was a differentiated approach to criminals, and a combination of coercion and corrective measures.

142

While firmly convinced that each and every crime must be punished, Dzerzhinsky believed in the need to make wider use of persuasion and preventive measures with respect to those Soviet citizens who had committed their first crime. He did not feel it was right to mechanically apply a particular article in the criminal code; rather, it was important to expose the roots and essence of the crime in the principled manner befitting a Party member, and take into account the opinions of the people who knew the accused well.

Dzerzhinsky was a resolute opponent of formalism in the punitive policy, and often lashed out against "supporters of articles and paragraphs". He also criticised those officials who seemed to be waiting for the enemy to strike in full force before "spectacularly" abolishing an entire organisation. He believed that these tactics reflected a serious flaw in such people's attitude to their duties. "We are not interested in creating an impression," he would repeat.

Dzerzhinsky could be merciless and determined when fighting against gangsters, recidivists and other serious offenders and insisted that they get what they deserve. If, however, the offender was a peasant or worker who had committed a crime through political immaturity or because he had been influenced by hostile propaganda, Dzerzhinsky advocated a totally different approach. He maintained that only those who were really dangerous to Soviet power should be imprisoned and wrote: "if a worker who has been caught stealing is made to work at his factory under the supervision of the rest of the workers, this being among other people waiting to see whether this Petrov or Sidorov is going to steal again, whether he will bring shame on the factory or become a truly conscientious and honest person—this sort of thing will work much better, will be much more effective and more sensible... A working-class environment will be able to set right weak-willed and unconscientious persons, while prison will only maim them."

In a decree passed on January 8, 1921, Dzerzhinsky proposed inspecting prison sites for the purpose of finding convicted workers and peasants and granting the trade unions the right to petition for their parole or to take them out on probation. Responsible officials in the bodies of state and public security were obliged to regularly visit prisons and interview workers and peasants to ascertain the motives of their crimes and assess the chances of their early release. Dzerzhinsky also requested Party workers to do the same.

Urging the appropriate bodies to step up educational and preventive work among the population, Dzerzhinsky was at the same time opposed to "dangerous extremes" in the corrective-labour policy towards criminals from among workers and peasants, the so- called "class approach" to the criminal which was used by those fighting against Soviet power.

In February 1924, Dzerzhinsky wrote: "I find it quite impossible to agree with proposals concerning the punitive policy... Their main idea is to grant privileges and concessions to the persons of proletarian extraction who have committed a crime as well as softer punitive measures."

Dzerzhinsky believed this sort of policy could lead to a higher crime rate and loss of moral standards among some of the workers. He thought that the campaign against crime should be boosted by attaining higher labour productivity and better material conditions for the people, a long and difficult process that demanded a great deal of discipline and a responsible attitude towards society.

Dzerzhinsky's work in the NKVD had many facets. He not only directed the efforts of the staff but, as the Commissar for Internal Affairs, headed many ad hoc commissions on the instructions of the Party Central Committee and the Soviet Government. Into each of these jobs, he put his boundless energy, persistence and discipline.

On February 3, 1920, the All-Russia Central Executive Committee and the Council of People's Commissars issued a decree on the procedure of the introduction of universal labour conscription, and approved the Statute on Corresponding Committees. On February 19, the Council of People's Commissars appointed People's Commissar for Internal Affairs Dzerzhinsky Chairman of the Chief Committee on Universal Labour Conscription.

The Committee was given the right to use Red Army units for reconstruction work at major enterprises and installations, recall skilled workers and specialists from the Military Department, and to re-distribute manpower in various industries. Under Dzerzhinsky's direct guidance, the industries were provided with the personnel they needed.

In fulfilling the assignments of Lenin, the Communist Party and the Soviet Government; Dzerzhinsky accumulated a great deal of experience in organisational work, which he later used when holding top positions in transport and industry.

Notes

[1] The New Economic Policy allowed of some free private enterprise and trade which promoted the country's agriculture.

Chapter Eight

AT THE CIVIL WAR FRONTS

Dzerzhinsky was mainly involved with the All-Russia Extraordinary Commission bodies to suppress numerous armed revolts, conspiracies, espionage and other hostile actions on the part of domestic counter-revolution and foreign intelligence services thereby greatly contributing to the successes of the Red Army in the Civil War. However, Dzerzhinsky made an even more direct contribution to the Army's final victory: he was twice put in command at the fighting front by Party Central Committee. One of Dzerzhinsky's trips to the front dates back to January 1919, when he, as a member of a commission of the

RCP(B) Central Committee and the Defence Council, was to investigate the causes of the surrender of Perm by the 3rd Army of the Eastern Front in the second half of December 1918. The loss of Perm and further retreat of the 3rd Army were fraught with serious military and political consequences for the Soviet Republic. The White army had captured a major industrial centre in the Western Urals with an ammunition factory, and regarded the seizure of the city as a decisive victory which would lead to the eventual capture of Moscow and elimination of Soviet power.

When the RCP(B) Central Committee learned of the enemy's plans, a Party investigation commission was sent to the Eastern Front to uncover the causes of the retreat and to build up the troops' defence capability.

At the time of the commission's arrival in Vyatka (now Kirov) on January 5, 1919, the units of the 3rd

Army were still retreating. The situation was extremely difficult, even desperate: all that remained of the 3rd Army (over 30,000 men) was about 11,000 exhausted and dishevelled men who were only just containing the enemy assault.

Considering the gravity of the situation and Lenin's instruction for the commission members to personally supervise the implementation of planned measures, the commission remained in the locality to try and build up the troops' capability and halt the retreat. Battle-worthy units were being drawn up to reinforce the 3rd Army, the headquarters received fresh personnel, and organisation in the rear was improved. The troops received winter clothes and provisions, and political and educational work continued. This produced a drastic change in the mood and morale of the troops. Kolchak's White Army had for several weeks been resisting the onslaught of the Red Army and was much fatigued. By midJanuary, the situation on the 3rd Army front had begun to improve.

Having taken the necessary steps to enhance the troops' combat capacity, the Central Committee commission also investigated the causes of the 3rd Army's defeat at Perm. It was found that the city had been abandoned due to the 3rd Army's heavy loss of troops and paucity of supplies. The Army had fought a long time without reinforcements; besides, its ranks included representatives of hostile classes. Other important reasons for the defeat were the absence of working contacts between the command and the troops, bureaucratic methods of leadership, and betrayal by a number of military specialists.

Dzerzhinsky was especially concerned about the presence on the staffs of a large number of officers of the tsarist army and other persons whose loyalty was, to say the least, questionable. He also found a predominance of uninterested and even hostile people in the local bodies of military and state administration, evidence of espionage, subversive activities and open treachery.

The commission took prompt steps to purge the government and Party bodies in the rear of the 3rd Army. The Vyatka Revolutionary Military Committee was set up to strengthen the ranks, and coordinate the activities of all government and Party organisations. Revolutionary military committees were also established in cities and towns, as well as strong revolutionary bodies in the countryside.

Analysing the situation, Dzerzhinsky realised that the entire system of fighting against espionage, counter- revolutionary activities and treason in the troops and army staffs on the Eastern Front needed to be re-worked. His proposals speeded up the formation of bodies of military counter- intelligence, special departments of the All-Russia Extraordinary Commission.

While working with the 3rd Army, Dzerzhinsky made a careful study of the composition and methods of work of local Cheka bodies. At his initiative, part of the personnel of the Vyatka Cheka was replaced, its contacts with the workers and rural poor were strengthened, and more extensive cooperation with Party and government bodies was initiated.

The commission did not restrict its activities to ascertaining and removing the causes that had led to the defeat of the 3rd Army. Studying the situation at the Eastern Front, the commission was able to take important steps in solving urgent problems in the military field. It carefully examined the practical leadership of combat operations, the organisation of political work in the Red Army, and the activities of local Party and government bodies.

These were highly important questions whose solution affected the situation not only at the Eastern Front but throughout the country.

In the course of the investigation, the commission laid bare the shortcomings in the drafting of the men and formation of units conducted by local military departments. Its report pointed to the need for a class approach when dealing with these matters.

The commission stressed the need to improve the formation, training and use of reserves. Citing the absence of 3rd Army reserves as one of the principal reasons for its defeat, the commission levelled justified criticism against the central military departments for underestimating the significance of this problem.

The commission made close study of political work conducted in the army, noting the exceptionally important role of experienced and competent political commissars, representatives of the Communist Party in the troops, and the personal example set by Communists fighting in the 3rd Army.

Having thoroughly examined the situation in the 3rd Army and in the rear at the northern flank of the Eastern Front, the commission came up with detailed report on the role of the rear under the conditions of civil war, the need to weed out hostile elements and the targets of the central body of authority in directing the daily activities of local Party and government bodies and extraordinary commissions.

The commission's work led to a turning point in the combat operations of the 3rd Army. In late January 1919, it assumed a counter-offensive thus foiling the plans of the Entente, which had been hoping that White Guard units would link up with the interventionist army in the North.

Dzerzhinsky's work on the commission allowed him to get a clear idea of the political and military situation prevailing on the Eastern Front and in the rear, and acquire valuable experience in organising the fight against domestic and outside counterrevolution on the front line.

At the final stage of the Civil War, Dzerzhinsky received another important assignment. On May 29,

1920, the RCP(B) Central Committee appointed him commander of the rear of the South-western Front.[1]

On April 25, 1920, the ruling circles of bourgeois landowner Poland, being dependent on Britain and

France and encouraged by the USA, began to move their troops, well armed and equipped by the Entente, against Soviet Russia. This treacherous action was undertaken under cover of preliminary peace talks. Commanded by Wrangel the White Guard troops, who had entrenched themselves in the Crimea, were also preparing for an offensive.

The Communist Party and the Soviet Government were aware of their plans, and back in February and

March, took steps to reinforce the country's Western borders, which at that time were defended by the Western and South-western fronts. However, by the time the Polish offensive began, the preparations and concentration of the troops had not been completed. As a result, by early May 1920 Polish troops had occupied most of the western part of the Ukraine, and on May 6 captured Kiev.

The Polish invasion stirred up domestic counter- revolution in the frontline zone and elsewhere. Foreign intelligence services also stepped up their activities. Within a short time, a number of subversive acts were staged at munitions depots and railways, kulaks terrorised the population, and cases of espionage became more frequent.

Given the gravity of the situation, it was imperative to build up the country's defences. Martial law was introduced in the western and central regions, and a plan was worked out to rout the enemy through offensive operations on the Western and South-western fronts, where fresh units were being sent.

However, the offensive launched on the Western Front on May 14 proved unsuccessful, although it did facilitate the offensive assumed by the troops at the South-western Front on May 26. Initially, this offensive was not particularly successful either. The enemy front was penetrated only on June 5. Then, under attack by the Red Army, the enemy began to roll back to the west. On June 12, Kiev was liberated.

Having lived in Kharkov since May 5, where he was assisting the local Party and government bodies crippled in the period of White terror, Dzerzhinsky had a good knowledge of the military and political situation in the Ukraine. As Commander of the Rear of the South-western Front, he, his staff and the troops under him were ordered to put an end to armed banditry and terror, suppress kulak revolts, provide conditions for the normal functioning of Party and government bodies and organisations, and guard communications and industrial enterprises.

Dzerzhinsky believed that a mass political propaganda and educational campaign among the population, particularly the peasantry, could make a substantial contribution to this work. The people had to be helped to understand the goals and character of the war with bourgeois Poland, and the policies pursued by the Communist Party and the Soviet Government in the countryside. Together with local Party and government bodies, the ideological and educational work in the rear was conducted by the political departments of rear guard units of the South-western Front, political sections set up on Dzerzhinsky's suggestion at logistical headquarters at the armies and at the front, and propaganda trains. There were talks, lectures, meetings, the distribution of leaflets, posters and newspapers, and reports to the people on the results of the campaign against banditry.

An important contribution to this campaign was made by extraordinary commissions and Vecheka special departments. They traced heads of active gangs and organisers of counter-revolutionary actions, found out their hide-outs, secret addresses, ascertained the gangs' strength, the weapons at their disposal, and the location of their principal forces and supply bases.

The Chekas operating in the districts where martial law had been introduced were granted the status of revolutionary tribunals and investigated both the actions of gangs and individuals involved in counterrevolutionary activities. Most of all they tried to acquire information about members of gangs and determine the degree of their guilt.

Army units were needed in the campaign against armed banditry. Displaying his usual resourcefulness and determination, Dzerzhinsky managed to concentrate in the Ukraine some units and formations of the Interior Guard Forces and railway guard units with a total strength of up to 50,000 men. Considering the fact that these were infantry troops which were poorly armed, Dzerzhinsky persuaded the Revolutionary Military Council of the South-western Front to provide them with a number of machine guns. To increase the mobility of the units, a cavalry brigade, several cavalry squadrons and an air wing were put at the disposal of the Front's Rear Commander and were used as the basis for the formation of mobile groups.

Dzerzhinsky also helped develop the tactics used in the struggle against bandits and kulaks. At that time, the general consensus was that small forces should be used to encircle and then eliminate the bands, but Dzerzhinsky considered this method inefficient. In Decree No. 36 of June 17, 1920, he outlined a new mobile and offensive tactics to combat bandits and kulaks in the rear of the South-western Front. He demanded that action be conducted according to an overall plan, instructed the units to pursue the enemy until its total elimination or capture and prevent its penetration into adjoining regions.

In view of the mobile warfare being waged, it was important to ensure the smooth and uninterrupted operation of communications and transport to maintain the combat capacity of the Red Army. In the areas where armed gangs were operating and where the length of railway lines servicing the South-western Front exceeded 10,000 km, this was not an easy task. Besides, the work of the railways was obstructed by speculators, among whom were quite a few gangsters, who attacked Red Army and Cheka men.

Dzerzhinsky took steps to guard railway lines, bridges and junctions, military depots, and telephone and telegraph communication lines. As a result, the transport system began to function more efficiently.

Though engaged in daily work to organise the campaign against banditry in the rear of the South-western

Front, Dzerzhinsky still managed to find time to take part in the work of the Central Committee of the Communist Party (Bolsheviks) of the Ukraine and spoke at meetings and conferences. He was virtually indefatigable, setting an example in selflessness and dedication.

Dzerzhinsky fulfilled the duties of Rear Commander of the South-western Front for six weeks; on July 13, 1920, he was summoned to Moscow by the Central Committee. But in that short time he managed to considerably strengthen revolutionary law and order in the rear.

* * *

By late July 1920, the Red Army had liberated Byelorussia and the Ukraine. Paying lip service to peace talks with Soviet Russia, the Polish government in fact sabotaged them. The Red Army was compelled to continue the offensive.

On July 18, 1920, a meeting of Polish Communists was held in Moscow. Dzerzhinsky announced to those present the decision on universal mobilisation of Polish Communists adopted by the RCP(B) Central Committee "in view of the possible entry of the Red Army into Polish territory". The meeting decided to form a mobilisation commission, Dzerzhinsky, who was one of its members, proposed to set up a body coordinating and controlling the preparatory work and distribution of the drafted men.

At July 19 session, the Central Committee Organisational Bureau discussed the establishment of a special body for the work on the Western Front, the Polish Bureau of the RCP(B) Central Committee, consisting of Julian Marchlewski, Feliks Kon, Edward Prochniak, Josef Unszlicht, and Felix Dzerzhinsky, who would serve as the Chairman. The purpose of the newly established body was to conduct propaganda work among the people in areas occupied by the Red Army, establish Party organisations, and work with prisoners of war. The Polish Bureau would also distribute leaflets, newspapers and pamphlets to the Red Army and populace.

That same day, the newly-established Polish Bureau held a meeting where it was decided to promptly despatch Dzerzhinsky and Marchlewski to the front, and to inform the Central Committee of the Communist Workers' Party of Poland about the work of Polish Communists in Russia.

At the July 23 meeting, the Polish Bureau discussed a number of important political, organisational and

Party issues. However, developments at the front compelled the Bureau members to immediately leave Moscow. That very day, Dzerzhinsky, Marchlewski and the others left by train for Smolensk, and from there to Minsk and Molodechno. Edward Prochniak temporarily stayed in Moscow to settle a number of matters involving the mobilisation of Polish Communists.

The situation in the areas liberated by the Red Army was grave. The railway lines past Molodechno had been destroyed and the Bureau members had to travel by car. Dzerzhinsky kept in regular touch with Moscow. In a telegram to the Polish Agitation and Propaganda Bureau of the RCP(B) Central Committee, he demanded the immediate despatch of mobilised Polish Communists (the Polish Bureau had mobilised 5,700 Polish Communists out of the 18,000 living in Russia), and in another, recommended setting up a mobile Polish printing press to service the South-western Front.

On July 28, 1920, the 15th Army units captured Bialystok, a major Polish industrial centre. Local government bodies had to be formed, and industry, transport and communication restored. On July 30, Dzerzhinsky, Marchlewski and Kon left Wilno for Grodno. Lenin closely followed the developments on the Western Front, and demanded information on the situation in the areas occupied by the Red Army.

On August 2, Dzerzhinsky used the hot line to inform the Western and South-western fronts about the formation of the Polish Revolutionary Committee (RC) in Bialystok, "which, in a Manifesto to the workers issued on July 30, declared itself the revolutionary authority and embarked on the work to establish Soviet power in Polish territory". Julian Marchlewski was appointed Chairman of the Polish Revolutionary Committee; its members were Felix Dzerzhinsky, Edward Prochniak, Feliks Kon and Josef Unszlicht.

In the Manifesto, the Provisional Revolutionary Committee, the first proletarian body of state authority in Poland, explained to the workers and peasants that the Red Army had entered Polish territory not as a conqueror but as a liberator of the people from the rule of landlords and capitalists fighting "for our and your freedom".

The Manifesto proclaimed the economic and political programme of the first Polish Provisional Revolutionary Government, calling on the people to seize state power immediately.

The Polish Revolutionary Committee began to introduce measures to promote the interests of workers and peasants: nationalisation of industry, confiscation of landed estates, and performing other socioeconomic and political changes.

The Manifesto evoked a broad response among the working people of the liberated areas of Poland. On August 2, a general meeting of workers and a meeting of railway employees were held in Bialystok. The assemblies voiced their support for the new revolutionary authorities, and on August 13, the workers of the

154

Bialystok railway junction passed a resolution confirming their solidarity with and loyalty to the Polish Revolutionary Committee.

The Provisional Revolutionary Committee launched a vigorous campaign to rebuild the shattered Polish economy on liberated territories.

Later, Feliks Kon wrote: "In those memorable historic days everyone was amazed at Dzerzhinsky's energy. He did ten people's work. The territories occupied by the Red Army did not have the smoothlyfunctioning state apparatus that existed in Soviet Russia. It had to be organised on the spot, and with great difficulty. These difficulties only served to double the energy of 'Iron Felix'." Dzerzhinsky despatched several requests to Moscow to send people to organise the economy. On August 9, a meeting of the Polish Bureau and the Polish Revolutionary Committee was held, where a decision was passed on the introduction of an eight-hour day at all enterprises and offices in Bialystok.

The Revolutionary Committee was greatly concerned with distributing food to the Polish population. On August 15, 1920, as the Red Army was approaching Warsaw, Dzerzhinsky telegraphed to Kharkov: "The wreckage worked by the White Poles threatens Warsaw and the other industrial centres with the disaster of famine. Your telegram on the despatch of 50 railway carriages of foodstuffs... presents a chance to put up a fight at the front of famine, too."

Dzerzhinsky also busied himself with the restoration of the railways. On August 11, the Polish Revolutionary Committee issued a decree to the Polish railway employees urging them "to take every revolutionary measure possible to prevent the destruction of railway lines and bridges."

It is typical that even under those harsh circumstances, Dzerzhinsky was anxious about the state of the famous natural reserve Byelovezhskaya Pushcha and instructed Stanislaw Bobinski to "look into the state of forestry" there.

Dzerzhinsky was personally in charge of billeting the Red Army troops in Bialystok. Through local revolutionary committees the

Polish RC supplied the wounded Red Army men with linen, food, tobacco and other necessities.

The task of rebuilding the economy on the territories occupied by the Red Army produced a great need for skilled personnel of Polish extraction, or at least those who could speak the language. Dzerzhinsky requested such personnel from Moscow, and personally recruited men for work at the Cheka and in the militia.

The Polish Revolutionary Committee was also engaged in forming Polish Red Army units. Dzerzhinsky was personally involved in this work. "We consider the organisation of a Polish Red Army a task of paramount importance," he telegraphed to Lenin on August 6, 1920. Such an army would be recruited, above all, from among the Polish working class. The Bialystok trade union conference stated that the workers were ready to defend the revolution with arms.

"We have a good relationship with the people," wrote Dzerzhinsky, "and will have a sufficient number of recruits, at least for now, from among the workers and the landless."

Dzerzhinsky considered it expedient to try and convince prisoners of war and deserters from the Polish Army to join the revolutionary army, believing that this matter should be approached as a major political objective. For this purpose, he proposed sending representatives of the Polish Bureau of the RCP(B) Central Committee and the Vecheka Special Department to POW camps.

The Bialystok Committee of the Communist Workers' Party of Poland and the recruiting bureau at the regional revolutionary committee made a significant contribution in recruiting men for the Polish Red Army.

Lenin constantly expressed his interest in the work of the Provisional Revolutionary Committee, gave recommendations, and requested detailed information on the situation in Poland. The Revolutionary Committee sent regular reports of its activities to Lenin.

In his letters to Lenin written on August 4-6, Dzerzhinsky described the situation in Poland, developments in the Polish Communist Party, the mood of Bialystok workers, and the needs of the Polish Revolutionary Committee. He also requested that Lenin arrange to send to Poland those mobilised Poles who could serve as instructors on Soviet political matters and work in the food and other branches of industry.

Lenin also expressed an interest in the situation in Bialystok, the prevailing mood of the people, and the plans for the future work of the Polish Revolutionary Committee.

On August 9, Lenin sent Smilga, Dzerzhinsky and Marchlewski a telegram which read: "Details about the temper of agricultural labourers and Warsaw workers are essential and urgently needed, as well as about political prospects in general."[2] Dzerzhinsky forwarded to Lenin greetings from the Bialystok proletariat, and a short while later, wrote about the situation in Warsaw stating that "The question of the land policy will be exhaustively examined in Warsaw".

The Provisional Revolutionary Committee maintained close contacts with the local revolutionary committees, which acted as provisional bodies of people's authority in the provinces liberated by the Red Army.

Having received approval of the Polish RC, leadership in the new bodies of state power in the frontline zone was temporarily exercised by the Soviet military command. Dzerzhinsky, who was also involved in the formation of local revolutionary committees, requested the military commander of the Western Front to inform him about all revolutionary committees set up on Polish territory and send copies of the orders and reports to the Polish Revolutionary Committee.

Immediately after it was formed, this body took steps to establish contacts with the Communist Workers' Party of Poland. This was no easy matter, for the messengers sent into the enemy rear (they had to travel illegally) seldom managed to make their way to Warsaw. In the end, the Polish RC failed to get in touch with the Party Central Committee. Besides, many of the Party's most prominent members were at that time in prison. Later, at a sitting of the Polish delegation to the Third Comintern Congress, the leadership of the Communist Workers' Party of Poland agreed with Dzerzhinsky that its failures were rooted, among other things, in the absence of coordinated action between the Party Central Committee and the Polish Revolutionary Committee.

Dzerzhinsky took a personal interest in the Communists' political prisoners deported to Poznan. He arranged to provide them with material aid and considered the chances for their release, believing that the issue of exchanging political prisoners should be postponed until the signing or a truce with the Polish government.

Refugees, POW and deserters from the Polish Army also served as important sources of information about the situation in Poland. Messengers brought back Polish newspapers, and their information provided the basis for reports on the situation in Poland, the plans of the Entente, stand of the Communist Workers' Party and other political parties. This information was passed on to Lenin, to the RCP(B) Central Committee.

When Red Army units began to rapidly advance towards Warsaw, Dzerzhinsky was full of optimism.

Josef Unszlicht later described Dzerzhinsky's mood and his activities at the time: "Dzerzhinsky is the most active member of the Polish Revolutionary Committee. He is brimming over with enthusiasm, and full of hope that the time of the emancipation of the Polish working class, the overthrow of bourgeoisie and the establishment of the dictatorship of the working class is not far off." On August 15, 1920, Dzerzhinsky, Marchlewski and Kon began their trip to Warsaw. However, the Red Army was forced to retreat from the city. Its failures at Warsaw were rooted in a number of factors, including grave errors made by the supreme command. Moreover, Wrangel's offensive on the South-western Front made it necessary to transfer some of the units there. Analysing the causes of the Soviet retreat from Warsaw, Lenin wrote: "Our offensive, our too swift advance almost as far as Warsaw, was undoubtedly a mistake... At any rate, the mistake is there, and it was due to the fact that we had overestimated the superiority of our forces."[3]

In view of the retreat of the Red Army, the Polish Revolutionary Committee had to suspend its activities. Dzerzhinsky personally supervised the evacuation of Bialystok, taking care to provide transportation for wounded and sick soldiers, and Party and government officials.

He took it very hard that the working people of Poland had been unable to shake off the yoke of landowners and capitalists. In his opinion, one of the reasons for the failure was that Polish Communists did not appreciate the role of the peasantry in revolution.

Another reason, he maintained, was the split in the working class. The Polish Communist Party, which was crippled by White terror and repressions, proved too weak to lead a popular revolution and render assistance to the advancing Red Army.

On August 23, Dzerzhinsky arrived in Minsk, where a few days later he was already working on the Revolutionary Military Council of the Western Front and continued to head the Polish Bureau.

At that time, Minsk was the venue of the Russian- Ukrainian- Polish peace conference, which began on

August 17, 1920. Dzerzhinsky kept Lenin informed about its work and helped in the organisation of the Soviet-Polish talks in Minsk, finding competent translators from among the Polish Communists working with the Polish Bureau. In September 1920, in a letter to the People's Commissar for Foreign Affairs, Georgi Chicherin, Dzerzhinsky requested that the exchange of civilian prisoners be placed on the agenda of the talks that had been resumed in Riga.

In late August, the Soviet army, which had been reinforced with fresh troops, stopped the advance of the

Polish White Army on the Western Front and began preparations for another offensive. On August 30, Dzerzhinsky wrote to his wife: "The situation at the front is soon to change to our advantage; army units have arrived from Petrograd, and brought colossal enthusiasm with them... However, I do not entertain illusions that victory will be ours again without difficulty—we shall have to strain all our resources for a long time to come."

In September 1920, the RCP(B) Central Committee Polish Bureau issued an address to the soldiers, workers, and peasants of

Poland denouncing hostile propaganda concerning the Red Army's alleged plans of conquest.

At that time, Dzerzhinsky demanded that the Polish Bureau in Moscow speed up the despatch of literature in Polish. In another letter, he asked for all editions of Polish pamphlets and books in Russian to be used at the political training course opened in Minsk at that time. He also arranged for leisure facilities and medical treatment for Polish Communists.

Despite the advantageous position of the Red Army at the front, on Lenin's initiative, the Government of the RSFSR offered to sign a peace treaty with Poland, wishing to avoid a winter campaign. On September

21 the talks, which had begun in Minsk, were resumed in Riga, and on October 12, 1920, a truce and preliminary terms of peace were signed.

Notes

[1]His functions were to maintain law and order in the Red Army rear.

[2]V. I. Lenin, Collected Works, Vol. 44, 1975, p. 410.

[3]V. I. Lenin, "Tenth Congress of the R.C.P.(B.), March 8-16, 1921", Collected Works, Vol. 32, 1977, p. 173.

Chapter Nine

GUARDING THE SECURITY OF THE SOVIET STATE

Led by the Communist Party, headed by Lenin, the Soviet people finally emerged victorious from the Civil War, having driven away the foreign invaders. Now it was possible to return to the peaceful building of socialism.

However, though defeated in open battle, the bourgeoisie did not renounce its plans to destroy the first state of workers and peasants. Adjusting to the new situation, the imperialist quarters merely changed their tactics. Now they hoped to bring about the country's economic ruin and hastened to take advantage of its desperate economic position.

Lenin repeatedly stated that the republic would have to steadily build up its defence potential and the might of the Red Army and Cheka bodies. He personally instructed Dzerzhinsky to draft a plan for the struggle against domestic counter-revolution under conditions of the peaceful building of socialism. Such a plan was prepared and presented to Lenin. It provided for the final annihilation of the White Guard, SR, Menshevik and other anti-Soviet organisations, the weeding out of the counter-revolutionary and criminal elements in some parts of the country, and consolidation of special purpose detachments and units whose duty was to fight banditry.

Dzerzhinsky introduced a number of effective measures to organisationally reinforce the Vecheka. He initiated the formation of new operation units, including the Economic Administration in the centre affiliated with the Vecheka Economic Department and with branches in the provinces, for the struggle against espionage, counter-revolution and sabotage in the various spheres of the economy.

Directed by Lenin's instructions and the decisions of the Central Committee, Dzerzhinsky consistently pursued the Party line in the work of the Vecheka and its local branches. The extraordinary nature of its activities as a body of proletarian dictatorship necessitated by the Civil War and foreign invasion no longer suited the changed conditions in the country—the aim of the peaceful building of socialism. In the report to the Ninth All-Russia Congress of Soviets held in December 1921, Lenin formulated an important theoretical thesis on the need for the prolonged existence in a socialist state of a body responsible for its security. He stated: "As long as there are exploiters in the world ... the power of the working people cannot survive without such an institution."[1] He insisted on the reform of the Vecheka and evolved a clearer definition of its competence and functions: "Prevailing conditions insistently demand that the work of this organisation be limited to the purely political sphere."[2]

On February 6, 1922, the All-Russia Central Executive Committee disbanded the All- Russia

Extraordinary Commission and formed the State Political Department (GPU) under the RSFSR People's Commissariat for Internal Affairs. The People's Commissar for Internal Affairs, Felix Dzerzhinsky, was appointed Chairman of the GPU.

That same day, the All-Russia Central Executive Committee confirmed the Statute on the GPU. Its functions were to prevent and suppress open counter-revolutionary actions, combat banditry, and uncover organisations and persons plotting to undermine the republic's economic apparatus. The GPU was charged with protecting state secrets, preventing espionage, guarding rail-and waterways and state borders, combating economic and political smuggling and the illegal crossing of borders, and fulfilling special assignments of the Central Executive Committee and the Council of People's Commissars in the field on preserving revolutionary public order.

When the Union of Soviet Socialist Republics was formed on December 30, 1922, a USSR Central

Executive Committee decree of November 15, 1923, endorsed the establishment of the Unified State Political Department (OGPU) at the USSR Council of People's Commissars as the body coordinating the efforts of all republics in the struggle against political and economic counter-revolutionary activities, espionage, and banditry. Dzerzhinsky was appointed head of the OGPU. The abolition of the All-Russia Extraordinary Commission and the formation of the GPU-OGPU signified more than a change of name for state security bodies. The gist of the reform of the Vecheka, according to Lenin, was the changed nature of its work to suit the new situation. The RCP(B) Central Committee pointed out that under the conditions of peace, the goals set before the GPU bodies would gain in complexity.

On May 6, 1922, Dzerzhinsky held a meeting of GPU representatives which discussed the functions of state security bodies and ways of consolidating socialist legality. He underscored the political significance of the Vecheka reform initiated by Lenin and of the establishment of the GPU, and the need to step up the campaign against economic counterrevolution and to further improve the Cheka apparatus.

The decree signed by Dzerzhinsky stated "Overt uprisings must be mercilessly suppressed, and the gangs are to be exterminated, but the struggle against SR underground organisations which are preparing revolts and terrorist acts, the capture of political and economic spies require subtle methods of work, etc... It is essential to know exactly what a particular person, a former officer or landowner, is engaged in, so that his arrest is justified; otherwise spies, terrorists and underground troublemakers will go scot- free." Headed by Dzerzhinsky, the state security bodies traced and eliminated British, French, Japanese and Polish spy nests.

The various White émigré centres supported by foreign intelligence services such as the Russian General Warriors' Union, the Supreme Monarchist Council, the Fraternity of Russian Truth, the People's Union for the Defence of the Homeland and Freedom, and the Russian Fascist Union closely collaborated with one another in coordinating their anti-Soviet plans. A so-called inter-union intelligence network was operating in Constantinople, and used White Guards who had fled to Turkey for intelligence purposes against Soviet Russia. A conference of the Baltic states convened in 1924 by the ruling circles of Britain and Finland called for the establishment of a united anti-Soviet centre and more vigorous anti-Soviet intelligence activities on Soviet territory.

Dzerzhinsky, his deputies Unszlicht and Menzhinsky, the central Vecheka—OGPU apparatus and local state security bodies kept close tag on the activities of the country's enemies and worked to foil their plans.

On July 24, 1921, the newspaper Izvestia VTsIK published materials from the Vecheka report concerning the discovery of anti-Soviet conspirational groups operating within the territory of the RSFSR in May and June 1921. These included the Petrograd Fighting Organisation, the Western Regional Committee of the so-called People's Union for the Defence of the Homeland and Freedom, and the Siberian Regional Union of Toiling Peasants, all of which were in touch with foreign intelligence services and with SRs and Mensheviks. The report stated, "The anti-Soviet movement in the past few months has shown that what we have now before us is the old close knit fraternity of counterrevolutionaries, from extreme monarchists to Mensheviks. Its ultimate goal is the restoration of the bourgeois and landowner rule, and its methods of struggle—banditry, terror and destruction."

Lenin repeatedly pointed out that the campaign waged by Cheka bodies against domestic and foreign counter- revolution would be successful only if the Cheka had a thorough knowledge of the enemy, its strength and weaknesses. "It would be very instructive," he wrote, "... systematically to watch... the most important tactical moves, and the most important trends of this Russian counter-revolution. It operates chiefly abroad..."[3]

Dzerzhinsky directly participated in or masterminded each major operation of the state security bodies against imperialist intelligence services, White émigré centres abroad, and domestic counter-revolution.

The Cheka's vigilance disrupted the plans of domestic and foreign counterrevolutionaries who had hoped to unite the foreign White Guard centres into a single system.

The OGPU operations masterminded and supervised by Dzerzhinsky provided good training for his men; they learned the subtle and meticulous art of discovering and thwarting enemy plans.

164

Dzerzhinsky directed the work of the principal operation departments of the Vecheka— OGPU. He personally supervised Operation Syndicate-2. Together with his deputy, Vyacheslav Menzhinsky, and the head of the counter- intelligence department, Artur Artuzov, he made a detailed study of the plan to lure Boris Savinkov, an émigré SR leader, to return to Russia to head the Liberal Democrats, an "anti-Soviet organisation" with which his emissary had established contacts. The Cheka men who were involved in the operation received many valuable suggestions from Dzerzhinsky through Artuzov. Savinkov had to become convinced of the strength of the "anti-Soviet organisation". He was a very ambitious man, and to cater to this trait, he was elected the organisation's Central Committee Chairman. This was done in his absence and at Dzerzhinsky's suggestion. A rabid enemy of Soviet power, he was thirsting for leadership in the anti-

Soviet movement. On August 15, 1924, accompanied by his closest associates, he "illegally" crossed the Soviet-Polish border, and was arrested in Minsk the next day.

The OGPU worked competently and resolutely to put an end to the existence of the People's Union for the Defence of the Homeland and Freedom.

On Dzerzhinsky's instructions, the OGPU bodies, working on Operation Trust, communicated to the British intelligence and the special services of some other capitalist states fictitious information which was thought to be highly valuable by the ruling quarters and the general staffs of Britain and France, and by the leaders of the White émigré circles.

In 1921-22, the underground White Guard, SR and Menshevik organisations staged arson and explosions in a number of the country's regions, destroyed railway lines, bridges and telephone and telegraph lines, and flooded mines. Taking advantage of the difficult economic situation that had evolved in the Soviet Republic, they sought to undermine confidence in Soviet power, instigated rebellions and strikes. They also tried to use the New Economic Policy to promote their illegal plans. Feigning support for the government, they infiltrated the Communist Party in an effort to split its ranks, as well as the Red Army and government bodies, and made their way in to a number of high positions in the various branches of the economy, seeking to cripple the country economically and militarily and obstruct the building of socialism.

The campaign waged by the GPU-OGPU bodies against the anti-Soviet activities of the Mensheviks, SRs and bourgeois nationalists was part of the overall fight of the Communist Party against counterrevolutionary parties and trends. Dzerzhinsky explained to his staff the new tactics in the struggle of Mensheviks and SRs against Soviet power and the need for more flexible and efficient methods of combating their activities and exposing their organisations. He believed that the bodies of state security should enlist the help of the people and use the press, workers' assemblies and meetings.

Dzerzhinsky headed the operation in which the records of the right wing SR Central Committee were found and seized. This group had masterminded and instigated a large number of kulak revolts and banditry in Siberia, Tambov Gubernia, the Ukraine, Byelorussia and some other districts.

In late 1921, the Cheka had acquired much new evidence of counter-revolutionary activities of the SRs.

On December 28, 1921, based on Dzerzhinsky's report on the activities of the SRs and Mensheviks, the

RCP(B) Central Committee Plenary Meeting passed a decision to try the SR Central Committee by the Supreme Revolutionary Tribunal, and instructed an ad hoc commission, to which Dzerzhinsky was appointed, to name the deadline for the publication of the necessary materials.

At Dzerzhinsky's suggestion, this information was printed by the Izvestia VTsIK. The report stated that the GPU had acquired evidence of terrorist and military activities of the Socialist-Revolutionaries in the years of the Civil War, and the crimes committed by this party towards the proletarian revolution. The Central Committee of this party and a number of other prominent members were tried by the Supreme Revolutionary Tribunal.

The trial, which took place in Moscow in June, July and August 1922, proved beyond any doubt that the SRs did engage in counter-revolutionary conspiracies and armed revolts against Soviet power, sabotage and individual terror, espionage for White Guards and interventionists. The sentence passed by the Supreme Revolutionary Tribunal noted that the activities of that party revealed that it was not socialist but bourgeois, that it was using its socialist name and the socialist elements it comprised to deceive the people, and that, in fact, it was a counter-revolutionary party and an enemy of the people.

The trial of SR leaders demonstrated that their actions were actually those of imperialist agents. Their collusion with the Western states helped trigger off the Civil War; SRs had instigated assassinations of Soviet political figures.

After the trial, the split in the SR party became more pronounced; many of its rank-and- file members parted ways with the leaders, which ultimately resulted in the party's disintegration.

To check the hostile activities of the Mensheviks, SRs and other anti-Soviet groups and organisations, on August 10, 1922, the All-Russia Central Executive Committee passed a decree on the administrative deportation of participants in counter-revolutionary actions. Many members of anti-Soviet parties and groups were deported from Moscow and other major cities.

At the same time, Dzerzhinsky seriously and attentively considered the letters and appeals of those people who had come to understand the folly of their previous behaviour and pledged to never again engage in anti-Soviet activities. After receiving a letter from SR Alexander Beilin, who wrote that he was determined to open a new page in his life, Dzerzhinsky wrote a memo stating that Beilin's case should be reconsidered.

Dzerzhinsky took an interest in the fate of former members of anti-Soviet parties who had gone over to the side of the Bolsheviks. On March 22, 1922, he wrote that for the GPU, the moral purity of these persons' motives was unquestionable, and that they ought to find a sympathetic response and full support in the Party.

The overall campaign launched by the Communist Party and the Soviet Government against law-breakers was also directed against banditry, which was flaring up in many of the country's regions.

The intelligence network of many capitalist countries knocked together criminal groups recruited from among the remnants of White armies and sent them into Soviet territory. Inside the country, such groups were comprised of kulaks, anarchists, bourgeois nationalists and criminal and déclassé elements. Banditry was particularly widespread in the Ukraine, the Kuban area, Tambov Region, Siberia, Central Asia, Karelia and the Caucasus.

It posed a major threat to the country. Thugs plundered entire regions, attacked Party committees and local Soviets, brutally killed Communists, Komsomol members and activists in the Soviets, robbed banks, trains, depots and shops, and terrorised the population. They tried to obstruct the measures introduced by the Communist Party and Soviet Government to promote the New Economic Policy and to reconstruct the national economy.

Their activities were often controlled by the intelligence networks of capitalist states and various foreign anti-Soviet and nationalist centres and organisations supported by this network, as well as SRs and bourgeois nationalists.

"In the banditry one feels the influence of the Socialist-Revolutionaries," wrote Lenin. "Their main forces are abroad; every spring they dream of overthrowing Soviet power... The SRs are connected with the local instigators."[4]

To direct the campaign against banditry, a special commission was set up. As head of the commission,

Dzerzhinsky rallied GPU—OGPU forces for decisive action. At his suggestion, Deputy Chairman of the GPU Unszlicht was sent to Byelorussia. The special GPU department for the struggle against banditry was being strengthened.

In view of the public threat posed by banditry, in October 1922, the RSFSR Central Executive Committee granted the GPU the right to execute participants in bandit raids and armed robberies without a court trial.

On January 29, 1924, Dzerzhinsky despatched a letter to the Politbureau of the RCP(B) Central

Committee suggesting that the leadership in the campaign against banditry should be assumed by the OGPU and its local branches and that the investigation departments and the militia be made accountable to them. When discussing ways to step up this campaign, the Politbureau and the Central Executive Committee Presidium accepted Dzerzhinsky's suggestion.

Dzerzhinsky believed that success in this work depended directly on the support of the working masses, the confidence of the toiling peasants.

Within a relatively short time, banditry was eradicated in a number of regions. The plans of the imperialists and domestic counter-revolutionaries to destroy Soviet power from the inside had fallen through. The overthrown exploiter classes lost all hope for the restoration of the old order. The eradication of banditry speeded up the reconstruction of the economy and socialist changes in the countryside.

Another major target of GPU activities was economic counter-revolution. The imperialist states and

Russian bourgeoisie abroad tried every means to disrupt or at least slow down the work to reconstruct the Soviet economy which had been severely undermined by the war. They also entertained hopes that their subversive activities in Soviet Russia would be more effective after the introduction of the New Economic Policy, and even believed they might completely restore capitalism and overthrow Soviet power. Associations of former Russian manufacturers, bankers and traders abroad, strengthened by their international contacts, played the leading role in staging acts of economic subversion in the USSR. Keeping in touch with various counterrevolutionary organisations on Soviet territory, they also financed foreign White émigré centres which conducted espionage and terrorist activities in Soviet Russia.

The prevalent forms of economic counter-revolution were economic espionage, wrecking and sabotage, smuggling, production and circulation of counterfeit money, speculation, and plunder of socialist property. It was imperative to suppress these activities in order to build a sound economic basis for the Soviet state, enhance its defence capacity and state security.

Dzerzhinsky wrote in a decree that one of the weapons of the bourgeoisie was foreign trade, attempts to "corrupt our foreign missions by bribery, pump away our gold reserves and mineral resources, and palm off on the Soviet state rubbish instead of engines, motorcars, spare parts and other things needed for the restoration of production".

The GPU-OGPU bodies uncovered dozens of major sabotage plots and conspiracy groups in various branches of the national economy whose subversive activities were directed from abroad. In 1924-25, sabotage groups were uncovered at a number of factories and mines, in bodies responsible for the provision and distribution of goods, and in cooperative organisations. It was found that intelligence data were also collected by the saboteurs and passed abroad.

Dzerzhinsky made it a point to expose the links between sabotage groups and their patrons abroad, and instructed the men at the GPU-OGPU Economic Department to pay due attention to this aspect of their work. He also explained to them the need to render aid to Party and government bodies in their work to improve the functioning of enterprises and organisations, to be more responsive to the letters and requests of citizens who wrote about acts of sabotage on the part of officials from among the prerevolutionary body of employees. He carefully reinforced the OGPU with skilled and experienced men.

Dzerzhinsky regularly informed the RCP(B) Central Committee and the USSR Council of People's Commissars about developments in the campaign against sabotage.

Dzerzhinsky had always regarded the state border as the front line of struggle. He personally headed and masterminded operations aimed at checking the flow of contraband which was doing a great deal of damage to the Soviet economy. Persons hostile to the Soviet system constantly tried to smuggle out of the country currency, gold, rare musical instruments, works of art and historical objects, and to flood the home market with contraband goods. Despite his extremely busy schedule, he regularly, and usually late at night, read reports of the Economic Department on the capture of smugglers and the goods that they were carrying. He offered recommendations on how best to guard the state border to prevent smuggling, and made it a point to inform Party and economic bodies about the type of goods in short supply inside the country and their smuggling from abroad. On April 26, 1925, in a speech at the All-Union Conference of Commanders of the OGPU Border Units, Dzerzhinsky stated: "The bourgeoisie was hoping that the Union of Soviet Socialist Republics would not be able to cope with the reconstruction of its economy and would come crying to the West, but we are advancing without its help... You, comrades, who are fighting contraband, must follow the economic development of our country... You could study contraband (which goods are smuggled and where) and the reasons for its filtering through, and pose before me ... the question: is it not possible to develop this or that branch, whose produce is getting inside the country as contraband?... Your suggestions based on the serious study of contraband may be useful for our economic bodies."

Dzerzhinsky regularly reported to the Party Central Committee and its Politbureau on the steps taken by the state security bodies to prevent and check contraband. He made suggestions directed at improving the legislation in force at that time. On February 2, 1924, the Politbureau discussed the question on the struggle against the smuggling of platinum and enjoined the OGPU to step up their efforts in the field. Dzerzhinsky supplied the materials for the discussion. On his instructions the OGPU set up special border zones at which travellers were checked for smuggled gold and foreign currency.

In 1924, the OGPU bodies confiscated over eight million roubles' worth of smuggled-in goods. In 192526, at the Western border alone, over 32,000 persons were detained carrying smuggled goods, currency and valuables worth about six million roubles. Within the same period, in Central Asia, the Cheka bodies detained over 51,000 smugglers and confiscated over six million roubles' worth of goods.

The concentrated efforts of state security bodies resulted in a sharp drop in the amount of valuables smuggled abroad.

Another dangerous form of activity of foreign and domestic counter-revolution, which was undermining the economic foundations of the Soviet state, was the manufacture and circulation of counterfeit money. The vigorous campaign launched by the state security bodies against this evil strengthened the Soviet credit and monetary system and Soviet currency, and enhanced the rouble's purchasing power.

On March 30, 1924, Dzerzhinsky requested the USSR Central Executive Committee to grant the OGPU special powers to suppress counterfeiters. In 1923-25, its bodies uncovered over 200 groups engaged in the manufacture and circulation of counterfeit money; about 2,000 counterfeiters were arrested and tried.

Another matter that lay within Dzerzhinsky's competence as Chairman of the Vecheka- OGPU was the organisation of guard duty at the country's state borders.

On November 24, 1920, the Labour and Defence Council proclaimed the Vecheka Special Department the body responsible for the security of state borders, providing it with military units operating under dual command. All issues involved in the protection of the state borders were to be settled by the special departments, while in other matters, these troops were under army command.

At Dzerzhinsky's insistence, on September 27, 1922, the Labour and Defence Council passed a resolution on entrusting the State Political Department with protection of the RSFSR land and water borders, and on forming an Independent Border Corps within the GPU forces.

Dzerzhinsky considered it vitally important to staff all army and border zone headquarters with competent and experienced commanders and political instructors. This alone could ensure the reliable protection of the state border and prevent its violations.

In a greeting to the delegates of the Second Congress of Political Instructors of the GPU Forces delivered on April 11, 1923, Dzerzhinsky stated that the issue of guarding the Soviet state borders was a particularly pressing one at the time, and that they must be closed to counter- revolutionaries and smugglers at whatever the cost.

In December 1923, at his suggestion, a Border Guard College was opened, which grew into the centre training commanders and political instructors of border units. Dzerzhinsky emphasised the importance of the students' military and political education! Addressing the first graduates of the College in September 1924 he said: "To protect the country from the agents of international capital, their spies, instigators of revolts, incendiaries and terrorists, and to stem the attempts to undermine the foreign trade monopoly by economic contraband—these are the main targets facing you and the border guards at large."

Dzerzhinsky believed that the personnel of the OGPU bodies and troops should be dedicated to the cause of the Communist Party and socialist Motherland vigilant and steadfast in fighting the class enemy to the end and strictly adhere to socialist laws. In a note to Ivan Ksenofontov written on January 19, 1921, he stated that the work of the Cheka was hard and thankless on the personal plane, extremely responsible and important on the state plane, and evoked the strong dissatisfaction among some persons and even bodies where sabotage was going on. At the same time, it offered temptations, as the very fact of being employed at the Cheka could have been used to promote one's personal ends. Dzerzhinsky stressed the need to weed out politically and morally unreliable employees, and condemned covering up for those who had abused their authority for selfish purposes as a triple crime.

Substantiating his conviction that the Soviet socialist state needed bodies of state security, Dzerzhinsky stated that their chief purpose was to uncover, prevent and check the subversive activities of imperialists and their secret services.

The Party Central Committee highly valued the work of the OGPU and repeatedly exhorted local Party committees to render them every assistance. It pointed out that the Vecheka and its local branches played the key role in the struggle against domestic and foreign counter-revolution and thus were the focus of attention of the entire Party, and that the GPU that had replaced the Vecheka, although working under more peaceful conditions, had to fight against no less great odds. The Central Committee stated that the Party should treat the GPU personnel just as it did the Vecheka, and that the GPU and its local bodies should remain one of the principal bodies of Soviet power.

Dzerzhinsky demanded that OGPU personnel keep in touch with Party and government organisations and inform them of the developments in the campaign against crime. He constantly worked to improve the functioning of state security bodies, remove everything that might serve as a breeding ground for dissatisfaction and hostility, inform more frequently the Moscow Party Committee about the OGPU activities, and keep up its prestige among the population.

Dzerzhinsky is still remembered as the Cheka man, a fiery revolutionary who was scrupulously honest and exhibited great courage; a man who was considerate to the people, merciless towards the enemy, and prepared to sacrifice his life for his country.

* * *

As Chairman of the Vecheka and, since 1919, the People's Commissar for Internal Affairs, Dzerzhinsky had from the first days of the Soviet state been involved in the campaign for helping homeless and hungry children. He was always dissatisfied with the amount of work done in the field in those hard times and, as his wife stated, was waiting for the end of the Civil War to be able to concentrate more on the communist education of children, of the youth. This was considered an important facet of the Vecheka activities to protect revolutionary law and order and prevent crime.

In 1921, the Soviet state was finally able to begin healing the wounds inflicted by the Civil War and foreign intervention. At that time, the country had over five million homeless and hungry children who desperately needed help, attention and care. Dzerzhinsky suggested that the appropriate bodies pool their efforts in the campaign against child homelessness. On his instructions, groups were recruited from among the Cheka staff to inspect children's homes and help their management take prompt measures to improve their work.

It occurred to Dzerzhinsky to involve all Cheka bodies from top to bottom in this campaign. Dzerzhinsky outlined his plan to Anatoly Lunacharsky, People's Commissar for Education. Later, Lunacharsky reminisced: "Felix entered the room as swiftly and urgently as ever. Those who had met him know his manner: he spoke as if in a great hurry, as if realising that time was running short and that everything had to be done promptly. The words chased each other like waves, as if in a hurry to be translated into action.

" 'I want to channel some of my personal strength and, what is more important, of the Vecheka forces, into the struggle against child homelessness,' he told me, and the familiar slightly feverish light of excited energy glowed in his eyes.

" 'I have arrived at this decision' he went on, 'proceeding from two considerations. First, this is a terrible thing! One can't help thinking when looking at the children that everything is really for them! The fruits of the revolution are not for us, they are for them! And yet how many of them have been terribly hurt by the fighting and the poverty. One feels like rushing to their help, as one would if they were drowning. The People's Commissariat for Education won't be able to cope on its own. You need assistance from the broad Soviet public. It is necessary to set up, under the All-Russia Central Executive Committee,... a commission that would incorporate representatives of all departments and organisations that can be useful. I have already talked to some people; I'd like to head this commission myself; I want to involve the Vecheka apparatus in practical work.' "

On January 27, 1921, the All-Russia Central Executive Committee Presidium appointed Dzerzhinsky head of the newly-established commission on the improvement of children's conditions, which came to be known as the Children's Commission It was instructed to investigate the state of affairs in the provinces and the condition of children's homes and institutions, to collect data on the number of homeless children and together with the bodies of Soviet state authority, find places for them in children's homes and in specially established children's and teenagers' communes.

That same day, Dzerzhinsky addressed a letter to all extraordinary commissions instructing them to take prompt steps to improve the children's conditions. It read: "The time has come when, breathing more easily on the foreign front, Soviet power can channel its energy into this matter, turn its attention above all to children, the future stronghold of the communist system.

"The extraordinary commissions, as bodies of proletarian dictatorship, cannot remain outside this project; they must render every assistance to Soviet power in its work to protect the children and provide for them. For this purpose, so as to involve the Cheka, the All-Russia Central Executive Committee Presidium has appointed me head of the abovementioned commission for the improvement of the children's conditions. Let this be a signal and an instruction to all extraordinary commissions."

The letter outlined a programme of work to be carried out by the Cheka to save and help bring up and educate children, and voiced its author's conviction that all Cheka men would come to realise the importance and urgency of this work and, as usual, give of their best. "Caring for the children is the surest way to eradicate counter-revolution. Having successfully dealt with the matter of provisions for children, Soviet power will have won supporters and defenders in each peasant and worker family, and with this, a broad basis in its struggle against counter-revolution," ended Dzerzhinsky's letter to the Cheka staff.

The news about the foundation of the Children's Commission headed by Dzerzhinsky was warmly welcomed by the people, and especially educationalists. From the start, the commission set to work with great enthusiasm. At Dzerzhinsky's initiative, a nation-wide investigation into the state of childcare institutions was conducted. Local Party, Komsomol and trade union bodies and all extraordinary commissions joined the campaign for saving children and improving their life. The noble example of Dzerzhinsky and his tremendous prestige in the Party and among the people was a major factor contributing to the success of this large-scale and difficult project.

Constantly overworked, Dzerzhinsky still found the time to attend the commission's meetings and personally direct its daily work. He initiated the establishment of work communes and colonies for children and teenagers, where former homeless children and juvenile delinquents received shelter, food and clothes, got an education and learned a trade, and finally became useful and worthy members of society. A great number of orphans were placed in children's homes or adopted by families or Red Army and Vecheka—GPU units.

The commission accomplished a great amount of work to help the children in the famine-struck Volga area in 1921-22. It suggested that children be evacuated to Siberia, the Ukraine, Byelorussia, Georgia, Turkestan and other areas where the situation was better. Dzerzhinsky, the Cheka and its local branches supervised this work. Dzerzhinsky personally read the reports on the possibilities of feeding and housing the starving children.

The Children's Commission and public organisations collected gifts for the children, sent sanitary and food trains to the famine-struck areas, and distributed state-granted rations among children's establishments.

But the focus of the commission's efforts was still child homelessness. Ragged, hungry and sick children swarmed railway stations, hid in cold and damp basements and attics of abandoned ramshackle buildings, begged, stole and sold things on the black market. They were particularly numerous in Moscow. The Moscow Extraordinary Commission for the Struggle against Child Homelessness set up nine reception points for 2,600 children, and two isolation centres for 600 children. However, that was far from enough; at times over 10,000 homeless children stayed there.

On December 21, 1922, the commission heard a report on the progress of the campaign against child homelessness in Moscow and passed the following decision: "To request Comrade Dzerzhinsky to report to the appropriate higher Party and government bodies on the desperate situation of the republic's child population, and, specifically, on the catastrophic increase in child homelessness."

Dzerzhinsky regularly reported to Lenin and the Party Central Committee on the children's conditions and the work being done to combat child homelessness, and always met with their support and sympathy. When they met before conferences, Lenin often asked Dzerzhinsky about the commission's work and the things being done to make the life of children better.

In August 1922, Dzerzhinsky sent a letter to the provinces suggesting that more should be done to open children's homes and render the children other urgent assistance. He insisted on being sent detailed information about the work of children's institutions in the provinces and the progress of the campaign to eliminate child homelessness, and had those who displayed carelessness in this field severely punished.

Gradually, the situation in this field improved, but the overall task was far from accomplished. Out of 5 million homeless, hungry and sick children, over a million were placed in children's homes, and about three million received aid from the Commission to Combat Famine, the Children's Commission and other organisations. However, about 1.5 million children still had not been reached by any form of aid. The network of children's institutions was not extensive enough to accommodate everyone, and there was no money to build new ones. Even those establishments that were already functioning were not provided with enough food, clothing or supplies.

In view of the desperate condition of a tremendous number of children and the formidable consequences of child homelessness, the Children's Commission, which enjoyed the vigorous support of Party, Komsomol and trade union bodies, held a Week of the Homeless and Sick Child throughout the country from April 30 to May 6, 1923.

On March 31, 1923, an address to the working people of the USSR "Everyone to the Aid of the Children" signed by Dzerzhinsky was made public.

"Be embarrassed neither by the form nor by the size of your donation. Remember that only the concerted effort of the broad worker-peasant masses can secure us success on the difficult front of combating child homelessness," the address read.

The Soviet people eagerly responded to the appeal of the Children's Commission. The Week of the Homeless and Sick Child was efficiently organised and brought in substantial funds. Thirty per cent of the money went to the already functioning children's institutions, and seventy per cent was used to build new ones.

In those years, such "weeks" were held more than once and were always successful, bringing in money and items for children. The forms of the people's aid varied and included gifts of money, clothes, shoes, food and linen, concerts given for the benefit of the children's fund, purchase of postal stamps issued by the Children's Commission, adoption of homeless children.

Dzerzhinsky was closely following the organisation and progress of education in the children's work communes and colonies. As a rule, they were set up in the countryside not far from towns and railway stations, and occupied former aristocratic country mansions or dachas, or were opened on the land of state-run farms. They were sponsored by Cheka bodies.

Dzerzhinsky believed productive labour could considerably help correct the delinquent behaviour of former homeless children and juveniles. The work communes and colonies combined education with work, and politics with morality.

The significance of the work communes and colonies was not only the fact that they had saved from death and gave tens of thousands of former vagabonds and young delinquents a start in life; they proved by practice the soundness of the new, Soviet system of communist education of children and teenagers.

A memorial to Dzerzhinsky's efforts in this field is the work commune named after him, which was established not far from Kharkov with the funds donated by the Ukrainian Cheka. For a long time the distinguished Soviet educator Anton Makarenko was a staff member of that commune, which the writer Maxim Gorky called "a window into communism". It was there that Makarenko shaped his educational theory.

Despite his many other duties, Dzerzhinsky frequently visited work communes, and colonies, and children's homes, had long talks with former delinquents, took an interest in their studies, work and daily life, rejoined at their progress and gave friendly advice.

In the autumn of 1923, having too much to do at the OGPU and the Commissariat for Transport, as well as in the RCP(B) Central Committee, Dzerzhinsky requested that the All-Russia Central Executive Committee Presidium allow him to resign from the commission. Since by that time it was already functioning quite smoothly, Dzerzhinsky's request was granted. But for the rest of his life, he continued to take a lively interest in educational matters, the work of schools and Young Pioneer and Komsomol organisations, and the daily life of Soviet young people. In the spring of 1924, he initiated a commission to inspect the Young Pioneer movement, seeing it as "a powerful means for creating an independent and strong nation of proletarians". He believed that the activities of Young Pioneers should blend independent ventures of children with sensible guidance of their elders. He often inquired about Moscow general education schools, and took time to analyse and criticise shortcomings in their work.

Janek, Dzerzhinsky's son, said years later that as a parent and educator, his father was both stern and demanding, kind and responsive. He taught Janek to love his country, be brave, hard-working, modest and honest. Dzerzhinsky never lectured him, was never boring; he relied more on emulation of worthy examples. "More than anything else," wrote Janek, "he hated lies and sentimentality which has nothing to do with sincere, real feeling."

Dzerzhinsky always knew how his son was doing at school, helped him whenever he had time to spare, especially in maths, listened with great interest about his stay at the Young Pioneer camp and the life of the Young Pioneer detachment to which his son belonged, about his friends.

Dzerzhinsky's relationship with his son is an example of sensible upbringing which shapes the young person into a worthy and useful member of society.

The country's children knew very well who Dzerzhinsky was and repaid his efforts with gratitude and affection. Touching letters were sent to him from all over the country. The children included photographs and, in a childishly touching manner, related events or their life and studies, thanked Dzerzhinsky for his concern and care. They promised their elder friend to be good and to study conscientiously. On an anniversary of the October Revolution, the residents of a children's home wrote him that his name had lit the fire of communism in their hearts, and that as young communards they would work to finish what their fathers had begun.

Warm, spirited letters were sent to Dzerzhinsky from children's homes, work communes and Young Pioneer organisations. "Dear Comrade Dzerzhinsky," read a letter from Voronezh, "we are sending you our warm Young Pioneer greetings, and want to tell you that we have named our detachment after you, and elected you an honorary Young Pioneer." The children asked Dzerzhinsky for his photograph and biography for the anniversary of their detachment.

Dzerzhinsky was, as always, very busy, but he sent the Young Pioneers a telegram on the day of the anniversary, July 6. He carefully preserved children's letters and, as his wife reported, frequently read them over and over again. Ingenuous and sincere, they helped assuage heartache and weariness, and filled him with fresh energy. Notes

[1]V. I. Lenin, "Ninth All-Russia Congress of Soviets; December 23-28, 1921", Collected Works, Vol.

33, 1973, p. 176.

[2]Ibid.

[3]V. I. Lenin, "Third Congress of the Communist International, June 22-July 1921", Collected Works, Vol. 32, 1977, p. 483.

[4]V. I. Lenin, "Speech at a Meeting of Moscow Party Activists, February 24, 1921", Collected Works, Vol. 42, 1971, p. 273.

Chapter Ten

THE PEOPLE'S COMMISSAR FOR TRANSPORT

After the end of the Civil War and suppression of foreign intervention, the country could begin to rebuild its economy. It was crucial to overcome economic dislocation and to reconstruct the transport system so vital to the state's economic life. Lenin wrote: "We must restore the exchange between agriculture and industry, and we need a material basis to do so. What is it? It is railway and water transport."[1] He also referred to transport as "the most important, or one of the most important sectors of our economy".[2]

The importance of this link prompted Lenin to suggest and the RCP(B) Central Committee to approve Dzerzhinsky's appointment to the post of People's Commissar for Transport. Dzerzhinsky held this position for nearly three years, until February 2, 1924. Vladimir Bonch-Bruyevich wrote in his memoirs: "Sometimes better, sometimes worse, in the beginning transport was severely crippled. Extraordinary measures were required to put it into working order. A man was needed who possessed a will of iron, experience in management, prestige among the workers, firmness in implementing measures and decisions, and the ability to combat sabotage and banditry which at that time was common on the railways."

Choosing Dzerzhinsky, Lenin and the Central Committee displayed complete confidence in his abilities, and at the same time vested him with the tremendous responsibility of organising the work of the People's Commissariat for Transport, which at that time was responsible for the normal operation of railways, the merchant navy and river and local transport. In addition to serving as head of this Commissariat, Dzerzhinsky also remained Vecheka Chairman and the People's Commissar for Internal Affairs. He accepted his new responsibilities having neither special knowledge in the field nor sufficient economic management experience. However, transport workers knew that the new Commissar was Lenin's closest associate, a staunch Bolshevik, a man of strong will, who placed the interests of the working class, of an the working people and of socialism above all else.

Dzerzhinsky was knowledgeable about the state of transport affairs: as Vecheka Chairman, he had helped to restore order on the rail- and waterways, and had frequently discussed issues pertaining to the functioning of transport with Lenin. Prior to being transferred to the Commissariat for Transport, Dzerzhinsky had carried out a number of important Central Committee assignments to improve the economy.

The work of rail and water transport and the industry was directly dependent on the availability of fuel. But in early 1921 the Soviet Republic was in the grip of a severe fuel crisis. The country was depending on the Donets Coal Basin to help solve this problem. Dzerzhinsky requested the Party Central Committee to send him to the Donets Basin, and received permission on January 26, 1921. He left for Kharkov, which at that time was the capital of the Ukraine, determined to see for himself what the situation was. Soon afterwards he made another trip to the Ukraine. Then, on February 19, the Council of People's Commissars of the Ukrainian Soviet Socialist Republic decided to set up a business fuel commission which would be headed by Dzerzhinsky.

In seeking to overcome the fuel crisis and economic dislocation, Dzerzhinsky also enlisted the help of local extraordinary commissions.

Back in Moscow, on March 5, he spoke on the fuel situation in the Ukraine at a Labour and Defence Council fuel commission session. The RCP(B) Central Committee Plenary Meeting held on March 7, 1921 decided to send Dzerzhinsky to the Ukraine once again.

On his third trip, Dzerzhinsky concentrated his efforts on introducing order into the work conducted at the Donets Basin and on the railways. The proposals he submitted to the Labour and Defence Council aimed at overcoming the fuel crisis were approved on March 23. Dzerzhinsky had suggested the urgent purchase abroad of equipment and machinery for the Donets Basin, organising regular supplies to that area, and recruiting miners to work there. The Labour and Defence Council approved Dzerzhinsky's candidacy for the post of Chairman of the Provisional Conference for the supervision of the supplies to the Donets Basin.

With time, the situation in the Donets Basin, the country's principal source of coal, began to change for the better. Fuel supplies to industry and transport started to improve. The extraordinary body—the Provisional Conference—was no longer necessary. Dzerzhinsky reported on the completion of its work at the Labour and Defence Council meeting of June 15, 1921.

At Lenin's suggestion, the Tenth RCP(B) Congress instructed the Central Committee to establish a special central commission for the purpose of introducing prompt measures to improve the workers' material conditions. Industrial regions set up their own sub-commissions. On March 20, 1921, the Second Session of the All-Russia Central Executive Committee of the eighth convocation approved the Statute on the Central and Local Commissions for the Improvement of the Working Population's Living Conditions.

The Commission for the Improvement of Workers' Living Conditions in Moscow and Moscow Region headed by Dzerzhinsky was formed on March 17, 1921. Speaking at the Moscow Soviet Executive Committee meeting that day Dzerzhinsky said: "We must acknowledge at present that, when after the expenditure of enormous effort by the working class, all foreign fronts have been eliminated, the most important task, whose solution will decide the further development of socialist construction, is improving workers' living conditions."

The Commission supplied workers with housing mostly by evicting persons who were not engaged in physical labour from the commune-houses (workers hostels). While Dzerzhinsky headed the Commission, 3,673 workers were given accommodations. The Commission was also engaged in providing communal services and medical aid to workers, improving the living conditions of children, organising kindergartens, finding accommodations in health-building and holiday homes for workers, and helping solve other problems of daily life. Its resolutions were obligatory to all bodies.

Dzerzhinsky chaired most of the Commission Presidium's meetings and frequently made speeches and reports. At his suggestion, on April 29, 1921, the Labour and Defence Council decided to inspect all Moscow storehouses, confiscate all unregistered items and distribute them among workers. Dzerzhinsky also suggested supplying the workers' organisations of Moscow and Moscow Region with 500 bicycles.

The Commission introduced reception hours for workers, and dealt with at least 80 applicants a day. Dzerzhinsky himself had reception hours every day.

Weighted down with the responsibilities or both Vecheka and the Commissariat for Transport,

Dzerzhinsky requested the Moscow Soviet Presidium to relieve him of his duties as Chairman of the Commission for the Improvement of Workers' Living Conditions. On May 20, 1921, his request was granted after he had served as Chairman for nearly two months. He had contributed to improving the Moscow workers' living conditions and was well appreciated by them.

The experience that Dzerzhinsky had accumulated as head of the Provisional Conference on the Donets Basin and the Moscow Soviet Commission, as well as his years at Vecheka, proved extremely useful for his work on transport. The Commissariat for Transport was at the time (since July 1921) divided into four

main departments: railway, river, sea and local transport. Each department and section of the Commissariat had a head and a commissar.

At the country's outlying regions, the Siberian, Southern, Turkestan, Caucasian (since May 1921) and, somewhat later Petrograd transport districts were set up to organise the work of transport on their territories. In all, the Commissariat was in charge of 30 railways headed by departments. The entire responsibility for the state of the railway and the movement of the trains was vested in its head and commissar. Sea transport was directed locally by the Baltic, Black Sea, Azov, White Sea and Caspian

departments.

An important document for the nearly two million transport workers was the circular "On the Immediate Tasks of the Republic's Transport and the Fundamental Principles of the People's Commissariat for Transport Further Work" signed on May 27, 1921.

Dzerzhinsky believed that the best way to learn about the transport system and its needs was to visit the localities. His first trip as the Commissar for Transport was to the Ukraine—the Southern Transport District, from May 25 to June 8.

Leaving Moscow on May 25, Dzerzhinsky held a meeting that same day with the administration of the Kiev-Voronezh railway in Kursk. In his speech, he talked about the ways to improve radically the work on the railway and demanded that transport workers be provided with adequate working conditions, citing this as "a matter of greatest importance".

On May 26, Dzerzhinsky arrived in Kharkov. The transport of the Ukraine, which had been liberated from foreign interventionists and the White Guards only a short while before, was in a state of complete dislocation and had to be promptly reconstructed. It was necessary to prepare the railways and waterways, as well as sea transport (above all the ports on the Black Sea and the Sea of Azov) to take out large amounts of food and fuel. The work of the transport system was greatly hindered by numerous robberies and acts of banditry. These issues were the subject for a detailed discussion Dzerzhinsky held with Ukrainian Cheka men in the early hours of May 27.

While in Kharkov, Dzerzhinsky met with the administrative personnel of the Southern Transport District to discuss the work of Ukrainian railways, and outlined the prospects for their development; in

Alexandrovsk (now Zaporozhye), he investigated ways to restore navigation on the Dnieper. Dzerzhinsky expressed his interest in Party and political work among the railway cadres, the activities of trade unions, the provision of food and other supplies, and the organisation of retail trade.

Dzerzhinsky kept a travelogue where he described the work of transport and industry, the political mood of the working people, the training of local personnel, and the campaign against banditry.

On May 30, Dzerzhinsky arrived in Nikolayev. At a conference on the work of the port and of river transport, he made a number of valuable suggestions concerning oil transportation, repair works on the barges, and hiring personnel. The next stop on the itinerary was Kherson, where questions of organising the work of water transport again came under discussion. Dzerzhinsky gave a critical analysis of the state of reconstruction works on the Dnieper, and proposed measures to speed them up.

On June 1, Dzerzhinsky arrived in Odessa, where he inspected the work of the Odessa department of the South-western railways, the department of Black Sea transport, the seaport, and Odessa Cheka. In the course of three days, he held a number of conferences with Cheka personnel, railway workers and seamen. He was mostly concerned with the work of the seaport, which had been destroyed in the war. When retreating in the spring of 1919, the English and French invaders seized 112 merchant vessels and plundered all depots and bases. Four months later, in August 1919, the city was invaded by Denikin's troops, who remained for six months and completed the destruction of the port and the fleet. Out of 62 piers, only 29 could still be used, and in the winter of 1920, when the Red Army entered Odessa, only one ship was in working order, and that a crew boat. Dzerzhinsky helped work out steps to restore the port, organise the repair of vessels, more rapidly put the oil barges in working order, strengthen discipline and secure better supplies for the workers. His fiery speeches before dockers and sailors made a great impression on his audiences, and they put their strength into rebuilding the ports and improving the work of the sea transport.

The last stop on Dzerzhinsky's tour of the Ukraine was Kiev where he arrived on June 6. There he helped the local authorities to restore the operation of the railways and the river fleet. On June 8, he left for Moscow.

Dzerzhinsky's two-week trip to the Ukraine had made an important contribution to the reconstruction of transport in one of the country's largest republics. Yuli Rudy, who at that time was head of the Southern Transport District, later wrote that the Commissar's vivid and emotional speeches and heart-to-heart talks injected the people with fresh energy and vigour, and improved their spirits. Dzerzhinsky personally supervised the placement of Party personnel sent to work on transport.

Back in Moscow, Dzerzhinsky reported on his trip at a meeting of the top personnel of the People's Commissariat for Transport. All members of the Commissariat's Collegium received the minutes of the conferences held during his visit. A synopsis of these minutes included notes on the work accomplished to carry out the proposals that had been made. The materials of Dzerzhinsky trip to the Ukraine were used by the Commissariat's higher-ranking officials to improve the management of transport throughout the country.

Dzerzhinsky's trip was also important for him in that, in the capacity of Commissar for Transport, he got his firsthand experience with railmen, examined the ruined stations and rolling stock, and decided upon measures to improve the situation.

In his work, Dzerzhinsky could always count on help from Lenin, who was personally involved in dealing with many transport problems. A large number of Lenin's speeches, articles and reports reflect his ideas in the field, and outline the main issues of its development. From April 1921 to December 1922 alone, Lenin sent Dzerzhinsky and his deputies and the heads of other transport departments over 50 memos dealing with various transport problems. Dzerzhinsky repeatedly appealed to Lenin when the latter's personal interference as the Chairman of the Council of People's Commissars was required. Telegrams from the provinces reporting on the progress of the work to rebuild the transport system were as a rule addressed to both Lenin and Dzerzhinsky.

Questions concerning the work on transport were regularly discussed at the Council of People's Commissars and the Labour and Defence Council; their conferences were chaired by Lenin and attended by Dzerzhinsky. Between May and December 1921, about thirty resolutions and decrees concerning transport matters were passed and made public by these two bodies. All of them were signed by Lenin.

During a six-month period in 1922, Dzerzhinsky took part in 24 sessions of the Council of People's Commissars and 26 sessions of the Labour and Defence Council where most of the questions considered were about the work of the transport.

In the summer of 1921, the Party Central Committee set up a commission for the improvement of the work of railways. Dzerzhinsky read a report at the Central Committee Organising Bureau's meeting which analysed the overall of transport situation, above all the ideological and political work among transport workers, criticised the work of a number of commissars and their biased attitude towards the trained professionals of the tsarist regime, and exposed the shortcomings in the work of some local Party organisations.

Dzerzhinsky did not try to conceal the fact that the overall condition of transport was grave. A number of his conclusions later entered in the draft resolution of the RCP(B) Central Committee. Among the measures he proposed were reinforcement of the People's Commissariat for Transport and the transport workers trade union with trained personnel, improving Party work, and organising better fuel and material supplies. On August 8, 1921, the RCP(B) CC Plenary Meeting approved Dzerzhinsky's conclusions and proposals with a number of corrections suggested by Lenin.

In the autumn of 1921, transport sub-sections were formed at the Party Central Committee and the local Party committees. Dzerzhinsky's experience and knowledge helped them considerably in their work.

After discussing Dzerzhinsky's report on December 19, the Central Committee Politbureau suggested a number of urgent measures to rebuild the Tashkent Railway, and on December 31, the Central Committee appointed Dzerzhinsky member of the CC Commission for the Supervision of the Transportation of Food and Seeds from Siberia, the Ukraine and Abroad.

In 1921-23, at Dzerzhinsky's suggestion, the Central Committee passed a number of important resolutions concerning the work of transport. Dzerzhinsky worked hard to see that they were implemented. In late 1921, he was instructed by the government and the Collegium of the People's Commissariat for Transport to make a detailed study of the work of the Petrograd port and railway junction, and render assistance in the improvement of the transport workers' political education. The work of the Petrograd port had more than once been under discussion at the Labour and Defence Council and the Commissariat's Collegium.

Dzerzhinsky arrived in Petrograd in the afternoon of December 12, and that evening took part in a conference of representatives of the local transport departments held in the management offices of the Nikolayev Railway. In his speech, he justified the need to form the Petrograd Transport District which was to begin functioning in late January 1922 and to take final shape by the beginning of navigation.

Next day, Dzerzhinsky made a report on the state and objectives of transport at the meeting of the Petrograd Soviet which was also attended by trade union activists, members of management boards of workers' cooperatives, and representatives of Red Army and Naval units.

Dzerzhinsky's appearance provoked a storm of applause. Petrograd workers knew well what an important contribution he had made to the October 1917 armed uprising in Petrograd and the campaign against counter-revolution conducted by the Vecheka. After describing, in general terms, the transport situation, Dzerzhinsky said that the reconstruction of transport would occur through the efforts and will of the workers, who, he hoped, would work in the economy with the same enthusiasm that they had displayed fighting at the Civil War fronts. He spoke about the international significance of Soviet Russia s economic development, stressing that the country's economic advances were compelling the capitalists to enter into a business relationship with the state of workers and peasants. "Not a single economic issue", he stated, "can be settled outside the ... global prospects of the class struggle... We have a great ally—the international proletariat." Dzerzhinsky's report outlined the problems of transport at the stage when the country initiated the New Economic Policy. All of his proposals were included in the resolution adopted by the Petrograd Soviet, which had mapped out steps to be taken towards improving the work of transport.

On December 14, 1921, Dzerzhinsky chaired an interdepartmental conference of top Party personnel working on the railways and on water transport of Petrograd. Reports on the transport situation and plans for its 1922 work schedule were made by Dzerzhinsky and his deputy V. Mezhlauk. Dzerzhinsky's stay in Petrograd boosted the organisational work under way on city transport.

* * *

One of Dzerzhinsky's most important contributions to improving the economy was his trip to Siberia in 1922 at Lenin's request and by decision of the Party Central Committee. The purpose of the trip was to organise the transportation of food and seeds.

By late 1921, the country had scored its first successes in the reconstruction of the economy, but the overall situation was still serious. The economic dislocation, which was still acutely felt in all fields, was further aggravated by a drought that affected a territory with a population of 30 million. Work was quickly begun to eliminate the effects of the drought and aid the starving people.

At that time, Siberia had large stores of food and seeds. The task was to organise their delivery to the famine-struck areas and the industrial regions despite harsh winter condition and the still inefficiently working railways. On December 31, 1921, the CC Politbureau decided to send Dzerzhinsky to Siberia to supervise the introduction of extraordinary assistance measures. Heading a delegation of 40 people Dzerzhinsky left on January 5 and returned on March 8, 1922.

Siberia was only beginning to rebuild its railway lines, bridges, stations and rolling stock which had been severely damaged during the Civil War. One hundred and sixty- seven bridges had been destroyed, and freight traffic on the Siberian Railway was only 10 per cent of pre-war volume.

After Kolchak's troops had been routed, Siberia was still a refuge for about 40,000 White Guard officers and other counter-revolutionary elements, who continued in their attempts to stage revolts, raid railway stations, and conduct subversive activities and sabotage.

The delegation headed by Dzerzhinsky arrived in Omsk, where the managing offices of the Siberian Transport District were located, some members were sent to inspect railway lines. It was important to promptly organise the transportation of foodstuffs to the famine-struck Volga area and the more industrially developed regions. On the first day of his stay in Omsk, January 10, 1922, Dzerzhinsky addressed the workers and office employees of the Siberian railways: "The life of our major industrial enterprises, our big industry which is financed by the state, depends on the timely deliveries of bread and meat that have been stored in Siberia."

Referring to the complexity of the international situation, he stated: "At this perilous time, when Japan in the East is trying to use our weakness and cripple us.... I appeal to all of you, from the rank-and-file worker to the high-ranking official, and urge that at once and by concerted effort, exemplary revolutionary order be established on the Siberian railways, that the assignments and requests of the republic to reconstruct the railways and rolling stock, and to transport foodstuffs be accomplished without fail."

Dzerzhinsky voiced his hope that Party, Komsomol and trade union bodies in the transport system would contribute to the effort, and that Siberian Communists, revolutionary youth and trade union transport workers would meet their commitments.

Dzerzhinsky believed that success hinged on the improvement of Party and political work, and proposed that experienced Party cadres be sent to Siberia. He requested the Central Committee to allow him to stay in Siberia until the personnel he had requested arrived. "I request you not to recall me from Siberia except in the ir.ost extreme necessity," he wrote to the Central Committee, which acceded to his request.

Dzerzhinsky initiated and directly assisted in the publication of the Siberian railwaymen's newspaper

Sibirsky Gudok (Siberian Whistle); his efforts resulted in more efficient work on the part of the transport workers' trade union and educational and cultural centres at railways.

Dzerzhinsky realised that in those difficult winter months of 1922, no work on transport would be successful without the wholehearted cooperation of the rank-and-file personnel—engine-drivers, stokers, switchmen, couplers. He managed to secure better conditions for transport workers and miners: he arranged for railway employees to be served hot meals while on the road; supplied winter clothes for railway workers; introduced order into the payment of wages and salaries; organised a campaign against epidemics, and obtained better housing conditions and leisure facilities for many workers. Needless to say, this promoted the efforts of transport workers, helped raise labour productivity, improved the transport efficiency, and, on the whole, helped meet the plan targets.

Dzerzhinsky and his delegation took care to adequately provide railway transport with fuel, making sure that the coal and firewood were thriftily used and not plundered. The delegation helped to strengthen the ties between the railways and the other branches of Siberian economy. Dzerzhinsky used to say in this connection that "transport is the main nerve of the country's economic life". He sought to provide the necessary conditions for the efficient transportation of food and seeds from Siberia, considering this a task of state importance. "Siberian grain and seeds for the spring planting—this is our salvation," he wrote to his wife.

Dzerzhinsky was always in contact with the RCP(B) Central Committee, the Labour and Defence

Council and the People's Commissariat for Transport. Telegraph offices in Omsk and Novonikolayevsk

193

(now Novosibirsk) frequently transmitted reports, memos and telegrams signed by Dzerzhinsky to Moscow. Day and night, these two Siberian cities and Moscow were in communication about each carload of meat and grain. Despite his illness, Lenin closely followed reports on the deliveries from Siberia. This work had been declared the key sector for all local bodies of Soviet power. Dzerzhinsky often reported on the targets set and measures introduced to speedily deliver foodstuffs at meetings of transport workers and Party personnel. Each railway line and junction sent in regular reports on the progress of the work, the condition of the labour force, and food and fuel reserves. The reports resembled war communiqués. And indeed this was a war, a war for food and for the reconstruction of transport.

Already by late January 1922, food deliveries rose nearly four times as compared to those of December 1921. However, the traffic was hampered by snowdrifts. Dzerzhinsky telegraphed: "The rails are completely snowed over... The local population, army units and workers have been commandeered to clear them up... Everything is being done for the railways to resume their work..." To prevent snowstorms from catching the railway workers unprepared, Dzerzhinsky asked the Petrograd Observatory to telephone in weather forecasts. Production of shields to protect against snow was launched. Communist subbotniks[3] were held to clean the rails from snow.

Thanks to the ceaseless efforts of the commission, Dzerzhinsky personally, the workers and engineering personnel of Siberia, the task set by the Party Central Committee and the Soviet Government was accomplished. As Dzerzhinsky wrote, "Transport met all commitments for deliveries of grain and meat by one hundred per cent and on time." During his stay in Siberia, over 65 million kg of seeds and large quantities of grain, meat and fish were delivered, helping to save hundreds of thousands of people from starvation.

Under Dzerzhinsky's guidance, Siberian transport was much improved and reconstruction proceeded apace.

Dzerzhinsky's work in Siberia increased his already invaluable experience, which made him such a competent head of the Commissariat for Transport.

194

Communist railwaymen and local Party bodies were instrumental in the difficult campaign to reconstruct the country's transport. "Transport will fail without dedicated Communists," wrote Dzerzhinsky in 1922. With his assistance, the Party Central Committee and the local Party bodies managed to reinforce the key sectors of railway transport with reliable and competent personnel. Subbotniks, which Lenin had called a great beginning", were often held and Dzerzhinsky himself took part in them. Guided by Lenin's advice, he did not rely solely on moral incentives but used material ones as well.

Another important factor influencing the work of transport was the press, especially the newspapers of transport workers. Dzerzhinsky initiated a number of such publications, and himself contributed to them, urging the workers to do their best to promptly rebuild Soviet transport. The People's Commissar studied every critical article concerning the work of the People's Commissariat for Transport or its local branches.

Reconstruction work on transport, as in all branches of the economy, met with opposition on the part of various opportunistic groups and advocates of capitalism, which were trying to transfer the control over Soviet transport to foreign capital. Dzerzhinsky said in this connection: "Those gentlemen who are trying to channel our thinking into enlisting foreign capital to transport have at heart not the interests of the country's economic development but political interests, that we are bound to reject."

Dzerzhinsky believed that it was both necessary and possible to promptly reconstruct the transport system, and sharply criticised those who dreamed only about attaining the 1913 standard. Defining the objectives of the reconstruction and further development of transport, Dzerzhinsky wrote: "Our programme must proceed from our poverty, dislocation and will for victory, i.e., producing maximum output with a minimum of means." But he also fought against setting unrealistic goals, and urged "proceeding not from artificially conjured plans but from plans that we are capable of fulfilling."

He believed that Soviet transport should operate as a single whole, resolutely opposed giving priority to local interests, and advocated a sensible fusion of centralism with local initiative.

* * *

Another field to which Dzerzhinsky made an important contribution as People's Commissar for Transport was the reconstruction of the merchant fleet. This matter was the subject of many discussions at the meetings of the Labour and Defence Council which were, as a rule, chaired by Lenin. On May 27, 1921, at Lenin's suggestion, the Labour and Defence Council decided to organise an expedition of the White Sea flotilla from Archangel through the Kara Sea to the mouths of the Ob and Yenisei, two great Siberian rivers, for the purpose of buying and bringing food and other provisions to industrial centres.

On June 15, Dzerzhinsky attended a Labour and Defence Council meeting which debated the plan targets in the field of ship-building for 1921-22. The resolution and decree of the Council of People's Commissars "On the Organisation of the Works to Repair the Ports and to Make Them Usable" were signed by Lenin.

The Collegium meetings of the People's Commissariat for Transport, which Dzerzhinsky chaired and in whose work he took an active part, regularly considered the rebuilding and work of sea transport, including work to repair old and build new ships, provide the merchant fleet with skilled specialists and necessary financial means, decrease personnel and introduce cheaper tariffs, increase freight traffic. It was considered most important to improve administrative structures and consolidate links between the merchant fleet and other branches of the economy. Dzerzhinsky personally supervised the work of many ports and steamship lines. He initiated measures to improve and develop the operations of the Black Sea, Baltic, White Sea and Caspian Sea fleets, and to reconstruct and expand the ports or Odessa, Petrograd, Nikolayev, Novorossiisk, Batumi, Poti and Sukhumi.

Even at that time, in the first years after the revolution, Dzerzhinsky accurately perceived the significance of the merchant fleet for the country. He noted in 1922 that "water transport, particularly the merchant fleet, has become an area with more than a purely Russian significance; it has assumed an international importance".

Dzerzhinsky devoted a great deal of effort to rehabilitating the Petrograd seaport. On June 21, 1922, he reported on its condition at a Labour and Defence Council meeting. It was decided to appoint him the Labour and Defence Council's representative with emergency powers at the Petrograd port, which gave him the authority to control and supervise its operations, take measures to improve work, reduce operational costs, appoint and dismiss personnel. His decisions were to be promptly carried through by all pertinent departments.

On June 25, Dzerzhinsky arrived in Petrograd and the next day convened a conference to discuss the work of the port. It was found that the number of cargoes brought in had fallen and that the port's efficiency was hampered due to the fact that the harbour was frozen over for an average of 139 days a year. The conference decided to extend the period of navigation and to accelerate the mechanisation of loading and unloading.

Back in Moscow, on July 5, Dzerzhinsky spoke at a Labour and Defence Council meeting concerning the measures he had introduced in Petrograd. In the course of the summer and early autumn 1922, the Council regularly discussed the condition of the Petrograd port, and Dzerzhinsky successfully dealt with many of its problems.

Dzerzhinsky made a large contribution to the work to develop the fundamental principles of the Soviet state's sea transport policy. In March 1923, at a meeting of the USSR State Planning Committee's Presidium, he reported on merchant fleet and merchant navigations-substantiating the need for "a comprehensive sea transport policy linked with the country's overall transport policy". The theses of his report were made public. Among the targets defined in Dzerzhinsky's report were improving the work of ports and establishing and developing the country's merchant fleet. He also suggested sensible ways to expand the merchant fleet, specifically by entering into talks for the return of the ships captured by the enemy during the imperialist and civil wars, purchasing vessels abroad, and building new ships at the country's shipyards.

The possession of a merchant fleet was politically significant in that it would ensure the country's independence in foreign trade operations. Transportation of cargoes by Soviet ships was also economically profitable, since it promoted the growth of the country s national income. Dzerzhinsky believed that to successfully pursue a comprehensive sea transport policy, management had to become centralised.

The persistent efforts of the Communist Party, of Lenin, and Dzerzhinsky towards developing the merchant fleet brought appreciable results at the early stage of the New Economic Policy. In 1921 and 1922, the monthly shipment on the Black Sea rose 2.7 and 3-4 times respectively as compared with 1920. In 1922, the Odessa and Archangel ports, which had grown shallow during the war, were already able to receive ocean liners. As Dzerzhinsky stated at the Sixth Ail-Union Congress of the Water Transport Workers' Trade Union in January 1924, the merchant fleet had accomplished its main task—the export of grain—in 1923. The ports' capacity had by that time already reached almost pre-war figures, and the tonnage of state steamship lines had increased. Dzerzhinsky of course had contributed greatly to this success.

* * *

Dzerzhinsky's efforts provided an example of effective transport management which was also meticulous. He closely watched fuel supplies and the campaign to keep railways free of snowdrifts, strengthened discipline, and searched for ways to raise labour productivity. Freight delays were reduced and the rate of turnover accelerated. Dzerzhinsky was kept informed of the condition of rails, security of railway traffic, safety of cargoes, provision of work clothes, payment of wages and availability of schools, clubs, hospitals and spas for railway employees. He made a thorough study of the operation of railways and water transport, often travelled to the provinces to help improve conditions on the spot, and demanded that each high transport official be held fully responsible for his sector.

198

For example, employees of the People's Commissariat for Transport had prepared a report on the condition and work of the Odessa port for the Labour and Defence Council. After he read it, Dzerzhinsky wrote on July 4, 1922: "According to the report, everything is fine and we are operating smoothly; but still there is no overall picture of the port's work. The thing to do is to inspect first, and then prepare a report."

In order to examine and analyse the work of the transport system and sum up and share valuable experience, in February 1923 at Dzerzhinsky's suggestion a Standing Conference for the Supervision and Assessment of the Work of Railway, Water and Local Transport was established under the People's Commissar. It was headed by Dzerzhinsky. Dzerzhinsky's speeches at its sessions reflected his thorough understanding of the transport system. His personal inspections of railways, junctions and stations served to uncover many instances of squandering, waste of capital, labour and time, and were followed by concrete measures to rectify matters.

Dzerzhinsky believed that skilled specialists and managers were important in the reconstruction and smooth operation of transport. He highly valued "people who thought, did their best, and were deeply concerned in the success of their work". He was merciless when it came to deliberate damage and sabotage but did not hesitate to offer work to the skilled professionals of the tsarist regime who had professed loyalty to the Soviet system. Dzerzhinsky also did his best to support the trained personnel from among the working class and peasantry who were dedicated to Party policy. He frequently spoke about the need to train them to operate sophisticated equipment and machinery and fill management jobs.

Dzerzhinsky opposed frequent and senseless shifts of responsible personnel and specialists, writing that this deprived the cadres of confidence in the stability of their position, introduced unnecessary agitation at work, reduced productivity, sometimes hindered a firm and businesslike approach, and prompted halfmeasures and compromise decisions. He believed that criticism and a self-critical attitude were the major conditions for combating shortcomings in the work of the transport system and promoting its progress. In a letter to the representatives of the People's Commissariat for Transport in the transport districts, he remarked: "The sooner and more thoroughly we lay bare all our shortcomings, the most striking facts of mismanagement and absence of a businesslike approach, the sooner we shall be able to eradicate them and achieve positive results in our work."

Dzerzhinsky fought against all manifestations of red tape, procrastination and empty talk. He personally kept a check on the amount of time spent by his Commissariat's top officials in meetings and conferences, carefully prepared each such assembly, drafted the agenda, read almost all the minutes, and checked over the implementation of decisions. In a note to the members of the Commissariat's Collegium, he stated the need to "more economically and efficiently organise the work of the Collegium itself" and recommended that its members write up a short weekly review of their activities and draft a plan for future work.

Dzerzhinsky insisted that the employees' business trips should be more effective. When dealing with practical matters, he enlisted the advice and help of a broad range of specialists and factory and office workers, yet at the same time used the power granted by one-man leadership once a collective decision had been reached. He played an important role in the struggle against bribery and plunder in transport, and involved a large number of employees in this campaign.

Dzerzhinsky was concerned with preventing accidents in transport and ensuring the safety of traffic. "Not a single accident, not a single case of disrepair of rolling stock, not a single crash must remain uninvestigated," he wrote in a decree. "The culprits must be severely punished."

Guided by Lenin's ideas about the need to improve all aspects of work of the state apparatus, Dzerzhinsky launched a reorganisation campaign in transport to cut down and streamline transport management bodies by reducing the number of personnel in the auxiliary services.

In 1922, at Dzerzhinsky's initiative, management boards were set up at rail- and waterways which were responsible for fuel and material supplies to be found locally, the administration of economic and commercial activities, and planned use of transport. This represented the most sensible form of contact between transport and other branches of the economy, and the most efficient way to reconstruct it under the conditions of the New Economic Policy.

Dzerzhinsky thought it important in the development of transport to introduce modern equipment and methods of work. He wrote that "the collective will, thought and creative endeavour of workers themselves ... can grow into a new factor promoting the unprecedented, gigantic growth of industry and transport". He urged management bodies to concentrate on developing the creative potential of the masses, and to provide innovators with material and moral incentives for fruitful work. A champion of technological progress, Dzerzhinsky wrote in 1922: "I keep thinking about the need to have an active body for introducing and finding technical improvements... This is the basis of our development and brighter prospects." A great deal of work in this field was accomplished directly through his efforts.

Dzerzhinsky assessed highly the brakes designed by Florenty Kazantsev, a worker at the Orenburg Depot's main workshop. Requesting the All-Russia Central Executive Committee to decorate Kazantsev with the Order of the Red Banner of Labour, Dzerzhinsky wrote on September 4, 1923: "The brakes invented by Kazantsev are of great practical interest. They are fully capable of replacing Westinghouse's brakes, and even have a number of advantages." On November 19, the All-Russia CEC approved Kazantsev's decoration. Dzerzhinsky also greatly encouraged Alexei Shelest and Yakov Gakkel in their work on the diesel locomotive. The chief targets in this field were defined in the letter "On the

Application of Inventions in Transport and Involvement of Workers in This Activity", which was signed by Dzerzhinsky and the heads of the transport workers' trade unions and sent to the provinces on January 16, 1924.

A great deal of work was accomplished by the commission on exemplary railways (set up under the People's Commissariat for Transport on Dzerzhinsky's recommendation), and by the Ad Hoc Conference for Combating Mismanagement and Unprofitable Operation of Railways of the USSR. Dzerzhinsky himself directed their work.

Dzerzhinsky had always displayed an economical attitude when operating with public funds. He personally analysed the Commissariat's estimates and monthly timetables of the entire transport and individual railways, and verified each item of receipts and expenditures. Wastefulness and deception were severely punished. The campaign against mismanagement and wastefulness brought in tangible results. While in late 1922, 40 per cent of the expenditures on transport were covered through state allocations, in 1923/24, the estimate drawn up by the Commissariat did not mention any such allocations. Transport had become a self- supporting and even profitable branch of the economy.

With Dzerzhinsky serving as the People's Commissar for Transport, the material base (railway lines, rolling stock, installations and buildings) of this section of the economy was restored.

Dzerzhinsky was the first to propose that a railway line be built between Siberia and Turkestan. He personally supervised the construction of the Semirechensk Railway, the first leg of the TurkestanSiberian Railway. In 1924 Dzerzhinsky had occasion to remark: "Do you remember foreign specialists predicting that our railways would be dead in March? Now everyone who comes here cannot stop talking about the way Russian transport has improved. Foreign prophets do not understand what collective will is, what it means to have the will to stand up for one's position."

Yan Rudzutak, who replaced Dzerzhinsky as People's Commissar for Transport, noted: "I think that Comrade Dzerzhinsky has attained this success because he was able, in the course of his three years' work, to concretely apply the methods of our unforgettable teacher, Comrade Lenin, including channelling collective will, collective thought and collective strivings into one focus, one point, one task—the reconstruction of bur transport. This is precisely Comrade Dzerzhinsky's greatest achievement, that he managed to unite all the creative, collective work of transport employees and the transport proletariat in the effort to attain one common goal."

Dzerzhinsky's work as People's Commissar for Transport terminated in early February 1924. It both promoted the reconstruction of Soviet transport and added to the store of Dzerzhinsky's experience in the economic and organisational field. Ahead lay even more strenuous work towards rehabilitating and advancing the country's industry as a whole.

Notes

[1]V. I. Lenin, "Speech Delivered at the All-Russia Congress of Transport Workers, March 27, 1921", Collected Works, Vol. 32, 1977, pp. 283-84.

[2]V. I. Lenin, "Ninth All-Russia Congress of Soviets, December 23- 28, 1921", Collected Works, Vol. 33, 1973, p. 152.

[3]Voluntary unpaid work on weekends or overtime.

Chapter Eleven

AT THE HELM OF SOCIALIST INDUSTRY

By early 1924, Soviet industry had scored its first successes. Its average annual increase in 1921-23 was 41.1 per cent, and Lenin's GOELRO[1] plan was being efficiently implemented. By 1922, the Kashira and Krasny Oktyabr Power Stations were operating.

However, the country's industry still faced grave difficulties. In 1923, its output had reached only 35 per cent of the level in 1913. Factories, blast and open-hearth furnaces stood idle, and labour productivity was still low: at a large number of factories, it was only 30-40 per cent of the 1913 level. The people were still deprived of main basic necessities. The goals were to reconstruct the basic industries, at the same time updating the factories by introducing modern Soviet and foreign technologies, equipment and machinery, enhance the involvement of the working class and all working people, tighten labour discipline, and raise labour productivity. These ambitious plans would require a great deal of effort on the part of the Communist Party and the working class, as well as considerable funds.

It was vitally important to have a man in charge of the reviving public industry who was both a talented and experienced organiser and a dedicated champion of Lenin's plan for building socialism in the USSR.

Industrial development could be capably directed only by a person who supported Lenin's principles of work, was innovative, perceptive, and firm and consistent in pursuing the Party line. The choice of the RCP(B) Central Committee was, appropriately, Dzerzhinsky.

On February 2, 1924, at the suggestion of the Party Central Committee, the first session of the USSR Central Executive Committee approved Dzerzhinsky's nomination for the post of Chairman of the Supreme Economic Council of the USSR. On February 5, he relinquished his duties at the People's Commissariat for Transport, and on February 11 began his new job. Thus he was placed at the helm of the entire socialist industry.

Another stage had begun in the career of this gifted and loyal associate and pupil of Lenin.

"I propose to pursue the same line at the Supreme Economic Council that I followed on transport," wrote Dzerzhinsky about his plans, "a clear state line, common to and obligatory for all economic executives, the unity in this sense, too, of Soviet public industry with the maximum of independence and initiative of the localities and departments and their public, not syndicate-like, amalgamations. It is a huge and difficult task."

Dzerzhinsky gave priority to raising labour productivity. In this he proceeded from Lenin's idea that "in the last analysis, productivity of labour is the most important, the principal thing for the victory of the new social system".[2]

This issue was closely linked with the policy of wages and salaries. It is therefore only natural that in the summer of 1923, when the gap between the prices for industrial and agricultural produce began to widen, the Central Committee considered the question of the factory and office workers' salaries and wages. A commission was set up, with Dzerzhinsky as one of its members. Its conclusions were incorporated in the decisions of the RCP(B) Central Committee Plenary Meeting held on September 25. They stated that the growth of wages could take place only in connection with higher labour productivity.

In February 1924, the CC Politbureau set up a standing CC commission for dealing with this question and Dzerzhinsky was elected a member. He did much to popularise and implement Lenin's ideas on the significance or labour productivity. In a note written on February 5, 1924, he stated that one of the main questions facing Soviet power was learning to balance wage increases against the growth of labour productivity and producing cheaper goods. A document drafted by Dzerzhinsky in March 1924 stated that the growth of real wages was possible only through increasing the output per worker, while production quotas had, in general, to be raised and calculated on the basis of a full eight-hour workday. A special body was set up at the USSR Supreme Economic Council Presidium, a Standing Conference on Labour Productivity. It was headed by Dzerzhinsky and functioned up to July 1925.

During this period, Soviet industry had no precise, scientifically substantiated criteria for establishing labour productivity. Various methods were employed, which not infrequently catered to narrow local interests. Statistical bodies were not very efficient either. The press carried contradictory information as to the labour productivity that had been attained. This hampered the search for ways to solve the problem.

The Communist Party naturally considered it a matter of top priority to introduce order into the calculation of manpower expenditure and to expose the anti-scientific basis of opposing forces' concept of a correlation between labour productivity and the size of wages and salaries. Dzerzhinsky greatly helped to solve these problems. He arranged for statistical studies to be initiated at the Supreme Economic Council (SEC), examined the wage and salary situation and the state of labour productivity at various enterprises, and consistently emphasised the significance of Lenin's idea of the role of labour productivity in the building of a socialist society. On June 4, 1924, speaking at a SEC session, Dzerzhinsky again stressed the need to raise labour productivity and increase wages and salaries by improving organisation of production and workers' control over this matter.

On June 12, 1924, the Central Committee Plenary Meeting formed a commission on wages and salaries, and approved its composition proposed by Dzerzhinsky, who was himself a commission member. Already at its first meeting on June 14, the commission instructed Dzerzhinsky to draft measures towards raising labour productivity. To focus public attention on this problem, Dzerzhinsky proposed to involve the press in the campaign. He believed it important for the press to report on steps taken which had secured an increase in labour productivity. He wrote a series of articles published by the central newspapers. On November 25, 1924, at a meeting chaired by Dzerzhinsky, the Standing Conference on Labour Productivity at the USSR Supreme Economic Council decided to establish a fund for the publication of literature concerning labour productivity. At Dzerzhinsky's initiative and under his general guidance, a collection entitled "On the Problem of Labour Productivity" was launched with the aim of analysing and summing up the experience accumulated in tackling the problem and promoting the results throughout the country.

An important part of the overall effort was to raise the efficiency of the work day. Dzerzhinsky believed that Supreme Economic Council employees should set the example here. With this end in view, he proposed conducting a survey of the structure and distribution of their working hours, and asked for suggestions and conclusions. "It is necessary," he wrote, "to take into account all general and individual breaks and idle moments. Going to breakfast, lunch, etc., should also be included."

On July 1, 1924, Dzerzhinsky chaired a conference on labour productivity. He requested each participant to make a profound and thorough analysis of the cause of low labour productivity, and to suggest ways of raising it by taking into account the specific conditions prevailing at each particular organisation or factory. It was decided to appoint commissions to study the actual state of labour productivity and wage and salary situation at factories.

On July 18, Dzerzhinsky held another conference on labour productivity, which was attended by representatives of economic management bodies and trade unions. On August 24, the thesis 'On Labour Productivity and the Steps to Increase It", which was approved by the USSR Supreme Economic Council Chairman, was published. It outlined ways and methods to raise labour productivity, measures to update factory equipment, mechanise production, introduce specialisation and standardisation, and bring the work of the factories up to full capacity. Of principal concern were, among other things, she scientific setting of output rates, intensification of labour, raising the efficiency of the work day, wider application of remuneration by output, and training of more skilled workers. The

Commission on Wages and Salaries stepped up its activities. After making a detailed study of the statistics and results of inspections in the major industries, it submitted proposals to the Central Committee Politbureau.

On behalf of the USSR Supreme Economic Council, Dzerzhinsky spoke "On the Policy of Wages and Salaries" at a Central Committee plenary meeting held on August 16-20, 1924. Drawing on Lenin's ideas on labour productivity, he convincingly explained why productivity must grow at a faster rate than wages and salaries under the socialist system, and that labour remuneration should be increased on this basis.

Dzerzhinsky's stand was shared by the overwhelming majority of the plenary meeting's participants, who approved his proposed resolution that "the growth of labour productivity must exceed wage growth".

Dzerzhinsky also discussed this question at a January 1925 plenary meeting. He stated that, having assumed power, the working class of the USSR thus shouldered responsibility for everything that was taking place in the country, especially for the condition of industrial production, and criticised the notion that the rates of production had reached their maximum. "If we fail to raise labour productivity," he said, "we shall be unable to exist as a Soviet workers' state." Dzerzhinsky was convinced that this task "calls for the indispensable support of the broad masses and full utilisation of their collective creative endeavour and initiative".

Speaking at an extended conference of the Supreme Economic Council Presidium and representatives of local economic councils held on December 2, 1924, Dzerzhinsky discussed the great international significance of the campaign for higher labour productivity. Higher figures have to be attained, he said, in order "to compete through our indices and labour organisation in a workers ' state under a workers ' dictatorship against the results of labour organisation under the capitalist system".

Dzerzhinsky spoke about the role of standardisation of industrial output as a major reserve for raising the efficiency of public production, and urged the participants in the conference to broadly introduce it "in order to rebuild our industry and the entire national economy". He considered it very important to introduce rational methods of production. "At present," he wrote, "the central and principal question of our industry is the question of rationalisation of our technology and organisation of production. The task must become a categorical imperative for the 'morals' and 'will' of all our economic management personnel, no matter which field they are engaged in." Dzerzhinsky believed in the need to study rationalisation set by industrially developed capitalist countries, and mapped out concrete steps to this end.

The Party Central Committee appreciated Dzerzhinsky's efforts and the work done by the Supreme Economic Council he headed to increase labour productivity. Dzerzhinsky spoke on the subject again at the October (1925) Plenary Meeting of the Central Committee. He also gave an account of the talk that a German workers' delegation had with Soviet workers at one of the factories. The latter were asked a number of questions but the one asked first was: "How do you work?", which was followed by: "What are you paid for your work, and how do you live?" Dzerzhinsky noted in tins connection: "A sound approach."

The Chairman of the Supreme Economic Council was concerned with fostering among the workers a conscientious attitude to their duties. Above all, this pertained to the younger generation of workers. In his opinion, many young workers still did not really understand that "the factory is in the hands of the state of workers and peasants, where the happiness of the working class is collectively shaped".

To raise labour productivity and improve the overall development of the economy it was becoming increasingly important to engage in sensible and efficient planning, which would take into account both the society's needs and its material potential. Dzerzhinsky was fully aware of this, and opposed both the planning dissociated from actually existing opportunities and the efforts to set the lowest possible targets in the economic growth and, specifically, labour productivity increase: "In the long run," he stated, "the basis of socialist economy is to draw up a sound plan." p Dzerzhinsky was convinced that a scientifically based and verified state plan should become law for each factory and each economic manager. His work was worthy of emulation in this respect. At one of the CC plenary meetings he remarked: "My entire work is geared towards implementing the plan." But he also believed that the state plan must not artificially restrict the work of a factory or economic amalgamation.

Dzerzhinsky repeatedly stressed Lenin's idea that improvement of the working people's material wellbeing and the growth of wages and salaries were attainable only through continuous technological progress, with due account for the state's financial potential. In February 1926, with a view to further raising the wages and salaries, the Party Central Committee formed another commission, of which Dzerzhinsky was a member. This commission provided information used in working out the resolution passed by the Council of Labour and Defence on May 18, 1926 , "On Raising Labour Productivity in Industry and Transport". The document emphasised the need to eliminate hold-ups and delays, to secure the timely supply of raw materials and fuel to factories, remove organisational inefficiency, improve the use of equipment, more carefully select top management personnel, and enhance the prestige and expand the rights of medium and lower-level operating personnel. Measures were mapped out towards consolidating labour discipline, making more sensible use of work time and manpower, and raising the skills of workers.

As a result of the joint efforts of the Party, the working class and the Supreme Economic Council apparatus headed by Dzerzhinsky, labour productivity in industry and wages almost approached the prewar figures. Higher labour productivity made it possible to improve the working people's material welfare, strengthen the alliance of the working class and peasantry, and form a major source of means for the country's socialist industrialisation.

* * *

Dzerzhinsky made an invaluable contribution to the implementation of Lenin's plan of building socialism in the USSR,

210

especially to the creation of heavy industry. Lenin observed that "the only possible economic foundation of socialism is large-scale machine industry.[3]

The principal branches of heavy industry, i.e., metallurgy and engineering, were both considered parts of the metal industry at that time. The Central Committee and the Soviet Government were doing their utmost to reconstruct it. In November 1923, Dzerzhinsky said: "We must become a metal Russia. Metallurgy is our whole future."

In March 1924, the CC Politbureau formed a commission on the metal industry headed by Dzerzhinsky. During its more than six months of work, the commission made a detailed study of the state of metallurgy and engineering, submitted a number of valuable proposals to the Central Committee and the government, and helped outline the basic trends in the further development of these major industries.

In his numerous speeches and memos to the Central Committee, the Council of People's Commissars, and the Council of Labour and Defence, Dzerzhinsky showed himself to be a staunch champion of Lenin's ideas on the role of heavy industry in the development of the socialist economy. He underscored the significance of metallurgy and engineering in enhancing the country's economic and defence potential, raising the standard of living, making cultural advances, and strengthening the alliance of workers and peasants. A great deal was being done to develop the larger heavy industry enterprises and the principal industrial centres.

The major topic discussed at the Supreme Economic Council conference held in May 1924 and chaired by Dzerzhinsky was the advancement of heavy industry in Leningrad. The conference also passed a resolution "On Tractor-building". The Central Committee formed a commission accountable to the Politbureau which was to deal with the industrial development of Leningrad. Dzerzhinsky was appointed its chairman. Leningrad's industrial development was closely linked with the economic renewal of the entire country and had considerable significance for consolidating the USSR's defence capability and enhancing the prestige of the world's first socialist state.

Fully aware of the importance of Leningrad's defence industry, the commission nevertheless pointed out that city factories must turn out an adequate amount of consumer goods. In this connection, it focused on the development of metal processing, electric machine engineering, aircraft and ship-building.

In July 1924, the Politbureau heard the commission's report on Leningrad industry and, drawing on its conclusions, made a statement on the significance of the city's industry in general, and defence industry in particular.

On September 12, 1924, the Politbureau considered Dzerzhinsky's report which contained a review of the metal industry. "If it is a must—and this is unquestionable—to advance the metal industry and place it on a sound foundation," the report read, "it is necessary to seriously warn each department that it is fully and unconditionally responsible for meeting its commitments which were either assumed by the department itself or were set by the Party and the government, with respect to the metal industry first and foremost." The Politbureau referred to this report when drafting measures towards developing this branch of the economy.

Dzerzhinsky stressed the importance of having a good idea of what was going on at each major enterprise. "The country and the Party," he wrote, "must know how each individual major factory is working. Each factory must have its own distinctive aspect."

On October 23, 1924, before the Congress of Transport and Industrial Workers was held, Dzerzhinsky wrote a letter to Abram Ginsburg, Deputy Chairman of the Chief Economic Department Collegium of the Supreme Economic Council. He spoke of the need to "analyse the opportunities for finding ... resources within our economy, the process of our organisation of production, labour and distribution". He maintained that the industry could make a big step forward if mismanagement in the production sphere was overcome, the raw materials and fuel were used more thriftily and their quality was raised, the work day was more efficient, and the number of employees correlated with the volume of production. He also believed it extremely important to stop mismanagement and overspending in distribution, and especially in retail and wholesale trade.

It was thought that the production of cheaper goods would help raise funds. Dzerzhinsky believed that cutting prices would lead to the accumulation of money in the country and provide an impetus for improving the organisation and technology of production. The lowering of prices for industrial goods and manufacture of more and lower-price means of production for agriculture would lead to the lowering of prices for agricultural commodities. "These means (tractors, fertilizers, etc.)," wrote Dzerzhinsky, "should in a few years give such a boost to agriculture that we will have enormous reserves for both exports and luxury domestic consumption." He recommended to draft a long-term plan for the development of production of the means of production for agriculture.

Dzerzhinsky also named such important sources of the accumulation of funds as utilisation of unused current capital, stepping up its turnover, granting lower-interest credit, accounting for and purposeful use of depreciation funds, an accurate estimate of fixed assets, and attracting personal savings to industry through state loans.

To more efficiently use financial and material means, Dzerzhinsky recommended more stress on planning and providing more favourable opportunities for developing the working people's initiative when searching and using domestic reserves.

Concentrating primarily on the sources of accumulation inherent in the socialist system, Dzerzhinsky did not reject the idea of foreign loans. He only opposed becoming dependent on them.

Dealing with this issue once again in his report at the Fifth, All-Union Conference of the Metalworkers' Trade Union (November 1924), Dzerzhinsky stated that the more stable the country's economic and political position, the sooner capitalists would be ready to render it assistance. "We shall obtain this loan only when we start to pursue a policy of independent development, make independent efforts, and only given such a policy will a foreign loan not ensnare us." Dzerzhinsky correlated the chances for getting foreign loans with the development of socialist economy, and the consolidation of its independence from foreign capital.

Heavy industry was beginning to grow at faster rates. A number of Leningrad factories which worked for the war switched over to the production of other goods.

When the Higher Government Commission on the Metal Industry finished its work, Dzerzhinsky requested the Politbureau to appoint him Chairman of the management board of the Chief Metal Industry Administration. This was done on November 13, 1924. He was in charge of 52 economic amalgamations and individual enterprises, as well as three syndicates responsible for the sales of the metal industry output. Dzerzhinsky held this post to the end of his life, remaining at the same time head of the USSR Supreme Economic Council and the OGPU (Unified State Political Department). Moreover, between November 23, 1925 and February 5, 1926, he was also Chairman of the RSFSR Supreme Economic Council.

The Central Committee decided to discuss at its January 1925 Plenary Meeting the state and prospects of the metal industry. Dzerzhinsky prepared a detailed report which outlined the prospects for the development of metallurgy and all branches of engineering, and contained clear ideas on the role and significance of heavy industry and the laying of socialism's material and technical foundation. This document was forwarded to all participants in the Plenary Meeting. In a speech delivered at the meeting in the evening of January 19, Dzerzhinsky discussed the need to speed up the development of the metal industry. "The problem of the restoration, updating and reconstruction of fixed capital, the means of production, is facing us in a large number of industries. If we ignore it now ... in the near future our position will be desperate—we shall have no technical foundation for further development. And this means that the growth of the metal industry, which is the technical foundation of the entire industry, transport, and agriculture, cannot be artificially obstructed."

The growth rates in heavy industry, as elsewhere, were closely associated with reducing the cost of industrial goods, which directly affected the outcome of the economic competition between the USSR and the capitalist countries on the world market. "If we do not secure prompt and adequate development of our own production," Dzerzhinsky's report stated, "we shall be doomed to being beaten by the lowerprice foreign goods."

Dzerzhinsky showed that it was possible and necessary to develop heavy industry at faster rates, but nevertheless warned against groundless hare-brained schemes, and considered it necessary to approach the issue with due account for the country's actual potential. His report contained suggestions for speeding up the development of non- ferrous metallurgy, engine-building, ship-building and agricultural engineering, and, above all, the tractor industry. Dzerzhinsky recommended trying to persuade noted specialists, including foreign experts, to lend assistance in developing the tractor industry. In a report to the January (1925) Plenary Meeting, Dzerzhinsky wrote: "This entirely new venture has, from the point of view of the country's needs, quite unlimited prospects." He pointed out that a new, completely modern tractor factory was badly needed. The meeting also discussed the question of diesel- locomotive building. The first effort in this field was a Gakkel diesel locomotive built at the Krasny Putilovets factory in Leningrad.

Dzerzhinsky's main proposals were supported by the participants in the meeting, who also approved his report, recognised the need to secure the further development of the metal industry, and instructed the CC Politbureau to secure increased budget allocations and credit to the industry. A plan was to be drafted for the reconstruction of the fixed assets and re-equipment of old and construction of new factories with due consideration for the needs of the entire economy. The Politbureau was instructed to discuss what could be done to improve metal supplies in the countryside. The General Committee Plenary Meeting unconditionally supported the proposal on the development of non-ferrous metallurgy using the country's own effort and resources. The Council of Labour and Defence was to examine urgently the question of building caterpillar tractors, automobiles and ships.

The decisions of the Plenary Meeting on accelerated development of metallurgy and engineering, the core of socialist heavy industry, were unanimously approved by the Party and workers.

In view of the growing importance of metal industry for the development of the national economy, the

Party Central Committee decided to discuss the prospects for its advancement at the 14th Ail-Union Party Conference. Dzerzhinsky was chosen as the speaker on the subject, and the newspapers published the major points of his report.

The delegates enthusiastically supported Dzerzhinsky's proposals on the accelerated development of metallurgy and engineering, the mechanisation of production and updating of factory equipment. Dzerzhinsky's concluding remarks met with a particularly warm response: "The Russia of workers and peasants—it can be none other than a metal Russia, precisely the base that can ensure the protection of our state and keep a firm hold on the achievements of the October Revolution. Only with metal, as with its own base, can it accomplish this, and raise the productive forces that are concealed in the depth of our land."

The conference unanimously approved Dzerzhinsky's suggestions and adopted them without alteration as a resolution, thus demonstrating its complete confidence in the Central Committee approach to heavy industry.

It was deemed necessary to increase the plans for metal industry for 1924/25 by 26 per cent as compared with the original programme, and to draft a plan for the building of new factories. The conference decisions laid the foundation for the practical efforts of the Party and the Soviet people directed towards promoting big industry.

Issues of industrial development were dealt with in detail at the Third Ail-Union Congress of Soviets held in May 1925, both in Dzerzhinsky's report and the delegates' speeches. "The question of the renewal of fixed capital," Dzerzhinsky said, "is already being replaced and supplemented by another issue, the question of expanding fixed capital. It is necessary to find the means to build new machine tools, new machinery, new equipment, new factories."

The delegates concentrated also on aircraft building. Even before the congress, Dzerzhinsky wrote: "Aircraft building must be put on a firm foundation." The country was beginning to shake off its dependence on foreign partners in this field; in 1925, all the planes required by the Red Army were built at Soviet factories.

Some of the results of the work in the metal industry were summed up at the Seventh All-Union Congress of the Metalworkers' Trade Union, which was held in November 1924. In 1924/25, the output of the metal industry more than doubled, while the growth of industry at large was 62 per cent. Dzerzhinsky's report and the speeches made by other Union members outlined measures to be introduced to further increase the growth rate of metallurgy and engineering.

Dzerzhinsky was a vigorous champion of Lenin's GOELRO plan, believing that the electrification of the country would pave the way for the technical re-equipment of the entire national economy. He urged "speeding up electrification" in order to deal with the principal problem—reducing the cost of industrial commodities.

In a report to the Third All-Union Congress of Soviets, Dzerzhinsky described the first successes in the work to implement the GOELRO plan and remarked, "Now, when the economy of our Union is firmly standing on its feet, the electrification of the country ... must become a top priority."

Dzerzhinsky's important memo of March 9, 1926, addressed to the Council of Labour and Defence, read, in part: "Energy will determine the success in solving the problem of industrialisation of the economy of the USSR and the further economic development of the Union." Dzerzhinsky pointed out the urgent necessity of state regulation of energy supplies and balanced planning of industry and transport with due consideration for the country's actual energy potential. Dzerzhinsky also stressed the importance of closely correlating the development of the fuel industry and electrification. He considered: the latter "a powerful means of distributing energy and making rational use of fuel". Dzerzhinsky worked towards organising electric power transmissions over long distances, and proposed the establishment of a Chief Energy Administration under the USSR Supreme Economic Council.

Dzerzhinsky took steps to improve the operation of Glavelektro, a special department, and Elektrostroi, an important sector of the department which was in charge of electric power station construction. He personally followed the progress of this work. Dzerzhinsky was particularly interested in the Volkhov Hydroelectric Power Station, which he visited on June 15, 1925, to inspect the progress of its construction. He conducted long talks with the project's chief engineer and other top personnel and workers.

Dzerzhinsky also supervised preparations for the building of the Dnieper Hydroelectric Power Station. In July 1925, he issued a decree concerning the station's project evolution procedures and correlating the building of the station with the national economy reconstruction plan. Dzerzhinsky instructed his subordinates to collect all materials pertaining to the project.

Late in 1925, the country marked GOELRO's fifth anniversary. By that time, the Shatura Power Station

(whose construction was initiated by Lenin) was completed. On December 3, Dzerzhinsky attended a Politbureau meeting when it was decided to name the station after Lenin. Four other stations were commissioned, and in 1926, two more. Lenin's plan for the electrification of Russia was leading to tangible results.

Dzerzhinsky was responsible for many of the successes in the reconstruction and development of the country's fuel industry, especially, the Donets Coal Basin. In the spring of 1923, the Basin was facing grave difficulties. On May 7, the Party CC Politbureau formed a commission to investigate ways to improve the Donets Basin's financial position and define a fuel policy. Dzerzhinsky was one of the commission's members. The situation was all the more serious since in 1923/24 this region was providing three quarters of the country's coal.

218

Dzerzhinsky's notes compiled during his work on the Politbureau commission contained suggestions concerning Party and political and cultural work. Dzerzhinsky proposed sending a group of experienced propaganda workers to the Donets Basin, expressed his attitude towards skilled specialists, mechanisation and electrification, raising the miners' labour productivity and wages, the activities of cooperative bodies, and the building of housing and public baths. Dzerzhinsky criticised a number of executives in the fuel industry. Unlike some top-ranking officials in the coal industry who pessimistically viewed prospects for development, Dzerzhinsky showed that it was possible to raise the production of coal.

Dzerzhinsky carefully thought out each of his suggestions and recommendations. He made notes on newspaper articles and books dealing with the fuel problem, and drew charts illustrating monthly coal production in the Donets Basin from 1920 to 1923. According to his calculations, it would be more economically expedient to use coal instead of firewood. Judging by his notes, Dzerzhinsky was interested in how fuel supplies were organised abroad, the links between the fuel industry and metallurgy, and their relation with railway transport;

Stored in the Central Party Archives are Dzerzhinsky's note pads devoted to "Fuel" which date back to his work on the commission. One important entry reflects the nature of the fuel problem and the ways of dealing with it: " Making fuel cheaper for the consumers and increasing its production must be an independent goal, unrelated to the other task, reconstruction of large coal mines, which will take years to accomplish and will require heavy state expenditure."

Dzerzhinsky subjected the materials received by the commission to a thorough analysis and gave a critical assessment of some of them. His participation in the commission's work was active indeed. He submitted a number of proposals, many of which were later accepted by the Politbureau. He recommended to put an end to the isolation of the fuel industry from the rest of the national economy.

On June 30, 1923, he submitted to the Central Committee a report which referred to a drop in the production of coal and the increase in its prime costs. Among the measures he proposed to increase the production of coal were: encouraging the development of small- and medium-scale coal .production (which before the war accounted for 43 per cent of the total coal output in the Donets Basin); reducing prices for coal to increase sales; granting more economic freedom to managing bodies; setting the issue of the miners' wages and taking steps to raise labour productivity.

On July 4, 1923, the Central Committee Plenary Meeting discussed the commission's report and approved the majority of its proposals.

Despite the measures undertaken to improve the work of the Donets Basin and to organise the sales of its coal, prices remained high. In a memo to the Politbureau of September 28, 1923, Dzerzhinsky outlined a concrete plan of action to reduce the prime costs of Donets Basin coal, and to improve the management of the fuel industry at large. His proposals were also discussed in the article "The Immediate Tasks of the Party in the Donets Basin" published in Pravda on January 22, 1924.

After being appointed Chairman of the Supreme Economic Council, Dzerzhinsky began to pay even more attention to the Donets Basin, the work of which was on the agenda of the Party Central Committee Politbureau meeting on February 9, 1924. The meeting recognised it as imperative to substitute mineral fuel for firewood. On March 2, Pravda carried the Address of the Central Committee, which stated that the great importance of the Donets Basin had prompted the Party to form a Central Donets Basin Assistance Committee. By decision of the Central Executive Committee and the Council of People's Commissars, the committee was to be headed by Dzerzhinsky, who wrote: "The Committee has set immensely important tasks. We must get things moving and greatly extend their scope." On March 28, the Central Donets Basin Assistance Committee considered the entire set of proposals pertaining to overcoming the crisis that was disrupting the sale of Donets Basin coal. The resolutions on its increased use were passed by the USSR Supreme Economic Council's Presidium at the meetings on March 22 and April 2, 1924, which were chaired by Dzerzhinsky.

The work under way in the field soon began to yield results. Already in August 1924, the USSR Supreme Economic Council Presidium noted that a great deal had been done to increase coal production, to mine higher-grade coal, raise labour productivity and improve the technical equipment of mines. When the targets set before the Central and local Donets Basin assistance committees had been reached, these bodies were abolished. However, Dzerzhinsky continued to keep an eye on that region.

Another solution to the fuel problem was the development of new coal-producing regions. On March 26,

1925, the Party Central Committee Politbureau granted the request of the USSR Supreme Economic Council to send a geological research party to examine coal and oil fields in the northern region of Sakhalin island.

On January 4, 1926, Dzerzhinsky chaired a meeting of the RSFSR Supreme Economic Council Presidium which discussed the industrial development of the Far East, and decided to launch large-scale preparations for coal mining there.

Another priority at the time was the reconstruction and development of oil production. In one of his notes Dzerzhinsky stressed that measures should be outlined to save fuel, introduce lower-grade types and evolve more rational methods of its production and burning. Thus, he advocated a more sensible use of oil as fuel and voiced doubts as to the expediency of its use on locomotives. "Oil is hard currency for us," he remarked.

The rapid advance of the national economy made it urgent to explore and develop new oil deposits. On February 24, 1926, the USSR Supreme Economic Council Presidium passed a resolution on the organisation of oil prospecting, calling it a matter of top priority.

The chemical industry was gaining increasing importance among the branches of heavy industry. Here, the principal goal was to increase production of mineral fertilizers. In a report to the Third All-Union Congress of Soviets held on May 15, 1925, Dzerzhinsky pointed to the high prime cost of such fertilizers as the principal obstacle for their production. The main difficulty was the expense of phosphoric acid which was used for the production of fertilizers. Dzerzhinsky reported that the Mineral Fertilizers' Institute had developed a cheaper technology for the production of phosphoric acid and that it was being introduced into industry. But it was soon apparent that this was an extremely slow process, and Dzerzhinsky requested that the reasons for the delay be investigated and reported to him.

Dzerzhinsky investigated many of the details of the functioning of the chemical industry. Learning that the prime costs and the retail and wholesale prices of chemical antiseptics were rather high, he immediately instructed the appropriate department to work out measures to reduce them.

Dzerzhinsky believed that the problems of the chemical industry should be made known to the public. "Only in this way," he wrote on October 30, 1925, "shall we be able to shake off our backwardness in the highly important field of the chemical industry... Our plans require the greatest concerted effort and common thought."

For the purpose of improving management in the chemical industry, on August 4, 1925, Dzerzhinsky signed a decree establishing a Chemical Committee affiliated with the USSR Supreme Economic Council Chief Economic Department. The steps introduced in this field promoted the development of the chemical industry.

Not long before the 14th Party Congress, in a report to the 14th Moscow Conference of the RCP(B) delivered on December 11, 1925, Dzerzhinsky spoke positively about the need to reconstruct Soviet industry on the basis of new technology: "We must at all costs find means allowing us to accelerate production and expand it."

The Soviet people were developing the country's large-scale industry despite great difficulties: Lenin was no longer alive to give guidance, petty-bourgeois elements were burgeoning, and opportunists inside the Party stepped up their activities. Moreover, money and materials were scarce, there was not nearly enough skilled workers and specialists, and the experience required to develop industry along socialist lines was still very meagre.

222

The need to launch socialist industrialisation was the principal idea of the overall work of the 14th Party Congress held in December 1925, which became known in the history of the Soviet Union as the industrialisation congress. It summed up the results of economic development and the experience of the work of Party bodies, and formulated the chief goal in the resolution "On the Report of the Central Committee"—"to secure the economic independence of the USSR that would prevent the USSR from becoming an appendage of world capitalist economy, for which purpose to pursue the line towards the country's industrialisation, the development of production of the means of production, and forming reserves for economic manoeuvring". These decisions were significant in principle. They raised the socialist industrialisation line to the status of Party policy.

Dzerzhinsky did not speak at the congress, but his previous work made a significant contribution to substantiating this policy, and later to its realisation. He was sometimes referred to as "the knight of industrialisation".

Dzerzhinsky demanded unswerving adherence to the decisions of the 14th Congress when drafting the plans for industrial development, above all, for heavy industry. He suggested that the Chief Department on Metal Industry at the USSR Supreme Economic Council redraft the plan for the development of metallurgy and metal-working industry, on the basis of the Party instruction "to turn the USSR into a country producing machinery and equipment".

On February 11, 1926, speaking in Leningrad, Dzerzhinsky said: 'We must find the resources and means inside the country to conduct socialist accumulation, the reconstruction and re-equipment of old and construction of new factories." In his speech delivered at the meeting of the USSR Supreme Economic Council Presidium on March 19, he noted: "We have arrived at a one-hundred-per cent use of our fixed capital, and we really must map out the complete reconstruction of our national economy."

Dzerzhinsky frequently spoke about the importance of finding practical application for science and technology in the course of socialist industrialisation. He wrote: "The country's industrialisation, which is becoming the foundation of our efforts to build socialism, can be accomplished only if we both make use of all scientific and technological advances, on the one hand, and develop scientific research, on the other."

The April (1926) Central Committee Plenary Meeting considered the issue "On the Economic Situation and the Economic Policy". It worked out measures to be introduced to promote the country's industrialisation in accordance with the situation and the decisions of the 14th Congress. Its resolutions stated that "the advance of the industries and industrialisation of the country in general are that vital target whose attainment will determine the further growth of the entire economy in the direction of the victory of socialism."

On May 8, 1926, while on a visit to Kharkov, Dzerzhinsky spoke at the Ukrainian Miners' Congress. A summary of his speech appeared in the papers under the heading "We Shall Accomplish Industrialisation Relying on Our Own Resources". That was the main idea of Dzerzhinsky's speech. "We can and must find means inside the country," he stated, and then proceeded to analyse the sources that could yield the means required for the industrialisation. One of the purposes of his trip to the Ukraine was "to form an idea or the progress of production processes in heavy industry". He then returned to Moscow for a short while, and on May 19 went back to the Ukraine. This time, he concentrated on the work of the Kerch Metal Works and tractor production at the Kharkov Engine- Building Factory, which he visited on May 28. That same day he left for Moscow. His last visit to the Ukraine gave a boost to the production in metallurgy and engineering.

In the course of his visit, Dzerzhinsky had a chance to form a more complete picture of the metal industry in the country's South. Its development was discussed on June 11, 1926, at a Labour and Defence

Council meeting, which Dzerzhinsky attended, and on June 14 at the meeting of the Central Committee Politbureau. These two bodies defined the measures towards further advancing metallurgy and engineering. Dzerzhinsky initiated many of them himself.

Dzerzhinsky's last speech at the July (1926) Central Committee Plenary Meeting, made three hours before his sudden death, also dealt with the future of socialist industrialisation and the search for the most efficient ways of accomplishing it.

The development of heavy industry opened up fresh opportunities for advancing light, especially textile industries. Dzerzhinsky stressed the need to boost the production of cotton and gain independence from exports in this field.

Dzerzhinsky outlined the principal targets before the textile industry at the Sixth Ail- Union Congress of the Textile Workers' Trade Union held in November 1924. He considered this industry an important field where the alliance of the working class and the peasantry could be consolidated: "Textile is one of the key sectors serving to strengthen the link between town and country." Dzerzhinsky stressed the need to reduce the prices of textile goods and to considerably expand production. In the course of his work, he made a thorough study of the operation of textile factories. With Dzerzhinsky as its head, the USSR Supreme Economic Council managed to significantly develop the textile industry, including textile engineering. Specifically, it was planned to build a large cotton mill in Leningrad.

The Party and the Government gave science an important role to play in the economy, and sought to provide adequate opportunities for scientific research. Dzerzhinsky was a vigorous supporter of this line, as is revealed in his letter of January 22, 1925 to the USSR Supreme Economic Council Scientific and Technological Department. Having earlier that day visited a department-sponsored exhibition, Dzerzhinsky wrote about the great achievements of Soviet scientists. At the same time, he noted that research institutes should and could do more to help rebuild industry and agriculture and consolidate the country's defences. He also said that they needed support from the Supreme Economic Council and other bodies. He suggested that the department prepare a report on the work of scientific research establishments to be discussed at the USSR Supreme Economic Council Presidium and address local economic bodies on behalf of the council concerning the activities of research establishments and the need to establish direct links with the former to ensure the more efficient introduction of scientific discoveries and achievements.

On February 4, 1925, the Supreme Economic Council Presidium discussed the work of its Scientific and Technological Department. Dzerzhinsky once more emphasised the importance of practical application of the results of scientific research in production. Stressing the significance of science in the country's economic development and technological progress, he stated at the Third All-Union Congress of Soviets: "When we, who are strong thanks to the alliance of the workers and the peasants and of the nations inhabiting our Union, will look for support to science, then and only then shall we be able to easily attain the goals which we have set ourselves."

This did not mean, however, that science automatically received the impetus it needed for development.

Dzerzhinsky noted that a great deal of effort of the Party and government bodies would be needed: "Encouragement of and assistance to scientific thought must be a top priority with us." These ideas were incorporated in the congress documents. On June 11, the USSR Supreme Economic Council Presidium discussed the ways to carry through the congress's decisions and instructed the Scientific and Technological Department to submit a report on improving the work 01 scientific- technical research establishments. Each of them was to be attached to a pilot-production plant, specialists were to be sent abroad, and a plan for the construction of scientific technical research centres was to be drafted.

Dzerzhinsky did his best to attract distinguished scientists to work in the industrial sphere. With this end in view, in December 1924, scientific and technological councils were formed under the Scientific and Technological Department of the Supreme Economic Council; new research establishments were opened, including the Institute of Mineral Raw Materials named after Lenin, the Laboratory of Hydraulic Installations, the Research Institute for the Study of the North, the Central Oil-Research Institute, and the Experimental Silicate Institute.

One aspect of the country's industrialisation was the drive for economising. In his time, Lenin repeatedly stressed the importance of economising under the socialist system: "If we see to it that the working class retains its leadership over the peasantry, we shall be able, by exercising the greatest possible thrift in the economic life of our state, to use every saving we make to develop our large-scale machine industry, to develop electrification, the hydraulic extraction of peat, to complete the Volkhov Power Project, etc."[4]

The drive for economising became particularly extensive after the 14th Party Congress, which signified the beginning of the work to practically implement socialist industrialisation. The initiator of the campaign was Dzerzhinsky. The decree signed by him on February 23, 1926, which came to be known as the "drive for economising" contained an order to reduce overhead expenses in the national economy. Since that time, this issue received extensive coverage in Dzerzhinsky's speeches, reports, memos and decrees.

In early March, the Moscow newspapers printed a press interview with Dzerzhinsky on his views on economising. "Under the conditions of Soviet reality," he observed, "economising is one of the principal Party trends in the field of the country's economic development... The emphasis on economising is thus ...

the struggle for authentic socialist construction." In one of his speeches, Dzerzhinsky referred to the slogan "economise" as the focus of the entire problem of the country's economic advance.

Addressing a conference of the audit commissions on March 8, 1926, Dzerzhinsky firmly stated that

"each intentional or unintentional unnecessary expenditure must be regarded as an offence against the

Soviet state". In order to foster deeper awareness of the need for economising, he proposed a meeting of Communists engaged in the economic field "for an open talk", and intended to make a report at the meeting.

The Party Central Committee, which greatly supported the campaign to economise, decided to send a letter to Party branches. Dzerzhinsky drafted a detailed memo which contained the major points to be included: "We need means... We are insanely wasteful. A rouble saved per person would give us 140 million a year. A small saving in each economic cubbyhole—thrift in everything that is absolutely necessary. The strict reduction of all extras and unproductive expenditure would save our economy hundreds of millions each year... Without economising, without doing our best in this field, we shall not be able to cope with the grandiose tasks facing us in the sphere of economic development, defence and satisfaction of the needs of the broad working masses. Dzerzhinsky's memo listed concrete examples of possible and necessary ways to reduce expenditures and save state funds. His proposals underlied the draft Address on the Thrift Economy Drive approved by the RCP(B) Central Committee and the Central Control Committee and to which Dzerzhinsky introduced some amendments. On April 25, it was made public under the heading: "The Address of the Central Committee and the Central Control Committee of the RCP(B) on the Thrift Economy Drive".

One of the objectives of Dzerzhinsky's trip to the Ukraine in May 1926 was to verify what was being done there to promote thriftiness. He arrived in Kharkov on May 6 and the next day was already chairing and speaking at the Ukrainian Supreme Economic Council Presidium meeting. The first question under discussion was the drive to economise. Dzerzhinsky spoke about the need to cut down overheads, filing and accounting, promote production rationalisation, raise labour productivity and enhance the role of production conferences in this matter. A few days before his death, on July 11, Dzerzhinsky wrote: "It is necessary to urge the trusts to promote the drive to economise by all available means and with great persistence." In the last months of his life Dzerzhinsky was primarily concerned with developing the economy by promoting thriftiness, and it was largely due to his efforts that progress was made in this area.

* * *

In dealing with the problems of economic development, the Party stressed improving the work of the state and economic apparatus and management bodies in industry and other branches of the national economy. At the basis of this work were Lenin's principles of economic management and of the work of the Party, state and economic apparatus: "We must reduce our state apparatus to the utmost degree of economy. We must banish from it all traces of extravagance."[5] Dzerzhinsky made an important theoretical and practical contribution to this effort.

On March 16, 1923, soon after the publication of Lenin's article "Better Fewer, but Better", Dzerzhinsky drafted a document which he himself called "a preliminary draft for a review", and sent it to the heads of a number of people's commissariats and departments requesting them to give their opinion. He wrote that a greater part of the administrative apparatus was composed of employees who used to belong to exploiter classes and bourgeois intellectuals, and voiced the opinion that they needed to be won over to the side of Soviet power after re-educating them. Suggesting that this question should be discussed at a Party congress, Dzerzhinsky mapped out a plan of concrete action comprising 15 items. Among other things, he recommended promoting to key positions workers and Communists who had long been Party members, had acquired some experience in organisational work, and still kept in touch with the rank and file. The Central Committee instructed Dzerzhinsky to make a report at the 12th Party Congress in the section dealing with organisational questions.

In his speech at a meeting of the organising section of the 12th Party Congress, Dzerzhinsky resolutely opposed bureaucratic methods of leadership and administration and the "monstrous centralisation", he dealt exhaustively with the goals set before the leading bodies. With respect to the reorganisation of the administrative apparatus, he observed: "We must follow Lenin's advice, 'better fewer, but better'." He was tireless in his efforts to improve industrial management and reduce the amount of red tape and unnecessary meetings.

His letter of June 3, 1925, addressed to the key Supreme Economic Council personnel, was typical: "Our greatest misfortune is at present an endless abundance of all sorts of meetings and conferences that eat up time without anything to show for the lost hours, that produce no tangible results." Dzerzhinsky considered it necessary "to hold people more personally responsible for their duties", and to "introduce the custom to always make the first item on the agenda the questions: is this meeting necessary, who of those present could and should be excused from it, and can the issue be dealt with outside of a meeting?"

Dzerzhinsky's letter was followed by a decree to the Supreme Economic Council which obliged the key personnel to draw up a list of commissions that could be abolished. A new procedure of holding conferences and meetings was introduced. They could now be convened only by the members of the USSR Supreme Economic Council Presidium, heads of departments and sectors, and chairmen of commissions. The meetings could start not earlier than 2.30 p.m., and were to be attended only by a limited number of persons who were directly involved with the matter under discussion. The agenda and materials for the conference with previously prepared suggestions were to be handed in to the participants no later than 24 hours before the opening. This procedure was discussed at the meeting of the Presidium held on July 13, 1925 and chaired by Dzerzhinsky.

"The basic evil that disorganises factories, trusts and economic management bodies," wrote Dzerzhinsky, "is the filing, reference, statistical and inspection deluge. Reports, reports, reports. Accounts, accounts. Figures, tables, endless rows of figures. Complete absence of competent people. Under this system, there is no time to examine the issue. The experts in the business are not people but references and reports. Mountains of papers, with nobody to read them and no physical opportunity for reading them."

Dzerzhinsky attempted to cut down all this paper work. On June 17, 1926, in a decree entitled "To Make the Management System Healthier", he demanded that each key official display precision and flexibility, and take more responsibility for his sector. This idea was formulated in the following way: "Decide, do and assume responsibility without wasting a minute, without unnecessarily appealing to authorities."

230

On June 23, Pravda carried Dzerzhinsky's article "On Improving the Work of the State Apparatus", which stressed that the campaign for a more flexible and thrifty state and economic management apparatus with a simpler structure and free from any bureaucratic outgrowths was an indispensable part of the drive to utilise more rational economic methods.

Dzerzhinsky again discussed this subject in his speech at the conference of the key Supreme Economic Council personnel held on July 9, 1926. High rates of economic development, he stated, depended to a not inconsiderable degree on the efficient functioning of the economic management apparatus. "The centre of gravity," said Dzerzhinsky, "should lie in the responsibility assumed by each working person; the counterposing of organisational fetishism to living people, conscientious people." Elaborating on this idea, he said: "We must introduce personal responsibility, know what each individual is doing, examine what he is studying, what he is responsible for, and to what extent." He proposed "introducing the regime of personal contacts with those who we are guiding and directing, and whom we entrust with a particular job".

On July 10, Dzerzhinsky issued a decree "On the Improvement of the USSR Supreme Economic Council Apparatus and Fighting Red Tape", which defined the organisation and content of business correspondence conducted by the various council divisions, and demanded that each document and suggestion be concrete and concise.

Dzerzhinsky believed that the best results could be attained when work was based on confidence in the employees. Two weeks after his appointment as the Supreme Economic Council Chairman, he observed that, "One cannot head such a huge body as the SEC other than through complete confidence in the employees." Further on, he stressed: "Those who have been entrusted with a department, the organisation of one local body or another, must have all possible confidence, all responsibility, and the opportunities for displaying initiative."

Having accumulated a great deal of experience while heading the Supreme Economic Council, Dzerzhinsky considered it expedient to reorganise the council. On March 3, 1926, he entrusted the council's personnel to draw up suggestions on the reorganisation of its structure and, in particular, on setting up the chemical, the power and the mining industry administration and the fuel department. In a memo of March 8, Dzerzhinsky advanced a well-grounded plan for the reorganisation of the Supreme Economic Council.

In the speech given on March 19 at a meeting of the Council Presidium, Dzerzhinsky spoke about the expediency of such reorganisation and outlined its principal trends. Criticising red tape and procrastination, he remarked: "I believe we shall have no procrastination if we reinforce our reorganisation with really efficient work, precision in the activities of apparatuses that will have no unnecessary links, no unnecessary intermediary bodies".

Following up on this, Dzerzhinsky issued a circular "On the Organisation of Industrial Management", which stated that clearly defining the range of functions of each employee and establishing the boundaries of his competence was a necessary condition of rational labour organisation. He pointed to the need to raise the prestige of administrative and technical personnel and not to burden it with unnecessary clerical work. This, in his opinion, would consolidate labour discipline.

Work on proposals aimed at improving the structure and functioning of the Supreme Economic Council continued. At a conference of public industry employees held in April 1926, Dzerzhinsky spoke about the need to reorganise the council apparatus but suggested that it continue as the central administrative body. When the draft statute on the USSR Supreme Economic Council was being written in its final form, Dzerzhinsky submitted a number of principled suggestions aimed at enhancing its role as a body or state authority. All of the documents he had written or helped prepare provided a detailed substantiation of his ideas concerning ways of improving the functioning of the economic management apparatus.

Untimely death prevented Dzerzhinsky from carrying through to the end the reform he had planned. This was accomplished some time later. On August 24, 1926, the USSR Council of People's Commissars heard a report delivered by Valerian Kuibyshev, who replaced Dzerzhinsky as Chairman of the USSR Supreme Economic Council, on the changes that should be made in its structure. Kuibyshev stated that Dzerzhinsky had planned to reorganise the council along three main lines in order to consolidate its role in the planning of industrial development, exercise more effective management over its individual branches, and expand the functions of the regulating body. "I completely support this idea of Comrade Dzerzhinsky," said Kuibyshev, "just as the plan for the reorganisation he had drafted." The Council of People's Commissars approved Kuibyshev's proposals and permitted work to begin on the reorganisation of the Supreme Economic Council apparatus.

Notes

[1]The state plan for the electrification of Russia was adopted in December 1920.

[2]V. I. Lenin, "A Great Beginning", Collected Works, Vol. 29, 1977, p. 427.

[3]V. I. Lenin, "Third Congress of the Communist International, June 22-July 12, 1921", Collected Works, Vol. 32, 1977, p. 492.

[4]V. I. Lenin, "Better Fewer, but Better", Collected Works, Vol. 33, 1973, p. 501.

[5]Ibid.

Chapter Twelve

DZERZHINSKY: A POLITICAL FIGURE OF LENINIST TYPE

Dzerzhinsky was one of the closest associates and loyal supporters of Lenin, a member of the leadership of the Communist Party which had been brought together by Lenin and which staunchly championed Leninism no matter how complicated and difficult the situation, and after his death remained loyal to the policies mapped out by him.

"Felix", reminisced Kliment Voroshilov, a prominent Soviet statesman and Party figure, "followed Lenin's example in everything he did. Like Lenin, he was humane and attentive to people, and extremely demanding and uncompromising towards the enemies of the revolution and their accomplices."

Lenin highly valued the work Dzerzhinsky was doing, trusted him implicitly, and, one may even say, looked after him.

In his memoires, Bolshevik Ivan Radchenko, a prominent economic executive, described his meeting with Lenin, at which Dzerzhinsky was also present. "After he [Dzerzhinsky] left, Lenin characterised him as a brilliant worker, speaking with a sort of joy, as about a loyal and dependable friend.

"Later, too, in tricky situations, when something was going wrong, Lenin used to say: 'We'd better entrust Dzerzhinsky with this, he's sure to cope.' "

Yelena Stasova, a secretary of the RCP(B) Central Committee, later wrote: "All of us who had come into contact with Lenin on business, saw and sensed the respect and support he gave to Dzerzhinsky. And that was only natural. Dzerzhinsky's courage, honesty and the purity of his life were known to everyone."

For his part, Dzerzhinsky repaid Lenin's trust and constant support with warm gratitude. "He displayed great attention and enormous confidence in Lenin's genius when listening to his advice, reading and rereading his works, to which he looked for answers to the most complicated questions posed by life," wrote Dzerzhinsky's wife. "When Felix spoke to Lenin over the telephone, I immediately knew to whom he was talking, even if I did not know what the conversation was about—Felix's voice was filled with great admiration and respect for Lenin."

Lenin constantly communicated to Dzerzhinsky all sorts of instructions, requests, advice and suggestions, and was sure to find an immediate and willing response.

He never forgot that Dzerzhinsky's health was not good, and was always urging him to take better care of himself.

"Learning that Dzerzhinsky was coughing blood but refused to take a rest," wrote Stasova, "Lenin rang me up and proposed that the Central Committee pass a resolution obliging Dzerzhinsky to take a two weeks' holiday. He had found a place where Dzerzhinsky could go, one of the state-run farms not far from Moscow, where food was good and which did not have a telephone: consequently Dzerzhinsky would be unable to get in touch with his subordinates and would get a good rest."

Lenin was worried about the harsh conditions under which Dzerzhinsky had to work in Siberia during his travel assignment there in 1922 and sent a telegram to Vecheka inquiring about his health. Moreover, Lenin issued instructions to somehow give Dzerzhinsky a medical check-up without telling him why this was being done. He demanded that the results of the check-up and the opinion of consulting doctors be communicated to him straight away.

Despite the unofficial nature of Lenin's telegram, Dzerzhinsky learned about it. In a letter to his wife written on February 7, 1922, and sent from Omsk, he remarked: "Of course my work here isn't very good for my health... But were I to be recalled earlier than I myself feel that my mission here has been to a large extent accomplished, I believe my health would suffer still more." Dzerzhinsky left Siberia only after his work there had been completed, displaying again the sense of duty that always motivated him in his work.

While in Siberia in 1922, Dzerzhinsky knew that Lenin was in poor health, and asked him for assistance only when absolutely necessary. He requested others not to bother Lenin either without extreme necessity.

On January 21, 1924, Lenin died. This was a great loss for Soviet Communists, all the Soviet people, the international working-class movement and the working people throughout the world. Soviet people rallied even closer around the Communist Party. Dzerzhinsky was terribly shaken by Lenin's death. His wife wrote later: "I had never seen Felix so grief-stricken as in those mournful days. He realised that the Party would find it difficult to carry on without Lenin. But he believed in the strength of the proletariat and its Party, and the victory of Leninism."

It was a token of appreciation of Dzerzhinsky as Lenin's loyal follower that the Party appointed him head of the USSR Central Executive Committee Presidium commission for the arrangement of Lenin's funeral.

* * *

Dzerzhinsky had many responsibilities as a member of the Party Central Committee. From July 1920, he was an alternate member of the Organising Bureau, and a member from August 1921; from June 1924 till the end of his life, he was an alternate member of the Central Committee Politbureau. He frequently made speeches and reports at Party congresses, Central Committee plenary meetings, and Politbureau meetings. Party congresses and the Central Committee frequently chose him to head major commissions or serve as one of the members.

Dzerzhinsky was also involved in important work in the field of foreign trade. On February 20, 1924, he spoke concerning a trade agreement between the USSR and Italy at a Politbureau meeting and was appointed a member of its commission for considering a draft agreement.

Speaking at the October 1925 Central Committee Plenary Meeting, Dzerzhinsky stated: "The rates of development of our foreign trade are still insufficient... All the problems of our national economy, which we are tackling with so much difficulty, have recently come up against the problem of foreign trade."

Some participants in the discussion spoke out in favour of relaxing the foreign trade monopoly.

Dzerzhinsky opposed this idea, for he considered it a means of protecting the country's industry. The Plenary Meeting appointed him to a commission to prepare proposals on the forms of exercising this monopoly by the state.

At the same meeting, Dzerzhinsky spoke on the work of trade unions, advocating the establishment of better working relations between trade union and economic management personnel, and criticising the bureaucracy in the activities of trade unions. He then touched on the attempts of the American automobile manufacturer Henry Ford to motivate the workers to increase production by introducing private enterprise, noting that the socialist system of production possessed more effective incentives which appealed to the hearts and the minds of the working people. He spoke highly of production conferences as one of the most efficient methods for allowing workers to freely discuss production problems and seek their solutions.

Dzerzhinsky set high standards for the work of each Communist and demanded unswerving loyalty to Party duty. In a February 28, 1923 memo he criticised the lack of cooperation between Communists working on transport and local territorial Party bodies, and proposed a number of concrete steps to consolidate the contacts between them. When the newly-appointed Chairman of the RSFSR Supreme Economic Council, Semyon Lobov, noted that the links between a number of economic executives, members of the Party, and the Moscow Party organisation were too weak, Dzerzhinsky supported him and drew up proposals towards involving the former in Party work.

Lobov wrote about Dzerzhinsky: "His constant wish was to establish a closer connection between Party members working at the Supreme Economic Council, trusts and syndicates, on the one hand, and the Moscow Party Committee and Moscow factories, on the other, and he was concerned that not everyone was yet involved in this work."

Dzerzhinsky's entire work was an example of selfless dedication to the cause of the Communist Party.

His character resume, kept at the Central Party Archives, states that as a member of the RCP(B) Central

Committee, he was an example of a true Communist working in close collaboration with rank-and-file Party members. This concise and yet exhaustive description reveals the principal aspect of Dzerzhinsky's work—his deep and sincere concern for the people.

Feliks Kon, who knew Dzerzhinsky well, reminisced: "Put at the helm of the national economy, he bent all his energies and prestige into preventing the smallest deviations from the line of the Central Committee."

Dzerzhinsky's writings contain pieces which reveal his profound understanding of the role of the

Marxist- Leninist Party and the ways of its development. Of considerable interest is his letter to the Central Committee of the Communist Party of Poland of January 20, 1925, in which he wrote: "The development of the Party means overcoming the mistakes, conscious advancement, i.e., overcoming conservatism, dogmatism... Party traditions, their strength mean ... moving unceasingly towards realising the ultimate goals of communism."

This was the policy he himself followed in his work.

* * *

Dzerzhinsky's views and convictions were profoundly internationalist. But he was also a Polish patriot who dreamed about a socialist, free Poland. Former General Secretary of the Central Committee of the Communist Party of Poland Lenski stated that "he [Dzerzhinsky] had always been the link connecting the revolutionary movement in Poland with the Russian revolution. He played that role ever since the formation of the Social Democracy of the Kingdom of Poland and Lithuania and until his death. It was his vision of a workers' and peasants' Poland that led him to urge Polish Communists to study the experience of the Russian revolution. He always displayed an interest in the Communist Party of Poland."

The Communist Workers' Party of Poland (the Communist Party of Poland since 1925) was formed on

December 16, 1918 as a result of the unification of the Social Democracy of the Kingdom of Poland and Lithuania and the Left wing of the Polish Socialist Party. The same kind of merger took place on the territory of Soviet Russia. A Central Executive Committee of the Communist Workers' Party of Poland in Russia was formed, and Dzerzhinsky was made a member. Through the Committee, he received information about the situation in Poland and the work of the Party. On July 12, 1919, the Central Executive Committee of the groups of the Communist Workers' Party of Poland in Smolensk sent him a resolution of the Central Committee on joining the Communist International. He also received illegal communist literature printed in Poland, leaflets, pamphlets, and books smuggled into Russia with great difficulty.

Back in Moscow after the cessation of hostilities on the Western Front in September 1920, Dzerzhinsky proposed to the RCP(B) Central Committee Orgbureau that Jakub Dolecki be sent to Berlin to establish communication with members of the Communist Workers' Party of Poland there, specifically, with Adolf

Warski, who in October 1920 was appointed head of the Central Committee Foreign Section of the

Communist Workers' Party of Poland. Via that section, the Polish Bureau of the RCP(B) Central Committee, in which Dzerzhinsky remained a member, received regular reports on the situation in Poland and on the work of the Party.

Like many other Polish Communists, Dzerzhinsky regarded work in Soviet Russia a good school for

Party cadres, and personally followed the training of members of the Communist Workers' Party of Poland On October 29, 1920, he requested the Central Committee Orgbureau to allow "50 men to come over from Poland to be put through Party courses". He never lost interest in his homeland and was always asking for firsthand information about Poland, the Party and its needs.

Dzerzhinsky took part in many -international forums and was the RCP(B) delegate to the First and Second congresses of the Communist International.

In July 1921, he attended the sessions of the Polish delegation at the Third Congress of the Communist International where a reunion took place between comrades-in-arms who had not seen each other for years.

One of the sessions of the Polish delegation discussed the results of the work of the Provisional Revolutionary Committee of Poland. Voicing the opinion of Polish Communists and former members of the Committee, Dzerzhinsky criticised the Communist Workers' Party of Poland leadership, which failed to establish relations with it. Expressing his views on the Party's activities, he advised Polish

Communists to make more extensive use of the opportunities for legal work and combine different forms and methods of revolutionary action. The Polish delegation also discussed Party membership. A number of Polish Communists residing in Russia were members of both the RCP(B) and the CWPP.

Dzerzhinsky's proposal on the issue was approved and the delegation took the following decision: Those who wish to be considered Party members must submit to RCP(B) discipline and render material and moral support to the CWPP. Dzerzhinsky was also present at the meeting of the Polish delegation held on July 14 after the congress was closed and devoted to the CWPP's work in the army. Like the majority of those who took the floor, he advocated thorough preparation for future revolutionary battles (this was also one of the resolutions of the Third Congress of the Communist International aimed at forming a single front against the advance of capital).

Closely following the progress of events in Poland, Dzerzhinsky made it a point to pass on information to the RCP(B) Central Committee. After receiving materials on the election campaign in Poland on September 13, 1922, he forwarded them to the Central Committee and requested that a report on this question be made by

Prochniak, representative of the CWPP at the next Central Committee Politbureau meeting.

As a result of terror and repressions, thousands of Polish Communists were arrested, and their families remained without any means of sustenance. Back in the summer of 1922, a group of Polish Communists living in the RSFSR issued an "Address to All Polish Communists in the Soviet Republics". It was signed by Dzerzhinsky and prominent members of Polish working-class movement Julian Marchlewski, Stanislaw Bobinski, Waclaw Bogucki, Stanislaw Budzynski, Feliks Kon, Jakub Hanecki, Josef Unszlicht and Edward Prochniak. The address read: "The way home is closed to us, and our ranks are supplemented with those who have been forced to leave it [Poland] due to fierce persecutions. We have only one right left, which no one can take away from us. It is the right to express solidarity with, the right to help the fighting Polish proletariat and its leader, the CWPP." The address ended with an appeal for donations to benefit the CWPP and political prisoners.

Dzerzhinsky thought it important that Polish Communists and Polish working people help build socialism in the USSR. As head of the People's Commissariat for Transport and then of the Supreme Economic Council, he tried to involve the Poles whom he personally knew well in the activities of these bodies, believing that work in the Soviet economy would prepare them for similar jobs in the future workers' and peasants' state of Poland. In 1923, Polish Communists who had been released from prisons arrived in the USSR on an exchange programme. Dzerzhinsky found one of them, Henryk Brand (Lauer), a job in the Supreme Economic Council apparatus. Jan Tannenbaum and Zdislaw Leder were also working there. Polish Communists initiated a campaign to raise funds for Polish schools. Dzerzhinsky as well as other Polish Communists contributed to it.

The Communist Workers' Party of Poland appreciated Dzerzhinsky' assistance and advice. In early 1923, the Party leadership decided to invite him, Marchlewski, Kon, and Unszlicht to its Second Congress, which was held in September 1923 in Bolshevo near Moscow. Taking part were also representatives of the

Communist International, of the RCP(B) Central Committee, and of other communist parties.

Dzerzhinsky's appearance at the congress provoked a storm of applause. Alexander Lenovich, veteran of the Polish communist movement and a delegate to the Second CWPP Congress, wrote later: "Felix Dzerzhinsky was for us all a legendary figure, the personification of the slogan 'For our and your freedom!' We were proud that our compatriot, a son of the Polish people, had become one of the jading figures in the Great October Socialist Revolution, a terror for counter-revolutionaries, one of Lenin's closest associates. We asked him to make a speech but he refused point-blank saying that he had lost touch with the current problems of the Polish workers' movement. He had absolutely no wish to speak from the congress's rostrum, but he talked with comrades Adolf Warski, Henryk Walecki, 'old Marcin' (Grzelszczak) and Kraiewski about the various issues that were vital for the Polish [workers'] movement. I remember him saying to the men surrounding him that we must drastically change our attitude to the agrarian question. He made a number of critical remarks about the stand taken by the Social Democracy of the Kingdom of Poland and Lithuania on this issue, saying that if we had recognised the significance of Lenin's slogan on the alliance of the workers and the peasants before and during the war, we would now have a socialist Poland independent of the imperialist states. Dzerzhinsky said that it was necessary to examine the nationalities question with great care for 'one must admit that we have blundered considering this question'."

Dzerzhinsky attended the Fifth Congress of the Communist International held in June- July 1924. As a member of the RCP(B) delegation, he was also a member of the Polish Commission under the Executive Committee of the Communist International.

Dzerzhinsky seriously examined the economic position of Poland and the condition of its working people. Seeking to determine the work to be done by the Polish Commission, in November 1925 Dzerzhinsky analysed the country's international position, its financial situation, the condition of the working class and the peasantry. On February 11, 1926, in a speech at the Extraordinary 23rd Leningrad Conference of the CPSU(B), Dzerzhinsky talked about the difficult economic condition of the Polish proletariat and peasantry which was due to criminal policies of the ruling circles.

On May 10, 1926, a government headed by Wincenty Witos, leader of the kulak party Piast, came to power in Poland. This provoked even greater discontent among the population. Capitalising on the situation, reactionary leader Josef Pilsudski, who was supported by the Polish Socialist Party and the peasants' parties Wyzwolenie and Stronnictwo chlopskie, effected a fascist coup in mid-May. The masses of workers, peasants and intellectuals were deceived by the leadership of the Polish Socialist Party and the Wyzwolenie party, which had built up Pilsudski's image as "the saviour of the motherland" and a "democrat". The leadership of the Communist Party of Poland and its activists, failing to realise that the coup was essentially fascist, supported it, and its organ Czerwony Sztandar even called for armed action to defend Pilsudski. Dzerzhinsky was gravely concerned over the situation in Poland. Back in April 1926, he wrote to Waclaw Bogucki, a representative of the Communist Party of Poland in the Executive Committee of the Communist International: "The slogan in favour of Pilsudski is in my opinion inadmissible and has nothing in common with the Bolshevisation of the party. The slogan of support for Pilsudski will signify the end of the Communist Party of Poland as a party of the working class."

Opposing Pilsudski in the days of the coup, Dzerzhinsky at the same time tried to show what the Polish workers and peasants could have attained in a country a socialist society. In his letter to the workers of Dovbysn he spoke of the significance of the effort made by working people in the Polish region in the Ukraine, and urged them "to work in such a way that we might send a delegation of Polish workers and peasants to visit you, so that they would have something to tell, upon returning to the country, the Polish workers and peasants."

Dzerzhinsky stressed the need to educate Polish Communists and the working people at large in the spirit of internationalism, and to help them strengthen their friendship with the Russians and other nations of the Soviet Union. He repeatedly reminded them about the traditions of the Polish-Russian revolutionary alliance, and urged them to draw on the illustrious past of the Polish working class.

* * *

Dzerzhinsky was involved in a broad range of activities as a statesman. He was a member of the All-Russia Central Executive Committee and the USSR Central Executive Committee, the Council of People's Commissars and the Labour and Defence Council, and headed a number of major government commissions or was a member.

Valerian Kuibyshev was accurate in writing: "There was not a branch of the economy or a sector of state activity at large which Dzerzhinsky did not know, in which he was not interested."

Dzerzhinsky made an important contribution to the work of public organisations, especially the trade unions. He frequently spoke at trade union congresses and conferences, and CC plenary meetings of the branch trade unions.

Together with Konstantin Tsiolkovsky, Friedrich Tsander and other distinguished scientists and engineers, Dzerzhinsky was elected to the Presidium of the Society for the Study of Problems of Interplanet Communications set up in 1924.

In November 1925, he greeted the inaugural meeting of the Society of Friends of Soviet Cinema: "Bring cinema and radio into the villages and workers' communities—let this be your motto, let the cinema and radio help to overcome promptly our cultural backwardness". Dzerzhinsky was elected Chairman of the Society. In a speech at the Society Council plenary meeting he spoke about the need to render practical assistance in promoting the construction of movie houses, especially in the country's outskirts, villages and areas with a predominantly working-class population, and to render regular financial assistance to the film industry.

For a number of years, until his death, Dzerzhinsky was head of the management board of the first transport joint-stock society, and in 1925-26, deputy chairman of the management board of the USSR Aviakhim society for assisting defence and aviation and chemical construction.

In answer to one of the questions on a questionnaire distributed among the delegates of the Tenth Party Congress: "What are your trades or professions?", Dzerzhinsky wrote: "I am only a revolutionary." And indeed, no matter what he did, he always remained a revolutionary, with a revolutionary's creative approach to all the work in which he was engaged. Clara Zetkin wrote about Dzerzhinsky: "One feature stood out—his revolutionary convictions, whose burning intensity developed Dzerzhinsky's outstanding qualities. These convictions were a sacred, primary obligation to him. Kind and sympathetic by nature, for their sake he could, and was even compelled to be, stern, hard and implacable towards others, for, even serving, them, he was incomparably sterner, harder and more implacable towards himself." p In his work Dzerzhinsky invariably looked for support to the working class, and also considered the promotion of its interests of primary importance. Strongly .believing in the power of collective creative endeavour, he always submitted questions of major importance for discussion by Communists, managers and workers; often, these discussions were more like open heart-to-heart talks. But Dzerzhinsky never tried to cater to the backward thinking typical of certain strata of the working population. When speaking before workers on the most topical issues, he was always frank and never tried to embellish the harsh conditions in the country in those years. Listening to Dzerzhinsky, they felt imbued with deep confidence in the worthiness of what they were doing, in the targets set by the Communists, and became even more conscientious and staunch supporters of the Bolsheviks.

Under the harsh conditions prevailing during the rebuilding of the economy, Dzerzhinsky still never neglected the questions of the workers' material conditions and their daily life. One thing he did was to open cheap canteens for them. He willingly agreed to become a member of the Council for the Assistance for the Narpit People's Catering Cooperative Society.

It was typical of Dzerzhinsky that one of the first USSR SEC Presidium meetings he chaired held on March 5, 1924, considered the question of opening cheap workers' canteens. The Presidium recognised the far-reaching significance of the Narpit's activities.

Dzerzhinsky also wished to build more housing for workers. On April 25, 1924, the Labour and Defence Council appointed him chairman of a commission to prepare a draft resolution for the promotion of cooperative construction of housing for workers and the establishment of a standing committee for this purpose. Its resolution was approved on May 21.

On August 21, 1924, the USSR Council of People's Commissars passed a decree which granted Dzerzhinsky the right to sell confiscated valuables, with the money raised to be used to open a fund for the building of housing for workers. On January 20, 1925, the Council of People's Commissars decided to give Dzerzhinsky control over this fund, and to form a bureau, headed by him, which would supervise the building of model- experimental housing for workers.

Since state allocations for housing were insufficient, Dzerzhinsky recommended developing individual and group housing construction by granting credits to workers for the purpose. He opposed unjustified expenditure in construction and advocated the use of cheaper materials, mechanisation, and foreign innovations. He suggested that standard model designs for housing be developed with due account for the price of materials, durability of houses, and their geographical location; he also insisted on the need for public control over housing construction.

Dzerzhinsky always kept in close touch with the people. Mazhimilian Saveliev, editor of the Torgovo- promyshlennaya gazeta (Trade and Industrial Newspaper) wrote: "Everyone knows about those 'new words' , those ambitious campaigns which he so passionately fanned up by the 'furnace' of his heart, a mighty effort of energy and will...

And he still managed to keep in close contact with broad masses of the revolutionary workers, appeal to the class consciousness of the proletariat on the basis of his truly Leninist approach to dealing with the principal problems of the revolution."

Rank-and-file workers sent Dzerzhinsky letters which contained heartfelt expressions of gratitude for the care and attention he invariably displayed and his courage and determination in the campaign against the enemies of the Soviet state. Many such letters were printed by newspapers and magazines. For example, here is a letter from the employees of the Mechanical Factory that was signed by 80 people.

"Dear Comrade Dzerzhinsky,

"We, workers and office employees of the Mechanical Factory which bears your distinguished name, address you, our comrade, who has dedicated himself to the defence of the rights of workers, peasants and all honest working citizens of the RSFSR.

"By your indefatigable work and inexhaustible energy, and with the support of all the working people, you have eradicated counter-revolution and thus given us an opportunity to devote ourselves to the reconstruction of our undermined economy, which we workers have inherited from the bourgeoisie, in particular, to rebuild our transport system, which you, dear Comrade Dzerzhinsky, are heading ...

"As a token of our respect, please accept our modest gift, a lighter with the inscription: 'To the sponsor of the Mechanical Factory, Comrade Dzerzhinsky, from the factory's workers'. We want you to know that at your first call, at any time, we are ready to rise to defend the workers' and peasants' rights, and to fill the key sectors of our production front, to rebuild the transport system which is so important to our young

Republic. We are sure that you will cope with our destroyed transport, rebuild it and completely restore it. We have this conviction because you have proven by deed your dedication to the working class when fighting against all enemies of the working people, and have already done a great deal to restore the transport system.

"Long live world revolution:

"Long live our leader in the struggle against economic dislocation in transport, Comrade Dzerzhinsky!"

Dzerzhinsky received letters not only from workers but from peasants, too. Their authors especially appreciated the campaign for thriftiness initiated by him. Here is an excerpt from one such letter: p "Dear Comrade Dzerzhinsky! On behalf of the peasants of a far-off village, allow me to express my proletarian gratitude for the thrift economy drive which will save us. Be healthy and in the future take more steps of this kind aimed at saving the gains of the revolution ... Be daring, we peasants are with you and for you. Proletarian greetings from peasant Ivan Zyuganov."

Dzerzhinsky had a rare gift for discovering just the right people to appoint to responsible jobs. An unerring intuition developed throughout years of Party work helped him to give accurate assessments of people's job capabilities and political convictions. "Work will be successful," Dzerzhinsky remarked in Kharkov in May 1926, "if it is entrusted to people who like the work and know how to set about it."

When staying in Siberia in 1922, Dzerzhinsky met Leonid Kazakov, who some time before was transferred from transport to another job. Talking to him, Dzerzhinsky became convinced that the man used to enjoy his work in transport and was eager to take part in its reconstruction. Dzerzhinsky wrote about him to the People's Commissariat for Transport, enclosing the man's short biography, "He produces a most favourable impression as an energetic, honest and responsible person. I request you to promptly collect information about him. In any case, I am sending him to Moscow ... for personal acquaintance". Dzerzhinsky never missed a chance to enlist the help of willing and useful people, but was at the same time very cautious when selecting new personnel. He was particularly considerate and thoughtful towards those who had rendered an important service to the revolution and the working class. One of the people he helped promote was Yevgeny Losevich, whom Kuibyshev had known well during the time of his exile.

248

Dzerzhinsky liked to spend time with his subordinates, and took care to give them' opportunities for advancement. Vladimir Knyazev, who was the secretary of the People's Commissar for Transport, said that the moment Dzerzhinsky spotted an able and gifted worker he made inquiries as to the conditions of his daily life and his needs, and continued to take an interest in him for a long time to come.

But, besides being considerate and kind, Dzerzhinsky was extremely demanding towards his staff. Apart from having talks with the men under him, Dzerzhinsky often sent them short notes. Archives have retained a great number of them. "I have adopted this form of contacts with the members of the Collegium," he explained, "because personal contacts and contacts at conferences are insufficient, and also because it is easier to give a more precise form to an idea and to affirm known instructions in a note, which helps to unite our huge Collegium in one strong fist."

Dzerzhinsky made it a point to investigate each case of abuse of official position or neglect and each difficult situation in a particular sector. Wherever he happened to be working, he managed to create an atmosphere of comradely confidence and openness in relations among employees, and took pains to encourage initiative. Vyacheslav Menzhinsky wrote that, "All his fellow-workers had extremely great scope in their work. This can be explained by the fact that as a gifted, daring organiser, he encouraged employee independence and for this reason preferred, in most cases, to conclude an argument with the words: 'Do as you think best, but remember you are responsible for the outcome'. "

It was usual with him, having heard a number of opinions on a complicated and controversial issue, to request postponing decision-making for two or three days so as to give it more thought. He was always fighting against " Window-dressing", outward show that detracted from real work, and criticised the unwillingness of an employee to thoroughly study a matter and acquire new knowledge.

In a memo of December 6, 1923, Dzerzhinsky named one of the most valuable qualities in a person, "to be honest above all else, and to be able to pick out honest people who are ready to promote the great cause by doing 'small things'."

Ivan Radchenko wrote in his reminiscences about Dzerzhinsky: "It was easy to work with him, he was so outspoken, sincere, hard-working, resolute and dedicated to what he was doing. Moreover, he was always polite, tactful and considerate."

Among Dzerzhinsky's many great qualities as a leader and a man of a new socialist system were his initiative and openness to everything new. It was he who raised many major economic, state and Party issues before the Party Central Committee and the Soviet Government. Dzerzhinsky vigorously supported each new and valuable idea, each useful initiative. He was responsible for launching a number of new promising industries. Himself a man of high principles and scrupulous honesty, he was intolerant to any abuse of Soviet laws, protectionism and nepotism.

Dzerzhinsky's sister Jadwiga described in her memoirs a college head, who at the same time held a highlevel post at the Moscow-Kazan Railway. He wanted to promote Jadwiga to a travelling inspector of that railway, which would have increased her salary. Jadwiga told this to her brother, who became very upset and issued an order: "In no case appoint my sister to this responsible position as she is unfit for it due to lack of necessary qualifications; immediately fire from this responsible position on the Kazan Railway the head of the college who is trying to show favouritism to an employee without even questioning her knowledge of the job."

Another of Dzerzhinsky's assets was his speaking ability and his gift as witty conversationalist. Engineer Ivan Bardin, later a distinguished metal scientist and Vice-President of the USSR Academy of Sciences, related his impressions of Dzerzhinsky speaking at a meeting in one of Kharkov's theatres: "For the first time in my life I was listening to such a fiery orator, a political fighter of this calibre, whose words, it seemed, originated in his very heart, emerged from the crystal depths of the human soul. I was looking around at people who had long had to go without a shave, who were exhausted and emaciated but confident of victory, drunk with the truth with which Dzerzhinsky scorched them as with a flame."

Dzerzhinsky lived a modest life. He contributed a silver ink-stand presented to him in 1922 by workers of railway workshops to the relief fund for the famished, considering it inadmissible to be using such an expensive article. Learning that the Semirechye Railway in Turkestan had been named after him without his consent, he wired his objection and also wrote to the Council of People's Commissars requesting that this decision be reconsidered.

"Felix was very unassuming in his private life," reminisced his wife. "More than once he said to me:' 'We Communists must live in such a way that the working people can say that we are using the victory of the revolution and power not for ourselves but for the happiness and welfare of the people."

He did not really look after his health at all, although his doctors demanded that he stick to a diet and a regimen. Here is one of the instances bearing out Dzerzhinsky's exceptional modesty which took place during his trip to Siberia in 1922. "Once," Dmitry Sverchkov wrote, "when Dzerzhinsky and I were sitting in his railway car, somebody brought him a glass of milk. Dzerzhinsky was acutely embarrassed... He considered milk an absolutely inadmissible luxury, an unpardonable extravagance under the harsh conditions of life prevailing at that time."

Dzerzhinsky hardly ever took time to rest. Even when on holiday he continued to work, drafted business letters and memos and requested Moscow to send him all sorts of documents. But in those rare moments when he allowed himself to relax he enjoyed the beauties of nature, liked to swim in the sea, went in for rowing, and was a good rider. He enjoyed fiction and had a good knowledge of Russian and Polish classics. He also loved and had a keen ear for music.

Everyone who knew him succumbed to his charm. Menzhinsky wrote about him: "By nature he was a very attracting, charming man with a tender, proud and pure soul."

As a rule, Dzerzhinsky refrained from complaining about his health. But once, when asked to write reminiscences about a Party member, he said: "I am so exhausted, overworked and ill myself that I am absolutely unable to write anything." And indeed, his strenuous, selfless work did affect his health, and he suffered frequent heart attacks. The Central Committee repeatedly passed resolutions obliging him to observe a regimen and to rest.

On December 11, 1924, when considering the question of Dzerzhinsky's health, the Central Committee

Politbureau ruled that he was to work only four days a week and to attend meetings of the Council of People's Commissars only when something of exceptional importance was being discussed. By a decision of the Central Committee Politbureau of December 18, Dzerzhinsky was granted a two weeks' leave of absence at the insistence of the doctors. Similar decisions were adopted later, too.

However, the tension in Dzerzhinsky's work continued to mount, reaching a climax on Tuesday, July 20, 1926, when he made an impassioned speech at the Central Committee plenary meeting. Representatives of the opposition were trying to paint a distorted picture of the country's economic development, and a well-substantiated rebuff was strongly needed to dash their hopes and expose their errors. Dzerzhinsky's report did just that. But even while speaking he felt a sharp pain in his heart. However he carried on to finish his speech and thus helped the Central Committee reach a sound assessment of the country's economic position.

After his speech, he went into the next room and lay down on a couch. Feeling desperately ill, he nevertheless summoned participants in the plenary meeting and questioned them about the progress of the debate. When he felt somewhat better, the doctors allowed him to walk to his flat, which was in a building next to the Armoury Chamber across from the Grand Kremlin Palace, where the plenary meeting was being held. Once in his bedroom, he fainted and died instantly. His death occurred at 4.40 p.m.

The Central Committee and Central Control Committee of the Party announced Dzerzhinsky's death with an address "To All Party

Members. To All Workers. To All Working People. To the Red Army and the Navy". "Today, the Party has sustained another heavy loss.- A heart attack has taken the life of Comrade Dzerzhinsky, a scourge to the bourgeoisie, a dedicated knight of the proletariat, the noblest fighter of the communist revolution, an indefatigable builder of our industry, the perennial worker and indomitable soldier of great battles...

"In him, the Party has lost one of its most outstanding and heroic leaders... His noble figure, personal valour, profoundly principled stand on all issues, his straight forwardness and exceptional honesty have given him enormous prestige. His service is tremendous. It cannot be overestimated.

"...His work was exemplary. His was a wonderful, magnificent life. His death, the death of a soldier on duty, was also magnificent.

"...We are lowering our battle standards over your body, our fearless friend! We call on all working people, on all proletarians, to pay their last respects to the fighter whose name will never be forgotten, whose cause will conquer the world.

"Long live communism;

"Long live our Party!"

The address issued by the Executive Committee of the Communist International in connection with Dzerzhinsky's death voiced the deep grief of the international community of Communists, of the world proletariat.

In the USSR, Party organisations and groups of employees sent to the Party Central Committee, the Central Executive Committee and the Council of People's Commissars letters and telegrams of condolence which expressed their profound grief and the sincere gratitude they felt towards Dzerzhinsky for everything he had done for the victory of the revolution and the building of socialism in the country.

^ Workers of Bryansk, who had assembled for a meeting of mourning, wrote in a telegram; "Let all enemies and slanderers remember that Dzerzhinsky will forever be an example of inexhaustible energy and indomitable will for the working class in realising Lenin's ideas."

^ One telegram justly called Dzerzhinsky "the symbol of revolutionary conscience and will of the proletariat". The telegram sent by the Central Committee of the Communist Party of Germany read: "For us German Communists Dzerzhinsky also was the symbol of revolutionary commitment to duty..." The telegram from the leadership of the Swedish Communist Party called him "one of the best leaders of the world proletariat."

Dzerzhinsky was buried in Red Square, next to Lenin's Mausoleum. To perpetuate Dzerzhinsky's memory, the USSR Council of People's Commissars decided to build a refuge for homeless children which would have the form of an industrial labour commune. The Moscow Institute for Transport Engineers was named after him. The People's Commissariat for Public Education was instructed to publish his works in collections suitable for a broad readership.

* * *

One hundred and ten years have passed since Dzerzhinsky's birth, over sixty years have passed since his death, yet he retains a place of honour in the community of fighters for social progress, for the victory of communism.

^ Dzerzhinsky was one of the fighters for the people's happiness whom Lenin described in 1910: "The proletariat needs the truth about political leaders, whether living or dead, for those who really deserve to be called political leaders do not become dead as regards politics upon their physical demise."[1]

The life and revolutionary work of Dzerzhinsky were examples of dedicated service to the cause of the working class and all the working people, examples for future generations of Soviet citizens.

Notes

[1] V. I. Lenin, "The Demonstration on the Death of Muromtsev", Collected Works, Vol. 16, 1977, p. 318.

CONCLUSION

All his life, Dzerzhinsky fought for the emancipation of the proletariat and all the working people from capitalist oppression. He served this cause with dedication, selflessness and honesty despite all manner of difficulty: exile and prison, ill health and danger, enemy intrigues and hatred.

Dzerzhinsky dedicated his life to the uncompromising and relentless struggle against tsarist autocracy, the oppression and exploitation of the working people by landowners and capitalists. He was motivated by a profound belief in the validity of the major tenets of Marxism-Leninism on the inevitable doom of capitalism and the need to emancipate the working class and build a new society.

His entire life was a never-ending heroic feat which demonstrates that Marxist-Leninist teaching is able not only to inspire and attract outstanding, progressive thinkers with its noble ideals, but can instil courage and determination in its champions. This is the strength of progressive ideas; they produce giants of thought and revolutionary action.

Dzerzhinsky greatly benefited from his contacts with Lenin. Lenin's very personality, his intelligence, unswerving dedication to the cause of the proletariat and principled stand against his opponents tremendously influenced Dzerzhinsky. From the start of their acquaintance in Stockholm in April 1906 at the Fourth Congress of the RSDLP and up to the last days of Lenin's life, Dzerzhinsky was his staunch supporter and loyal associate, and later became a close friend.

Under Lenin's guidance and together with other revolutionaries Dzerzhinsky made a direct contribution to the establishment of a revolutionary party of the working class, the party of a new type, a real vanguard of the proletariat. He was indefatigable in his work to strengthen its unity and ensure that only the most dedicated people loyal to Marxist-Leninist teaching and the spirit or proletarian internationalism joined it. His campaign against opportunism was based on deeply-rooted principles; he had always resolutely opposed renegade and divisive activities both in the ranks of the Social

Democracy of the Kingdom of Poland and Lithuania and in the CPSU(B);

Dzerzhinsky was directly involved in the three Russian revolutions. In each, he was in the front ranks of the fighters, and in the October Revolution, a leader and direct participant in the armed uprising in Petrograd. He supervised the seizure of key sectors, including the telephone exchange, railway stations and bridges.

Immediately after the victory of the revolution, Dzerzhinsky was entrusted with maintaining revolutionary law and order in the capital. This was considered a matter of paramount importance, for it was necessary to reinforce the confidence of the population in the new authorities and to set up a new state apparatus.

Dzerzhinsky greatly contributed towards building the Soviet state, the world's first state of workers and peasants, a state of proletarian dictatorship which was instrumental in suppressing the opposition of the overthrown exploiter classes, defending the gains of the revolution, and building a new society.

A prominent professional revolutionary, an internationalist, immediately after the victory of the revolution Dzerzhinsky was put in charge of a key organ of the dictatorship of the proletariat—the AllRussia Extraordinary Commission to Combat Counter-Revolution, Sabotage and Profiteering (Vecheka), which served as a strong shield and an avenging sword of the revolution. Dzerzhinsky was nominated for the post of its chairman by Lenin and approved by the Council of People's Commissars. That highly responsible job, which required courage and iron will, but also kindness and consideration, showed Dzerzhinsky to be a "knight" of the socialist revolution. He was a fearless and vigilant guardian of its interests, and at the same time a deeply humane and just arbiter with the power to decide a person's fate. Until the end of his life, he remained head of the Vecheka-OGPU (the State Political Department). For years, he combined his work there with holding other major Party, government and political posts. Often the Party would send him to accomplish important tasks which required organisational talent, energy, decisiveness, and the ability to rally the people to the struggle against economic dislocation, famine and child homelessness. His keen sense of responsibility for the future of the revolution and profound knowledge of the situation, specific conditions and circumstances, allowed him to tackle any Party assignment, any type of Party or government work with selflessness, persistence and courage. He educated and trained a fine group of Cheka men who were deeply committed to the cause of the revolution, who displayed valour and dedication when fighting against counter-revolutionary plots, espionage, subversive activities and profiteering both in the years of the Civil War and at the time of peace.

Cheka employees proudly referred to themselves as "Dzerzhinsky s men". Dzerzhinsky liked to repeat: "A Cheka man must have a cool head, a warm heart and clean hands." He fostered in his men loyalty to the Party line, persistence, readiness to promptly obey orders, courage, vigilance and the ability to keep state secrets. And their efforts were not in vain: they made an invaluable contribution to the triumph of the revolution and dealt a strong blow to counter-revolutionary elements.

Dzerzhinsky's service to the country in the campaign against counter-revolution and sabotage can hardly be overestimated. However, this is not the sum total of his contribution to the reconstruction of the transport system the building of the Soviet state. He headed many other major branches of Party and government work, and his contribution to the reconstruction of the transport system that had been crippled by the imperialist and Civil War and the development of industrialisation was invaluable. In the years of peaceful work, "the first Cheka man" became one of the most distinguished organisers of the economy. His name is associated with the construction of the first large factories in the new socialist society and the discovery and mining of many important types of mineral resources. He stood at the base of Soviet tractor-building, agricultural machine-building, the chemical, radio-technical, defence, aircraft and other branches of Soviet industry, and made a major contribution to the strengthening of the country's economic and defence capability.

As head of the USSR Supreme Economic Council, Dzerzhinsky exercised capable leadership over the country's industry, improved business management, promoted the economy drive. He also succeeded in reducing overheads, raising labour productivity and improving the quality of output. He displayed unparalleled talents as an organiser capable of seeing state interests behind each economic issue. Close ties with the people, a profoundly scientific approach to dealing with economic matters, the ability to tackle any problem from a Party stand, the striving to grasp the laws of economic development and to make them serve the construction of a socialist society—those were all features of Dzerzhinsky's style as a statesman and economic manager of the Leninist school. He waged an uncompromising struggle against deceit, unprincipled attitudes, fawning, bribery and flattery. Invariably truthful, self-critical and principled himself, Dzerzhinsky demanded that his fellow-workers display the same qualities.

Dzerzhinsky's many responsible positions and ranks did not go to his head. To the end of his life, he retained the simple habits he had evolved when working underground. Jams Peters, Deputy Chairman of the Vecheka, wrote: "Even holding top government posts, Dzerzhinsky remained a model of temperance and modesty in his private life. And not because he prided himself on his simple tastes, as some people did, but because it came natural to him."

Energetic and active by nature, Dzerzhinsky was always eager to learn something new. However, his extremely busy schedule left him little time for extensive studies and meditation. Like Lenin, he had to deal with many issues and find time to cope with the tasks that he had been assigned or had undertaken himself.

Dzerzhinsky's dedication to the cause in which he believed, honesty, keen sense of duty, warmheartedness and enthusiasm earned him prestige and great popularity in the Party, among the working people and in the international communist and workers' movement. This is how his fellow workers and Party members remember him and how posterity thinks of him.

The Soviet people, the peoples of the entire socialist community, the world communist and national liberation movement, the working people in the capitalist countries have not forgotten this great internationalist and fighter for communism.

Towns, schools, factories, farms, ships, cultural centres, squares, streets, and Young Pioneers'' groups in the Soviet Union and other socialist countries nave been named in his honour. But the best memorial to Dzerzhinsky, as it is to other loyal sons of the people, is the building of a developed socialist society in the USSR.

In a Resolution on the Political Report of the Central Committee, the 27th Party Congress charted a strategic line towards the country's accelerated social and economic development, confirmed the dedication of the Communist Party to Marxism-Lenin ism, and showed its ability to assess a situation realistically, to learn from experience and to discard that which no longer meets the requirements of the day. The documents of the congress have made a new contribution to the theory and practice of scientific communism, and given the people fresh vigour and creative energy.

Headed by its time-tested vanguard, the Communist Party and its Leninist Central Committee, the Soviet people have begun work to implement the congress' decisions and attain the targets set for the Twelfth Five-Year Plan. The cause launched by professional revolutionaries, the Leninists, lives and goes on.

"In my revolutionary work," said Dzerzhinsky, "under harsh conditions, I have always looked for support and a source of new strength in the realisation of the fact that this work serves the cause of emancipation of the working masses and leads to communism." His selfless and sincere service to the revolution provides an inspiring example for new generations of the Soviet people.

On September 9, 1977, on the occasion of Dzerzhinsky's centenary, Yuri Andropov stated in a report entitled " Communist Convictions: A Great Source of Strength of the Builders of the New World": "In labour and in combat, in our entire life we are inspired by immortal Leninist ideas. We learn how to passionately and selflessly fight to realise these ideas from the Bolsheviks of Leninist calibre, one of whom is Dzerzhinsky. For us, they remain the embodiment of commitment to communist principles and of revolutionary fervour. They are forever with us in our work towards the triumph of communism."

The heroic life and selfless work of Dzerzhinsky will always provide a source of inspiration for thousands of revolutionaries all over the globe who are fighting for emancipation from exploitation bravely championing independence, peace, equality, justice, and the security and happiness of all peoples.

NOTABLE DATES IN DZERZHINSKY'S LIFE AND WORK 1877-1926

1877

August 30 (September 11)

Felix is born into a small landowner's family on the Dzerzhinovo estate

1887

August

Dzerzhinsky is enrolled in the first form of Wilno secondary school

1894

Autumn

Dzerzhinsky joins a social-democratic group in Wilno

1895

Autumn

As a pupil in the eighth form of the Wilno secondary school, Dzerzhinsky joins the Left internationalist wing of the Lithuanian Social Democracy

1896

April 2(14)

Dzerzhinsky leaves the school and becomes a professional revolutionary

1897

March 18 (30)

Dzerzhinsky is sent to Kowno by the Wilno Social-Democratic organisation to conduct revolutionary work

April 1 (13)

Dzerzhinsky publishes the first issue of the Kowienski Robotnik, an illegal Polish paper July 17 (29)

Dzerzhinsky is arrested and put into the Kowno Prison

1898

June 13 (26)

Dzerzhinsky is deported to Vyatka Gubernia for three years, first to Nolinsk, then to the village of Kaigorodskoye

1899

August-December

Dzerzhinsky escapes from exile, illegally returns to Wilno, then moves on to Warsaw. There, he gets in touch with the most politically active workers and launches a campaign against the petty-bourgeois nationalists Polish Socialist Party. He sets up the Working-Class Union of Social Democrats and makes trips to Wilno to address the Wilno organisation on the unification of the Polish and Lithuanian Social- Democrats; he is elected to the Organising Centre (Central Committee)

1900

January

Dzerzhinsky writes a draft programme for the unity congress of the Social Democracy of Poland and Lithuania; takes part in the work of the Social-Democratic Working-Class Union's congress

January 23 (February 4)

Dzerzhinsky is arrested and incarcerated in Warsaw Citadel No. 10 Block

1901

April

Dzerzhinsky is deported and put into the Siedlce Prison

October 20 (November 2)

The authorities sentenced Dzerzhinsky to exile for five years to Eastern Siberia

1902

January-April

Dzerzhinsky is transferred to the Moscow Central Deportation Prison, then is sent on to a deportation prison near Irkutsk

May 6-8 (19-21)

Dzerzhinsky heads the political prisoners' demonstration of protest at the deportation prison

June 12(25) En route to the town of Vilyuisk to begin his term of exile, Dzerzhinsky escapes and returns to Warsaw in July and then goes abroad

August 1-4 (14-17)

Dzerzhinsky takes part in the conference of the Social-Democracy of the Kingdom of Poland and

Lithuania in Berlin. At his suggestion, the conference decides to set up a SDKP and L Committee Abroad and to publish the Czerwony Sztandar newspaper. Dzerzhinsky is elected to the Committee; moves to Krakow, where he engages in underground work under the alias of Yuzef.

1903

July 12-16 (25-29)

Dzerzhinsky takes part in the Fourth Congress of the Social Democracy of the Kingdom of Poland and
Lithuania in Berlin convened at his suggestion. The congress passes a decision on a merger with the RSDLP. Dzerzhinsky is elected to the Main Board of the Social Democracy of the Kingdom of Poland and Lithuania 1904

Late December

Dzerzhinsky illegally moves from Krakow to Warsaw to exercise leadership in Party work and the revolutionary movement

1905

January-April

Dzerzhinsky conducts illegal work in Warsaw, organising strikes, issuing leaflets and appeals in which he calls on Polish workers to rise up against the autocracy

April 18 (May 1)

Dzerzhinsky is instrumental in organising a mass May Day demonstration in Warsaw

May

Dzerzhinsky drafts the Rules of the Social Democracy of the Kingdom of Poland and Lithuania June 9-11 (22-24)

Dzerzhinsky issues leaflets urging a universal strike of solidarity with the workers of Lodz fighting at the barricades

July

Dzerzhinsky leaves for Lodz and Pobianitsa to help organise the work of the local Social- Democratic branches

July 17 (30)

Dzerzhinsky chairs a Party conference of the Warsaw City
Organisation of the Social Democracy of the Kingdom of Poland and
Lithuania and is arrested
October 20 (November 2)
Dzerzhinsky is released under the October amnesty following the
tsar's manifesto of October 17, 1905 November 15-17 (28-30)
Dzerzhinsky takes part in the conference of the SDKP and L in
Warsaw
December 14 (27) Dzerzhinsky speaks at the metal works in the
Dabrowa coal-mining basin urging the workers to stage a general
strike of solidarity with the Moscow workers who had launched an
armed uprising. The general strike began on the same day
1906
April 10-25 (April 23-May 8)
Dzerzhinsky takes part in the work of the Fourth (Unity) Congress of
the RSDLP in Stockholm where he first meets with Lenin
June 5-12 (18-25)
Dzerzhinsky takes part in the Fifth Congress of the Social-Democracy
of the Kingdom of Poland and Lithuania
July
Dzerzhinsky is elected to the RSDLP Central Committee as the
representative of the Social-Democracy of the Kingdom of Poland
and Lithuania; leaves Warsaw for St. Petersburg
August-September Dzerzhinsky works in St Petersburg, meets with
Lenin; resolutely supports the Bolsheviks in the struggle against the
Menshevik Central Committee; sends Bolshevik literature to Poland
November 3-7 (16-20)
Dzerzhinsky takes part in the Second RSDLP Conference in
Tammerfors
December 13(26)
Dzerzhinsky is arrested and put into the Paviak Prison in Warsaw
1907
May 19 (June 1)
At the Fifth RSDLP Congress in London, Dzerzhinsky is elected to
the Party Central Committee (in his absence)

May 22 (June 4)
Dzerzhinsky is released from prison on bail
July 21-23 (August 3-5)
Dzerzhinsky takes part in the Third RSDLP Conference in Kotka
(Finland)
November 5-12 (18-25)
Dzerzhinsky takes part in the Fourth RSDLP Conference in
Helsingfors
1908
March 30 (April 12)
Dzerzhinsky chairs the general conference of the Social-Democracy
of the Kingdom of Poland and Lithuania
April 3 (16)
Dzerzhinsky is arrested and imprisoned in No. 10 Block of the
Warsaw Citadel
April 30 (May 13)
Dzerzhinsky makes the first entry in his prison diary
November 22-30 (December 5-13)
Prague hosts the Sixth Congress of the Social Democracy of the
Kingdom of Poland and Lithuania, which elected Dzerzhinsky to the
Main Board in his absence
1909
January 15 (28) and April 25 (May 8)
By court decision, Dzerzhinsky is stripped of all property rights and
sentenced to life exile in Siberia
November, second half
Dzerzhinsky escapes from the village of Taseyevo, his third escape
from exile
December
Dzerzhinsky illegally returns to Warsaw, then moves on to Berlin
1910
January
The Party sends Dzerzhinsky to Capri (Italy) for a cure
March-December

Back in Krakow, Dzerzhinsky heads underground Party work, opposes conciliatory tactics towards opportunism in the Main Board of the Social-Democracy of the Kingdom of Poland and Lithuania

1911

January 31-February 1 (February 13-14)

Dzerzhinsky sends a letter to the Main Board stating his solidarity with the policy pursued by the Central Organ and by Lenin

May 28-June 4 (June 10-17)

Dzerzhinsky takes part in the conference of the nine RSDLP Central Committee members convened in Paris at Lenin's suggestion

July-December

Dzerzhinsky works to consolidate the Party organisations in the Kingdom of Poland, several times visits

Warsaw, Lodz, Czestochowa, and the Dabrowa Basin

1912

January

Dzerzhinsky moves illegally to Warsaw

January 19-23 (February 1-5)

Dzerzhinsky travels across the Dabrowa Basin, visits Czestochowa, organises deliveries of literature to Party organisations

April

Dzerzhinsky engages in propaganda and agitation work in connection with the shooting of workers at the Lena goldfields in Siberia

September 1 (14) Dzerzhinsky is arrested for the sixth time and locked up in No. 10 Block of the Warsaw Citadel

1913

Dzerzhinsky is detained in No. 10 Block of the Warsaw Citadel

1914

April 29 (May 12)

Dzerzhinsky is sentenced to three years' hard labour by the Warsaw District Court

July 28 (August 10)

Dzerzhinsky is deported from Warsaw to the Mtsensk Prison, from there to the Orel Prison and to the Orel Central Convict Prison

1915

Dzerzhinsky serves his sentence in Orel
1916
Late March
Dzerzhinsky is transferred to the Moscow Prison in connection with
the institution of new court proceedings
May 4 (17)
Dzerzhinsky is sentenced to six years' hard labour
1917
March 1 (14)
Dzerzhinsky is released as a result of the February revolution. He
speaks at the meeting of the Moscow Soviet of Workers' Deputies
warmly welcoming the revolution
March, first half
Dzerzhinsky is elected to the Moscow Committee of the RSDLP(B)
March 26 (April 8)
Dzerzhinsky takes part in the conference of the Moscow group of the
Social-Democracy of the Kingdom of Poland and Lithuania which
confirmed the decision adopted at the March 3 (16) meeting and
passed a resolution on unity of action with the RSDLP(B) and joining
its ranks
April 3-4 (16-17)
Dzerzhinsky takes part in the Moscow City Conference of the
RSDLP(B)
April 11 (24)
Dzerzhinsky is elected a member of the Executive Committee of the
Moscow Soviet of Workers' and Soldiers' Deputies
April 19-21 (May 2-4)
Dzerzhinsky takes part in the Moscow Region Conference of the
RSDLP(B); makes an opening speech April 24-29 (May 7-12)
Dzerzhinsky takes part in the Seventh (April) All-Russia Conference
of the RSDLP(B) June-July
Dzerzhinsky takes treatment for tuberculosis
June, first half

Dzerzhinsky is elected to the Central Executive Committee of the Social-Democratic groups of the Kingdom of Poland and Lithuania in Russia
July 26-August 3 (August 8-16)
Dzerzhinsky takes part in the Sixth RSDLP(B) Congress, at which he is elected a member of the Party Central Committee
August 6 (19)
Dzerzhinsky is elected to the RSDLP(B) Central Committee Secretariat
August 14 (27)
Dzerzhinsky is appointed to the Information Bureau by the Party Central Committee
October 10 (23)
Dzerzhinsky takes part in the RSDLP(B) Central Committee meeting which approves Lenin's resolution on the armed uprising
October 16 (29)
At the enlarged meeting of the RSDLP(B) Central Committee Dzerzhinsky is elected to the Revolutionary Military Centre heading the armed uprising
October 21 (November 3)
By decision of the RSDLP(B) Central Committee, Dzerzhinsky is appointed to the Executive Committee of the Petrograd Soviet
October 25 (November 7)
Dzerzhinsky is directly and actively involved in the October armed uprising
October 25-26 (November 7-8)
Dzerzhinsky takes part in the Second All-Russia Congress of Soviets; welcomes the Decree on Peace on behalf of the Social-Democrats of Poland and Lithuania; is elected member of the All-Russia Central Executive Committee
November 16 (19)
The All-Russia Central Executive Committee meeting of the second convocation elects Dzerzhinsky a member of the All-Russia CEC Presidium
December 7 (20)

Dzerzhinsky receives Lenin's message concerning measures to be taken against sabotage and counterrevolution. Dzerzhinsky holds the first (organising) meeting of a commission to combat sabotage and counter-revolution. The Council of People's Commissars passes a decision to name it the All-Russia Extraordinary Commission to Combat Counter-revolution and Sabotage; Dzerzhinsky is appointed Commission Chairman

1918

January 10-18

Dzerzhinsky takes part in the Third All-Russia Congress of Soviets; the congress elects him to the AllRussia Central Executive Committee

March 6-8

Dzerzhinsky takes part in the Seventh Party Congress and is elected a member of the RCP(B) Central Committee

March 14-16

Dzerzhinsky takes part in the Extraordinary Fourth All-Russia Congress of Soviets and is elected a member of the All-Russia Central Executive Committee

August-September

Under Dzerzhinsky's supervision, Vecheka uncovers and suppresses a major anti-Soviet plot of imperialist states organised by Robert Hamilton Bruce Lockhart, head of the British Mission in Moscow

November 6-9

Dzerzhinsky takes part in the Extraordinary Sixth All-Russia Congress of Soviets and is elected a member of the All-Russia Central Executive Committee

November 25-28

Dzerzhinsky chairs the Second All-Russia Conference of Extraordinary Commissions

December 3

Lenin and Dzerzhinsky take part in the session of the government commission on Vecheka bodies

1919

January 3

As a member of a commission, Dzerzhinsky leaves for the Eastern Front
February 17
Dzerzhinsky speaks at an All-Russia Central Executive Committee meeting on the reorganisation of Chekas and revolutionary tribunals
March 18-23
Dzerzhinsky takes part in the Eighth RCP(B) Congress, which elects him a member of the Party Central Committee
March 30
The All-Russia Central Executive Committee approves Dzerzhinsky's nomination for the post of the People's Commissar for Internal Affairs of the RSFSR
March
Dzerzhinsky takes part in the First Congress of the Communist International as the RCP(B) delegate August 18
By decision of the Party Central Committee Organising Bureau, Dzerzhinsky is appointed head of the Vecheka Special Department
September 24
Dzerzhinsky speaks at the Moscow Conference of the RCP(B) on the uncovering of the conspiracy conceived by the National Centre, a counterrevolutionary organisation in Moscow
December 5-9
Dzerzhinsky takes part in the Seventh All-Russia Congress of Soviets, and is again elected a member of the All-Russia Central Executive Committee
1920
January 15
Izvestia newspaper prints the Vecheka resolution signed by Dzerzhinsky on the termination of the use of capital punishment (execution by firing squad) by Vecheka and its local branches
January 24
The All-Russia Central Executive Committee Presidium passes a decree to award Dzerzhinsky with the Order of the Red Banner
February 3-6

Dzerzhinsky takes part in the Fourth All-Russia Conference of Extraordinary Commissions February 19
The Council of People's Commissars appoints Dzerzhinsky Chairman of the Head Committee for Universal Labour Conscription
March 29-April 5
Dzerzhinsky takes part in the Ninth RCP(B) Congress and is re-elected a member of the Central Committee
April 5
The RCP(B) Central Committee Plenary Meeting elects Dzerzhinsky an alternate member of the Central Committee Organising Bureau
April 26
The Party Central Committee decides to send Dzerzhinsky to the Ukraine
May 29
Dzerzhinsky is appointed Commander of the Rear of the South-western Front July 16
The Party Central Committee appoints Dzerzhinsky a member of the RCP(B) delegation to the Second Congress of the Communist International
September 22-25
Dzerzhinsky takes part in the Ninth All-Russia Conference of the RCP(B) which elects him to the Central Control Commission
October 20
The Labour and Defence Council appoints Dzerzhinsky Chairman of the Moscow Defence Committee December 22-29
Dzerzhinsky takes part in the Eighth All-Russia Congress of Soviets and is re-elected a member of the All-Russia Central Executive Committee
1921
January 15
Dzerzhinsky chairs the conference on the organisation of frontier troops
January 27

The All-Russia Central Executive Committee Presidium appoints Dzerzhinsky chairman of the CEC commission for the improvement of the life of children
March 7
The Moscow Party Committee appoints Dzerzhinsky chairman of the commission for the improvement of the workers' living conditions
March 8-16
Dzerzhinsky takes part in the Tenth RCP(B) Congress, and is re-elected a member of the Party Central Committee
April 14
On Lenin's proposal, the All-Russia Central Executive Committee Presidium appoints Dzerzhinsky
People's Commissar for Transport in addition to his duties as head of the Vecheka and the People's Commissariat for Internal Affairs
June 22-July 12
Dzerzhinsky takes part in the Third Congress of the Communist International as a member of the RCP(B) delegation
August 8
Dzerzhinsky makes a report "On the Condition of the Transport" at a Party Central Committee plenary meeting chaired by Lenin
November 15
At a meeting of the Council of People's Commissars Dzerzhinsky makes a report on the Collegium of the Commissariat for Transport
December 13
Dzerzhinsky speaks on the condition and goals of the transport system at a meeting of the Petrograd Soviet of Workers' and Peasants' Deputies
December 23-28
Dzerzhinsky takes part in the Ninth All-Russia Congress of Soviets and is re-elected member of the AllRussia Central Executive Committee
1922
January 2
The All-Russia Central Executive Committee Presidium decides to send Dzerzhinsky to Siberia as the special representative of the

Committee for introducing extraordinary measures for the transportation of foodstuffs from that region
January 5
Dzerzhinsky leaves for Siberia
February 6
Dzerzhinsky is appointed Chairman of the GPU (State Political Department) under the RSFSR People's Commissariat for Internal Affairs
March 13
Dzerzhinsky makes a report on the condition of the transport system and the political situation in Siberia to the Party Central Committee Politbureau
March 27-April 2
Dzerzhinsky takes part in the Eleventh RCP(B) Congress, and is re-elected a member of the Party Central Committee
May 10
Dzerzhinsky speaks at a conference at the Party Central Committee about the transport situation September 2
By a decision of the Labour and Defence Council, Dzerzhinsky is appointed Chairman of the Council's Commission for the Struggle Against Bribe-taking
December 23- 27
Dzerzhinsky takes part in the Tenth All-Russia Congress of Soviets, which elects him a member of the
Congress Presidium, a member of the All-Russia Central Executive Committee, and delegates him to the First USSR Congress of Soviets
December 30
Dzerzhinsky takes part in the First USSR Congress of Soviets, and is elected a member of the Central
Executive Committee of the Union of Soviet Socialist Republics
1923
January 23
As head of an ad hoc commission, Dzerzhinsky arrives in Kharkov to inspect the work of railways February 8

Dzerzhinsky makes a report on the situation of the transport system at a Central Committee plenary meeting of the Railway Workers' Union
March 31
Izvestia carries the address, "Everyone to the Aid of the Children!", by Chairman of the Children's Commission under the All-Russia Central Executive Committee, Dzerzhinsky
April 17-25
Dzerzhinsky takes part in the 12th RCP(B) Congress and is re-elected a member of the Party Central Committee
June 12-23
Dzerzhinsky takes part in the Third Extended Plenary Meeting of the Communist International's Executive Committee as a member of the RCP(B) delegation
July 6
The Second USSR Central Executive Committee session of the first convocation appoints Dzerzhinsky People's Commissar for Transport
July 17
The USSR Council of People's Commissars decides to appoint Dzerzhinsky to the Labour and Defence Council
November 15
The Council of People's Commissars appoints Dzerzhinsky Chairman of the USSR OGPU (Unified State Political Department) Collegium
November 20
Dzerzhinsky sends a report to the USSR Labour and Defence Council on the metal industry
December 3
Dzerzhinsky makes a report on the work of the Commissariat for Transport at a conference of the Railway Workers' Union
1924
January 16-18
Dzerzhinsky takes part in the Thirteenth RCP(B) Conference
January 19-22, 29
Dzerzhinsky takes part in the Eleventh All-Russia Congress of Soviets, and is elected a member of the Congress Presidium and the All-Russia Central Executive Committee

January 22

The USSR Central Executive Committee Presidium appoints Dzerzhinsky Chairman of its commission for the arrangement of Lenin's funeral

January 26-February 2

Dzerzhinsky takes part in the Second USSR Congress of Soviets and is elected a member of the Congress Presidium and a member of the Central Executive Committee of the Union of Soviet Socialist Republics

February 2

The First Session of the USSR Central Executive Committee of the second convocation appoints Dzerzhinsky Chairman of the Supreme Economic Council of the USSR while he continues to hold the post of Chairman of the OGPU

March 20

The Party Central Committee Politbureau sets up a Higher Government Commission for the Metal Industry, and appoints Dzerzhinsky its chairman

March 21

The USSR Supreme Economic Council forms a Central Donets Basin Assistance Committee under Dzerzhinsky's chairmanship

April 15

Dzerzhinsky chairs a session of the standing conference on labour issues at the USSR Supreme Economic Council Presidium

May 23-31

Dzerzhinsky takes part in the work of the Thirteenth RCP(B) Congress, which re-elects him a member of the Party Central Committee

June 2

The Party Central Committee plenary meeting elects Dzerzhinsky an alternate member of the RCP(B) Central Committee Politbureau and Organising Bureau

June 17-July 8

Dzerzhinsky takes part in the work of the Polish Commission at the Fifth Congress of the Communist International

276

June 21

Dzerzhinsky makes a report on the prospects for the development of metal industry at the Fourth Plenary Meeting of the Central Committee of the Metalworkers' Union

September 1

Dzerzhinsky speaks about transport requirements for metal at an extended conference of the Higher

Government Commission for Metal Industry

September

Dzerzhinsky greets Cheka commanding officers, the first graduates of the Higher Frontier Troops' College

November 13

By a decision of the Party Central Committee Politbureau, Dzerzhinsky is appointed Chairman of the Glavmetal (Chief Administration of Metal Industry) Management Board

November 21

Dzerzhinsky reports on the state of metal industry and its goals at the Fifth Ail-Union Conference of Metalworkers

November 25

Dzerzhinsky speaks about the goals of the commissions for raising labour productivity at a meeting of the standing conference for raising labour productivity at the USSR Supreme Economic Council 1925

January 19

Dzerzhinsky makes a report on the situation and prospects for development in metal industry at the Party Central Committee plenary meeting

March 31

Dzerzhinsky speaks about the goals of the cooperative movement at an extended Labour and Defence Council meeting

April 27-29

Dzerzhinsky takes part in the Fourteenth RCP(B) Conference; makes a report "On Metal Industry" May 7-16

Dzerzhinsky takes part in the Twelfth All-Russia Congress of Soviets, and is elected a member of the Congress Presidium

May 13-20

Dzerzhinsky takes part in the Third Ail-Union Congress of Soviets; makes a report "On the Situation in
Industry of the USSR"; is elected a member of the Congress Presidium and a member of the Central Executive Committee of the Union of Soviet Socialist Republics
June 14-16
Dzerzhinsky stays in Leningrad where he inspects the work of industrial enterprises July 4
Dzerzhinsky speaks about the situation in the Communist Party of Poland at a meeting of the Polish Commission of the Executive Committee of the Communist International
July 20
Dzerzhinsky took the chair at a special Supreme Economic Council conference devoted to the aircraft industry
November 4
Dzerzhinsky makes a speech at the All-Union Conference on Introducing More Efficient Methods in Production
November 17-26
Dzerzhinsky takes part in the Seventh All-Union Congress of the Metalworkers' Union
December 18-31
Dzerzhinsky takes part in the Fourteenth Party Congress and is re-elected a member of the Central Committee
December 28
Dzerzhinsky speaks at a Party Central Committee plenary meeting on questions of Party unity
1926
January 1
Dzerzhinsky makes a speech at a Party Central Committee plenary meeting; is elected an alternate member of the Politbureau
January 25
Dzerzhinsky makes a speech on the fuel supplies to the industries at a meeting of the USSR Supreme Economic Council Presidium
April 6-9
Dzerzhinsky takes part in a Party Central Committee plenary meeting

278

May 28
Dzerzhinsky visits the Kharkov Locomotive Factory
June 11
Dzerzhinsky takes part in a meeting of the Labour and Defence
Council
July 14-20
Dzerzhinsky takes part in a united plenary meeting of the Party
Central Committee and Central Control Committee
July 20 4.40 p.m.
Dzerzhinsky's sudden death

Printed in Great Britain
by Amazon

27171138R00156